Library of
Davidson College

The Military, the State, and Development in Asia and the Pacific

edited by

Viberto Selochan

Westview Studies in Regional Security

The Military, the State, and Development in Asia and the Pacific

Westview Studies in Regional Security
Wm. J. Olson, Series Editor

The Military, the State, and Development in Asia and the Pacific, edited by Viberto Selochan

The Comandante Speaks: Memoirs of an El Salvadoran Guerrilla Leader, edited by Courtney E. Prisk

Uncomfortable Wars: Toward a New Paradigm of Low Intensity Conflict, edited by Max G. Manwaring

The Military, the State, and Development in Asia and the Pacific

EDITED BY

Viberto Selochan

Westview Press
BOULDER • SAN FRANCISCO • OXFORD

Westview Studies in Regional Security

Chapter 2 is reprinted from *The Pacific Review*, Vol. 1, No. 4 (1988), by permission of Oxford University Press (copyright © 1988 by Oxford University Press). A revised version was published in Wolfgang S. Heinz, Werner Pfennig, and Victor T. King, eds., *The Military in Politics: Southeast Asian Experiences*, Special Issue (Hull, England: Centre for South-East Asian Studies, University of Hull, 1990); the cooperation of the Centre for South-East Asian Studies is gratefully acknowledged.

This Westview softcover edition is printed on acid-free paper and bound in library-quality, coated covers that carry the highest rating of the National Association of State Textbook Administrators, in consultation with the Association of American Publishers and the Book Manufacturers' Institute.

All rights reserved. No part of this publication may be reproduced or transmitted in any form or by any means, electronic or mechanical, including photocopy, recording, or any information storage and retrieval system, without permission in writing from the publisher.

Copyright © 1991 by Westview Press, Inc.

Published in 1991 in the United States of America by Westview Press, Inc., 5500 Central Avenue, Boulder, Colorado 80301, and in the United Kingdom by Westview Press, 36 Lonsdale Road, Summertown, Oxford OX2 7EW

Library of Congress Cataloging-in-Publication Data
The Military, the state, and development in Asia and the Pacific / edited by Viberto Selochan.
 p. cm.
Includes bibliographical references.
ISBN 0-8133-1111-X
 1. Civil-military relations—Asia. 2. Civil-military relations—Pacific Area. I. Selochan, Viberto.
JQ26.C58M55 1991
322'.5'095—dc20   91-8908
                                                                                           CIP

Printed and bound in the United States of America

The paper used in this publication meets the requirements of the American National Standard for Permanence of Paper for Printed Library Materials Z39.48-1984.

10 9 8 7 6 5 4 3 2 1

Contents

Abbreviations	ix
Foreword, *R. J. May*	xiii
Acknowledgments	xv
About the Editor and Contributors	xvii
Map	xix

1 Introduction: The Military, the Developmental State and Social Forces in Asia and the Pacific: Issues for Comparative Analysis, *Robin Luckham* — 1

2 Military-Civilian Relations in Indonesia in the Late Soeharto Era, *Harold Crouch* — 51

3 The Thai Military and Its Role in Society in the 1990s, *Suchit Bunbongkarn* — 67

4 The Armed Forces of the Philippines and Political Instability, *Viberto Selochan* — 83

5 The Military in Malaysia, *Harold Crouch* — 121

6 The Military in Myanmar: What Scope for a New Role? *Robert H. Taylor* — 139

7 The Military in Pakistan Politics: Direct or Indirect Participation? *Samina Yasmeen* — 153

8 The Military in Bangladesh, *Chowdhury R. Abrar* — 179

9 The Military Factor in South Korean Politics, *James Cotton* — 203

10 Military Roles and Relations in Papua New
    Guinea, *Yaw Saffu*   221

11 The Politicization of Military Professionalism in
    Fiji, *Jim Sanday*   239

References   271

Abbreviations

AFP	Armed Forces of the Philippines
AL	Awami League
ASEAN	Association of Southeast Asian Nations
AUCs	Armed Unified Commands
BCP	Burma Communist Party
BKSAL	*Bangladesh Krishak Sramik Awami League* (Bangladesh Worker's and Peasant's Awami League)
BSPP	Burma Socialist Program Party
CA	Commission on Appointments
CAFGUs	Citizen Armed Forces Geographical Units
CENTO	Central Treaty Organization
CHDF	Civilian Home Defense Force
CJS	Chief of Joint Staff
COAS	Chief of Army Staff
COMELEC	Commission on Elections
COP	Combined Opposition Parties
CPC	Constitutional Planning Committee
CPP	Communist Party of the Philippines
CPT	Communist Party of Thailand
DFI	Defence Field Intelligence
DJP	Democratic Justice Party
DRP	Democratic Republican Party

FEER	Far Eastern Economic Review
FSC	Federal Shariat Court
GDP	Gross Domestic Product
GHQ	General Headquarters
GNP	Gross National Product
ICS	Indian Civil Service
IJI	*Islami Jamhuri Ittehad*
IMET	International Military Education and Training Program
INP	Integrated National Police
IPG	Independent Parliamentary Group
ISI	Inter-Services Intelligence
JP	Jatiya Party
JTU	Japanese Teacher's Union
JUSMAG	Joint US Military Advisory Group
KBL	New Society Movement (*Kilusang Bagong Lipunan*)
KCIA	Korean Central Intelligence Agency
KMA	Korean Military Academy
KNU	Karen National Union
LDP	*Labang Demokratikong Pilipino*
MAP	Military Assistance Program
MBA	Military Bases Agreement
MCP	Communist Party of Malaysia
MND	Ministry of National Defence
MNLF	Moro National Liberation Front
MQM	*Muhajir Quami* Movement
MRD	Movement for Restoration of Democracy

NBC	National Broadcasting Commission
NCO	Non-Commissioned Officer
NICs	Newly Industrialized Countries
NISA	National Intelligence and Security Authority
NKDP	New Korea Democratic Party
NLD	National League for Democracy
NPA	New People's Army
NSC	National Security Council
NSI	National Security Intelligence
NUP	National Unity Party
OPG	Official Parliamentary Group
OPM	*Organisasi Papua Merdeka*
PC	Philippine Constabulary
PCO	Provisional Constitution Order
PDI	Indonesian Democratic Party
PETA	*Pembela Tanah Ayer*
PFF	Police Field Force
PIM	Pacific Island Monthly
PKI	Communist Party of Indonesia
PMA	Philippine Military Academy
PML	Pakistan Muslim League
PNA	Pakistan National Alliance
PNG	Papua New Guinea
PNGDF	Papua New Guinea Defence Force
PNI	Indonesian National Party
PPP	Pakistan People's Party
PSI	Indonesian Socialist Party

RAM	Reform the Armed Forces Movement
RCO	Revival of Constitution Order
RFMF	Royal/Republic of Fiji Military Forces
ROK	Republic of Korea
RPIR	Royal Pacific Infantry Regiment
RUCs	Regional Unified Commands
SACs	Security and Administration Committees
SAP	Social Action Party (Chat Thai)
SEATO	South East Asia Treaty Organization
SIPRI	Stockholm International Peace Research Institute
SLORC	State Law and Order Restoration Council
UMNO	United Malays National Organization
UN	United Nations
UNP	United National Party
USAFFE	United States Armed Forces in the Far East
WAFP	Civilian Home Defense Force
YOURS	Young Officers Union at Your Service

Foreword

As the "winds of change" swept across Africa, Asia and the Pacific in the late 1940s and 1950s, colonial powers, for the most part, strove to create viable post-colonial states in more-or-less their own image. Independence constitutions provided the frameworks for participatory democracies in which there was, typically, a clear separation of powers and in which armies were subservient to civilian authorities. Within a comparatively short space of time, however, many post-colonial states had abandoned such models in favour of one-party-dominant states or military regimes. In the words of Gerald Heeger (1974) there was a general shift "from the politics of development to the politics of order". Reactions to this tendency among students of political change varied: what for one was a (regrettable) "decline of constitutional democracy" (Feith 1962, on Indonesia) was seen by another as "the river of Asian history [returning] towards its original and natural course" (Benda 1964, reviewing Feith). On at least three points, however, there seems to have been general agreement: first, that the military is seldom a monolithic organization operating as an independent agent; second, that there is no simple relationship between militaries and regime types; and third, that in most Third World countries the military has the potential to initiate, or to prevent, substantial regime changes, and that such actions are not always predictable.

The countries of Asia and the Pacific provide a variety of case studies on the role of the military, ranging from repressive military regimes to small states without armies. In many, the military has either displaced a civilian government, has become a partner in government, or remains a potential threat to civilian rule. And in most it seems likely to have a significant influence on future political developments. Yet, surprisingly, the literature on the military in Asia and the Pacific is sparse, and such analyses as there have been are mostly particularistic, eschewing a comparative approach.

It was in this context that in November-December 1989 a conference was organized by the Department of Political and Social

Change in the Research School of Pacific Studies, Australian National University, to consider "The Armed Forces in Asia and the Pacific: Prospects for the 1990s". The conference was organized within the framework of the department's research program on Regime Change and Regime Maintenance in Asia and the Pacific, by Viberto Selochan, then a Ph.D. scholar in the department completing a thesis on "Professionalization and Politicization of the Armed Forces of the Philippines". The conference drew together scholars from Australia, Indonesia, Malaysia, Thailand, Japan, Papua New Guinea and the UK. A dozen papers looked at the recent political history, and future prospects, of those countries in Asia and the Pacific in which the military had played a significant recent role in government or in which it seemed possible that it might do so in the future. Not all the papers presented at the conference are included here, and some have been added; but most of the contributions to this volume were first presented in draft form in Canberra in 1989, and Luckham's lengthy introduction had its genesis as a brief conference overview.

There is still much to be investigated, reflected upon and written about concerning the diverse roles the military has played, and is likely to play, in the politics of Asian and Pacific countries and the comparative perspectives which Asian and Pacific countries have to offer to the broader literature on the military in politics. In part this will be a continuing interest of the Regime Change and Regime Maintenance project. In the meantime, this volume makes a substantial contribution to a sparse literature.

R. J. May
Senior Fellow and Head of the Department
of Political and Social Change,
The Australian National University

Acknowledgments

Organizing a conference and editing the papers are time consuming and lengthy processes in which many people take part. It is therefore impossible to thank everyone individually.

I must, however, acknowledge the following. My thanks to the authors for being prompt in returning their revised chapters.

The staff at the Department of Political and Social Change at the Australian National University, Canberra, were supportive during the planning of the conference. My thanks to all of them.

Special thanks are due to Dr. Ron J. May, without whose support and assistance the conference and book would not have eventuated. Thanks to Alex Bellis for her assistance in the organization of the conference. Thanks are also due to Claire Smith, whose help I was constantly seeking.

Bev Fraser knows the story of putting the papers together for publication. Bev has given unflinching support in this process and has done much to bring this book to fruition. I am therefore most grateful to her.

Viberto Selochan

About the
Editor and Contributors

Chowdhury R. Abrar is an assistant professor in the Department of International Politics, Dhaka University. He is a graduate of Sussex University, England, and completed his Ph.D. on the authoritarian state in Bangladesh at Griffith University, Queensland. Abrar has published articles on Bangladesh politics and society.

Suchit Bunbongkarn is professor and head of the Department of Government at the Political Science Faculty, Chulalongkorn University, Bangkok. He was an adviser to former Prime Minister Prem Tinsulanoud from 1981 to 1987. He has published widely on Thai politics. His most recent publication is: *The Thai Military in Politics 1981-1986* (1987).

James Cotton (Ph.D., London School of Economics) is a senior research fellow in the Northeast Asia Program, Department of International Relations, Australian National University, Canberra. He is author of *Asian Frontier Nationalism: Owen Lattimer and the American Policy Debate* (1989) and editor of *The Korean War in History* (1989), as well as various studies on Asian Pacific politics and international relations and political theory. His current research is concerned with the politics of the Asian NICs.

Harold Crouch is a senior fellow in the Research School of Pacific Studies, the Australian National University. Previously he was associate professor of political science at the National University of Malaysia. He is the author of *The Army and Politics in Indonesia* (1978) and co-editor of *Military-Civilian Relations in Southeast Asia* (1985).

Robin Luckham holds joint appointments at the Peace Research Centre of the Australian National University and at the Institute of Development Studies at the University of Sussex, England. He has published *The Nigerian Military* (1971) and edited *Soldiers and Politicians in Ghana* (1976), as well as other books and articles on the military, Third World security issues and disarmament and development.

Jim Sanday held the rank of lieutenant colonel in the pre-coup Royal Fiji Military Forces. He was a visiting fellow at the Strategic and Defence Studies Centre at the Research School of Pacific Studies at the Australian National University. He is presently a Canberra-based regional defence analyst. Sanday has published widely on the post-coup Fijian military. His most recent publication is *Fiji: Anatomy of a Crisis* (1990).

Yaw Saffu is a professor of politics at the University of Papua New Guinea and head of the Department of Political and Administrative Studies. He has published widely on the politics of Papua New Guinea. Since 1984 Saffu has written the PNG 'Political Chronicles' in the *Australian Journal of Politics and History*.

Viberto Selochan is a research fellow at the Centre for the Study of Australia-Asia Relations at Griffith University, Queensland. The subject of his doctorate was the Armed Forces of the Philippines and he has since published several articles on the Philippine military; his most recent book is *Could the Military Govern the Philippines?* (1989). His current research is on Asia-Pacific security.

Robert H. Taylor is a professor of politics at the University of London and head of the Department of Political Studies at the School of Oriental and African Studies. His recent publications include *The State in Burma* (1987) and *Marxism and Resistance in Burma* (1985). He teaches both comparative politics and international politics with reference to Asia.

Samina Yasmeen is a lecturer in international politics at the University of Western Australia. She has published articles on South Asian politics, Chinese policy towards Pakistan and other issues in international relations. She is currently examining the strategic implications of the Kashmir dispute.

xix

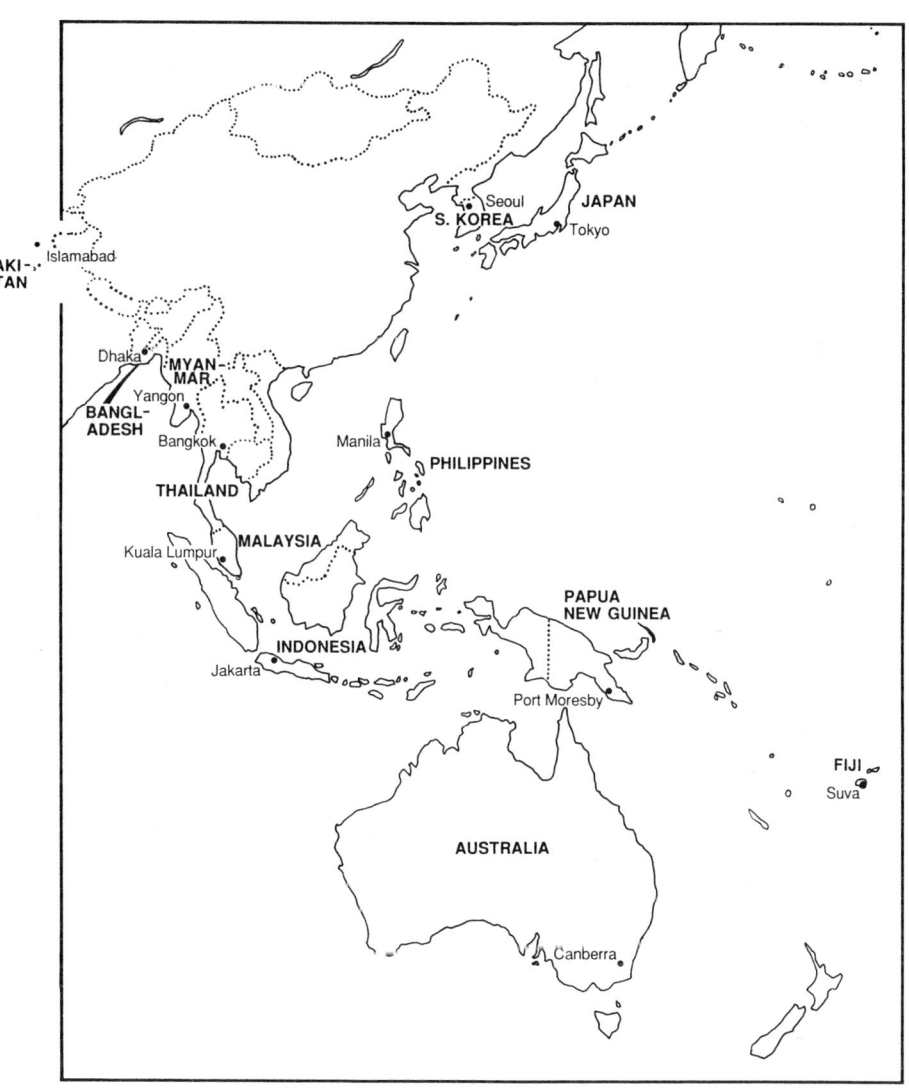

Map of Asia and the Pacific

1

Introduction: The Military, the Developmental State and Social Forces in Asia and the Pacific: Issues for Comparative Analysis

Robin Luckham

In this chapter I present some ideas about the analysis of the military and its relations to the state, social forces and development. As a longtime observer of Third World and African, rather than Asian and Pacific military establishments, I paint with a broad brush, relying on my reading of the chapters in this book and other secondary sources.

Nobody can fail to be impressed by the immense historical and cultural diversity of the region. The armed forces of the smaller and more impoverished states, such as Papua New Guinea (PNG), Fiji or indeed Bangladesh, can be readily compared with African armies. On the other hand those of states like South Korea Thailand, Malaysia, Indonesia, Pakistan and India are qualitatively different in size, equipment and professional competence. Moreover they draw (in varying degrees) upon the resources of dynamic industrializing market economies and relatively autonomous, effective state machines.

I shall focus on eight major issues, or groups of issues, which in my view any serious analysis of the military must address. Some are considered at length in the chapters below, others less fully. Some are the standard fare of the existing literature on Third World military establishments, others point up gaps and contradictions in that literature. Throughout I shall emphasize the problematic and contested nature of the military as a distinct object of study. The more one looks at it, the more it decomposes, like the vanishing smile of the Cheshire cat, into the turbulent social and political forces that swirl round it. Yet the more one seeks to explain its role in relation to those forces, the more its military specificity is brought (like the smile) back into focus.

1. Historical Contexts: End of Empire, Cold War and State Formation

The states of Asia and the Pacific, and their armed forces, are the product of very particular historical conditions. Demands for independent statehood and for national armies to act as its standard bearers arose, as in other postcolonial states, from the confrontation between a process of state formation which began under colonial rule, and struggles for national self-determination waged outside, indeed against, the colonial state, and sometimes continuing against its post-colonial successors. In other words, they were born from fundamentally contradictory processes, establishing different syntheses between state and nation in each national case.

The great historical watershed was World War II. It was even more of a watershed in Asia than in other Third World regions, for four main reasons. First, because Japan had driven its armies deep into the heart of the colonial empires, and in the process had fractured their monopolies of organised force and claims to legitimate authority. Second, because from the moment of victory the United States had turned its efforts to containing communism, establishing a hegemonic "grand area" on the Pacific rim (Cumings 1988: 71), exporting its capital, and restructuring the military establishments of strategically situated Asian states. Third, because the War had at the same time catalysed national liberation and revolutionary movements, which continued their struggles during the post-war period, especially in the former French and Dutch colonial empires, where colonial credibility had been most severely called in question. And fourth, because the consolidation of socialism in China, North Korea, and eventually Indochina, confronted US and European imperial control. In sum, the end of empire and the onset of the Cold War were inextricable; and both together shaped the military institutions and security arrangements of post-colonial states.

Yet analyses of Asian military establishments have tended to abstract them from these formative historical experiences, to measure them against ideal-typical models of modernity, military professionalism and civil-military relations.[1] Such ideal-types must be treated with more than a little caution, since they have typically been extrapolated (often with insufficient respect for the historical record) from the historical experiences of Europe and the United States. Moreover, they have been used to establish blueprints for the managed transfer of military institutions to the region after independence. In this sense, they have not just been analytical tools, but also aspects of the phenomena which require analysis.

A broad distinction can be made between military establishments which arose out of colonial state-formation, and those which sprang from struggles for national emancipation; in other words from each of the two terms of the contradiction referred to earlier. Those established under colonial tutelage were indoctrinated (seldom successfully) "to accept the Western liberal concepts of apolitical professionalism and civilian supremacy" (Crouch 1985a: 288). Those which originated from anti-colonial armies and took part in struggles for national independence, were overtly political from their inception.

In the former category are the great majority of the ex-British states, including India, Pakistan, Sri Lanka, Malaysia, Singapore, Fiji and most Pacific island countries, together with Papua New Guinea (sharing a similar, ex-Australian, colonial heritage), and the Philippines (whose armed forces were developed on an American professional model, devised by a 1935 US Military Mission headed by General MacArthur). Bangladesh arguably belongs in the same group, despite having fought a war of national independence against Pakistan, since the national military establishment created after the war drew on the professional traditions and the former soldiers of the Pakistan army, largely excluding the former partisan forces.

The armies of these post-colonial states, even more than the state structures they defend, have been deeply influenced by their colonial origins. They were established in the colonial bureaucratic mode, as the ultimate custodians of domestic law and order, more than for external defence. Most were indigenised through a planned, though often in practice hastily improvised, process of "institutional transfer", aimed at cloning professional military establishments from the metropolitan model. After independence that model was reproduced through military assistance programs, professional training schemes and transfers of weapons and political technologies, both by the former colonial countries and by other powers. This assistance contributed to the expansion of military influence, thus contributing to the pathology of the "overdeveloped" state. However, from this common colonial matrix there developed quite different relations between armies, states and social forces, owing at least as much to local circumstances as to the imposed colonial frame.

The second category includes most former French and Dutch colonial possessions, along with the former British territory of Burma (now Myanmar). It subdivides between those states where nationalist movements, in alliance with anti-colonial armies, took control of the state after relatively limited confrontations with weakened colonial powers, as in Indonesia and Myanmar; and those in which there were protracted liberation wars, developing into struggles for socialist transformation as well as national emancipation, as in Vietnam, Laos and Cambodia.[2] The latter belong within a wider family of post-revolutionary socialist states, including China and North Korea. However, their distinctive party-controlled military establishments are not dealt with in this book.

Two countries fit into neither category, namely Thailand and South Korea. The former can be conveniently grouped with Indonesia and Myanmar, despite the fact that it was never colonised. Its military establishment lays claim to a legitimacy myth extending back to the 1932 coup, when it intervened to support a popular uprising against the absolute monarchy; although only to replace it with a military-dominated oligarchy, which continued to rule in partnership with the palace. South Korea's armed forces, on the other hand, emerged out of a largely discredited (Japanese) colonial tradition. The most decisive influence by far on their professional role and attitude to politics was their wholesale reconstruction, with US assistance, as the lynch-pin of an anti-communist garrison state.

How much significance can be attached to such historical differences? This is not an easy question to answer, because of complex changes since independence. One way of summarising them might be to say that they have consisted of double movement. In most post-colonial states, political, economic and social forces have corroded the apolitical professionalism of the armed forces, though in varying degrees from country to country. However, in states brought to independence through national revolutions the reverse has occurred. The state has reclaimed the nationalist revolution with the assistance of the military establishment; the latter meanwhile having been reprofessionalized with the assistance of external powers. At the same time post-colonial and anti-colonial armies have *both* been inserted into a neo-colonial security framework, whose contours have been jointly defined by the Cold War and by the place of the national economies of the region in a changing international division of labour.

Indeed it seems to be in countries which most explicitly severed their colonial links, where the state has become most militarised. The armed forces of both Indonesia and Myanmar forged their identity in the course of national independence struggles and civil wars during and after World War II. They played an important role in helping to establish the structure of civil administration during the transition to independence. Their founding generations of military "freedom fighters" still to this day claim guardianship of the independence revolutions. And even if the historical veracity of this claim is open to debate, there is little doubt as to its ideological appeal. In each country the military has used the past to legitimize both its own appropriation of the state, and the state's reassertion of itself over the social forces competing with each other in the nation's name (on Indonesia, see Anderson 1983a). It has been as "nation-builders" as well as architects of state security, that the armed forces have staked out a developmental mandate.

Before the armed forces could seize the state and restructure it in a military image, they had to consolidate their professional and material base. In Indonesia the armed forces slowly built up their competence during campaigns to subjugate a rebellious periphery; with military assistance from outside powers, including the USA (for the army) and the USSR (for the navy and air force). Their economic position was consolidated when they were made responsible for nationalised enterprises taken over from Dutch firms after 1957. Not only did their commercial operations make them to a significant degree self-financing, they also enhanced their political autonomy. The armed forces also acquired a direct stake in class relations, becoming (indirectly) major employers of wage labour. As such they suffered from the hyper-inflation and economic stagnation of the early 1960s, and had to cope directly with labour unrest. President Sukarno's attempts to counterbalance them by strengthening the Indonesian Communist Party (PKI), only antagonised them further.

The military's seizure of power was thus triggered by the failure of Sukarno's "Guided Democracy" to produce either development or national unity. However, shifts in power within the military establishment itself were also crucial, deriving from its professionalization and its new roles in the process of capital accumulation. After an abortive coup attempt by left-wing officers in 1965, another faction in the army staged a counter-coup, and systematically destroyed the PKI, organising the massacre and incarceration of hundreds of thousands of the latter's alleged supporters, including large sections of the non-communist left; at the same time isolating President Sukarno, and then removing him from office in 1967.

The "New Order" instituted by General Soeharto was founded upon military control of the state, capitalist development funded initially by foreign aid and oil rents, anti-communism and close military and security ties with the United States. It was in this manner that the military's revolutionary generation became flag-bearers for a counter-revolution and shifted the country from non-alignment, into effective Cold War partnership with the West.

In Myanmar, however, the equivalent "revolutionary generation" of officers headed by General Ne Win charted a somewhat different historical course. The Burma Independence Army formed by nationalist politicians participated in Japan's invasion of Burma in 1942; but its leaders were soon secretly organising resistance to Japanese occupation under the banner of the Anti-Fascist Peoples' Freedom Movement. After the War fresh armed conflicts arose from the exclusion of the Burma Communist Party from power and the government's insensitive handling of ethnic minorities. At the height of these conflicts in 1949-50 the military was elevated to partnership in the government. It was called in again by the politicians to form a caretaker government and hold the country together in 1958; and subsequently took power in its own right in a 1962 coup.

Yet in contrast to the Indonesian junta, the Burmese military government attempted to coopt and outflank the left by establishing its own Burma Socialist Programme Party (BSPP). The new military order was state socialist, autarkic and non-aligned. And though external powers did not rush in with military and economic support as in Indonesia, they did not actively destabilize the regime either. Instead it was treated as a strategic buffer between the Indian subcontinent and the communist regimes on its borders.

In both Southeast and Northeast Asia, the Cold War overshadowed decolonisation. In China, North Korea, Vietnam, Laos, and Cambodia anti-imperial struggles eventually brought communist regimes to power, with their own brand of socialist militarism. In the remaining countries, anti-communist regimes were installed, most of them supported by large-scale Western military and economic assistance.

Some of the latter were in effect garrison states. South Korea was one of the most clearcut instances, arising from the subdivision of

Korea between the communist North and non-communist South after World War II. The Korean War, which both resulted from and confirmed this subdivision, turned both Koreas into permanent armed camps. The consolidation of South Korea's state machine, accumulation in the economy, and the build-up of a formidably well equipped army, were facilitated by massive injections of US military and economic aid. Military influence, even in periods when the military did not formally hold power, became rooted both in the state structure, and in latter's pursuit of rapid industrial growth.

Thailand and the Philippines were also pulled into the Cold War, whilst not being quite as close to its vortex as Korea. The former was the only country in South and South-East Asia never directly colonised. The Philippines was the sole country which came to independence under American tutelage. In each of these states World War II, together with periods of direct (in the Philippines) and indirect (in Thailand) Japanese over-rule, catalysed a modernisation of both the state and the armed forces. Thailand was dragged into the Cold War by its geographical proximity to Indochina and Malaysia, the anti-communism of its military and political elites and its own home-grown communist insurgency. The Philippines also faced major left-wing revolts, beginning with the Huk rebellion soon after World War II. At the same time it was central to US strategic planning, due to the presence of large American naval and air force bases. Its armed forces, like those of Thailand, were enlarged and restructured for counter-insurgency operations, receiving substantial US military assistance. Yet at the same time their professionalization was hindered by the political nature of counter-insurgency, and by the manifold personal interconnections between the military elite and other fractions of the political class.

Malaysia was placed on the front line of the Cold War by the eruption of the anti-communist Emergency soon after World War II. However, the main military operations were concluded before independence in 1957. Although the communists fought on, the Cold War did not dominate the political process quite as directly as in South Korea. Furthermore, anti-communism was mediated through ethnic differences between Malays, Indians and Chinese, on which the colonial administration played skilfully during its counter-insurgency campaign. Britain handed over an army in which the political privileges of the Malay Bumiputra elite were entrenched in military recruitment. The army's anti-communism was subsumed within its support for a Malay-dominated ruling class. It was correspondingly less tempted to make itself a state within the state, as in South Korea.

Colonially managed transitions to statehood were far from uniform in their timing and results. India, Pakistan and Sri Lanka acceeded to independence soon after World War II. Malaya had to wait until 1957; Malaysia was formed as a federal state in 1963; and Singapore withdrew from it to become independent in its own right in 1965. In Fiji, PNG, and the other Pacific island states, the transfer of power took place still later, and to states which remained considerably more dependent for their survival on different forms of international support.

Most former colonial states have reverted in one form or another to the colonial practice of non-representative, bureaucratic governance. In some, military coups have swept aside the representative parliamentary democracies established by independence constitutions. In others, democratic procedures and practices have been eroded from within, through the accumulation of power in the hands of ruling classes, and the gradual erosion of constitutional protections.

Fiji provides an especially striking example of the continuing influence of colonial structures. From the time paramount chief Ratu Seru Cabokau's Royal Army was formed under British officers in 1871, the military has supported "the authority and interests of the chiefly establishment as well as defending structures created by the state to support a capitalist economy" (Sanday, chapter 11, below, p.242). The coups of 1987 once again enlisted the military in support of chiefly power, although in the process it emerged as a political force in its own right.

Nevertheless in some countries—India, Sri Lanka, Malaysia, Papua New Guinea (PNG) and most other Pacific island states—the colonial principle of the subordination of the military and police to the civil power, along with one version or other of parliamentary democracy, have precariously survived. However, democracy has been qualified by periods of emergency rule, restrictions on human rights, manipulations of the franchise, and use of the police and military to enforce public order and repress dissent. As during the colonial period, military establishments have upheld systems of rule based on varying mixtures of force, cooptation and exploitation.

Independence has also produced a significant, though by no means uniform, pluralisation of statehood and of the military establishment. Indeed in the Indian subcontinent this pluralisation led to a partition of the state and of the armed forces: between India and Pakistan in 1947, and between the latter and Bangladesh in 1971. From these partitions there emerged divergent relations between armies and states. In Pakistan and Bangladesh fragile states succumbed to military rule. Yet in India the military has never once attempted to displace the country's ramshackle and tumultuous representative democracy[3] despite politico-economic crises at least as severe as those in states where armies have seized power. Elsewhere in the region, post-colonial states have held together, though often only as a result of *force majeure*, including the coercion of dissident minorities. At the same time the pluralisation of statehood has been reproduced in the recruitment quotas and intricate ethnic politics of the military establishment (discussed in section 7 below).

2. Military Coups, Regime Change and Democratisation

The literature on the military has tended to make a fetish of the coup. It contains long shopping lists of factors said to "explain" intervention. Some of these emphasise the structure and behaviour of the armed forces themselves: their professionalism, or lack of it; discontent about having to repress civil unrest; corporate ambitions and grievances; breakdown of discipline; career dislocations; regional, ethnic or class divisions; cliques and factions; and personal ambitions and career disappointments, such as those which allegedly motivated Lieutenant Colonel Rabuka to seize power in Fiji.

Some consider military intervention a product of social forces external to the military itself: those brought into being by macro-societal crises of modernisation, political disorder or decay, economic dislocations, foreign intervention, or external dependence. Others focus on the interplay between such external factors and military structures and arrangements (Luckham 1971a) on the armed forces' organisational boundaries; their relationships with the police and other security bureaucracies; state-military relations; and the complex pathologies of "praetorianism", "bonapartism", or "caesarism".

Checklists of these explanations are sometimes useful, as much to eliminate factors which do not apply in individual cases as to identify those which do. In chapter 5 below, for instance, Crouch goes through such a list to ask why the military has not staged coups in Malaysia, despite the presence of some of the normal correlates of intervention (and the absence of others). However, the literature has seemingly come up with more explanations, at varying levels of analysis, than there are coups to be explained. It is all too tempting to pick out from this array of factors those which seem *ex post facto* to provide plausible answers in each national case, whilst neglecting comparative and causal analysis.

Various attempts have been made to assemble different variables, or groups of them, into broad-guage explanatory frames. Yet it seems we are little closer than we were quarter of a century ago to producing a parsimonious body of theory that would "adequately explain why coups happen in some countries and not others" (Horowitz 1980: 3), whilst taking account of the genuine diversity of interventions in different national situations.

Some of the difficulty arises from making the coup as such the primary focus of enquiry. The very frequency of coups, and the difficulty of making sharp distinctions between countries where they have and have not occurred, undermines the notion that they are in all cases politically significant events. If most regimes in developing countries remain vulnerable to military intervention, what purpose is served by analysing why the army has intervened in one instance rather than another?

Rather than analysing coups as such, we might do better to consider them as part of a much wider process of transformation: firstly as a subcategory of a broader class of regime changes or political transitions; and secondly as one among several different channels through which military power can influence politics.

Indeed this would seem to be the direction in which the case studies presented in this volume take us. Some describe the circumstances in which military interventions have occurred (Thailand, Pakistan, Bangladesh, Indonesia, Myanmar, South Korea, Fiji), some those in which they have been attempted (Philippines), and some those in which they may or may not occur at some future time (PNG, Malaysia).

Yet it is far from certain that all these coups and potential coups have been the same kind of event. Some have been coups in office, orchestrated by existing governments to change their own personnel, policy direction or constitutional status. An example is General Park's suspension of the South Korean constitution in the name of the *Yusin* or revitalising reform program in 1972. Some have effected transitions from one military-dominated government to another, like the transfer of power in Pakistan from General Ayub Khan to General Yahya Khan in 1969 (although formally General Ayub was an elected President). Some have replaced military governments by civilians, as after the assassination of General Ziaur Rahman during an army revolt in Bangladesh in 1981 (though it is not clear that this was the outcome intended by the conspirators; and in any case the new civilian regime lasted no more than a few months). In some instances the military has helped remove one civilian government, to replace it with another, as in the Armed Forces of the Philippines' (AFP) participation in the 1986 "People's

Power" rebellion against President Marcos. And in other cases the armed forces have staged proto-typical coups, displacing civilian governments, including the 1958 and 1977 coups in Pakistan; the 1961 coup in South Korea; the 1962 coup in Burma; the 1965-8 military takeover in Indonesia; the 1975 coup in Bangladesh; the 1987 coups in Fiji.

However, in virtually all these cases the words "coup" or "military intervention" are impoverished characterisations of the totality of a complex train of historical events. The advent of the military to power in Indonesia, for instance, was spread out over three years: including an aborted coup by left-wing officers in 1965, a counter-coup, the wholesale slaughter of members of the PKI, General Soeharto's effective assumption of power in 1966, and only then the formal replacement of President Sukarno by General Soeharto in 1967. The 1961 coup in South Korea, the 1962 coup in Burma, the 1977 coup in Pakistan and the 1975 coup in Bangladesh all took place against a background of major civil unrest, which played as central a part in the historical drama as the coups themselves.

The 1975 Bangladesh coup was brought to a head by the assassination of Bangladesh's first President, Sheikh Mujibir Rahman, by rebel army officers cooperating with dissident members of the Awami League Party, though it had been preceded by what had been tantamount to a civilian coup in office, under which Sheikh Mujib's government had declared a State of Emergency, curtailed fundamental rights, established a one party state and stepped up coercion by the paramilitary *Rakkhi Bahini*. Six years later the new military President, General Ziaur Rahman, was also cut down by the bullets of rebellious soldiers, to be succeeded by an elected civilian government, in turn dismissed in 1982 by General Ershad after only three months in office. Ershad's regime itself was overthrown by major civilian demonstrations and strikes toward the end of 1990, which the military and police were unable or unwilling to suppress. There was no coup as such, yet the dismissal of the regime ultimately hinged on the fact that the armed forces did not carry out the orders of an established government.

Not only have the interventions been diverse and complex events, their consequences for the exercise of state power have differed greatly, and not always in proportion to the trauma and violence inflicted. A broad distinction may be made between interventions which have merely changed the composition of the existing government; those which have removed the government without changing the regime (the latter being distinct from the former because it refers to the ensemble of norms and practices which regulate the exercise and distribution of political power, rather than the particular governing circle which exercises that power); those which have replaced both government and regime; those where the armed forces have brought regimes down in order to abort major political, social or economic changes; and those where, to the contrary, they have intervened to both change the regime and transform the prevailing balance of social and economic forces.

On the face of it coups displacing elected civilian governments to install military juntas can be described as regime changes; and likewise with transitions in the opposite direction, from military or authoritarian rule to democracy. For military takeovers not only transfer the institutional locus of power from the state's ideological apparatuses (parties, legislatures, civilian politicians etc.) to its repressive apparatuses (the military, police, security bureaucracies etc.). They typically alter the rules of the political game, for instance by introducing martial law, banning political activity, abolishing constitutional checks and balances, curtailing press freedom, disregarding human rights and using coercion.

Nevertheless the installation of a military government by no means always adds up to a change of regime. The military may already have established itself as the power behind the throne in advance of the coup. The displaced civilian government may itself have been ruling arbitrarily, perhaps even more so than the soldiers replacing it. Or conversely the military government may preserve the trappings of constitutional rule, representative institutions and party politics, seeing itself as an arbitrator between contending civilian claimants on power. The point is that it cannot be assumed that regime change has taken place without detailed scrutiny of how political norms and practices have actually been altered in particular national circumstances.

Coups may also be staged to *conserve* a regime, the existing socio-economic order, or both together. The Fiji interventions of 1987 are a case in point. The first coup initiated a conservative counter-revolution, reversing the verdict of an election which had produced the first major realignment of political forces in the country since independence. The second was staged to put pressure on the conservative alliance of politicians and chiefs, whom the military had installed, not to compromise with the politicians it had ousted, to provide stronger constitutional guarantees for ethnic Fijian interests, and to institutionalise the military's role in the political process. Both interventions were intended to restore an *ancien regime* in which the norms and practices of ethnic Fijian chiefly power would operate in tandem with the constitutional procedures of representative democracy. This implied preservation of the structure of class, ethnic and regional domination on which that regime had rested. Yet in the process the framework of constitutional government itself was impaired, perhaps irretrievably; and the balance of social forces was tilted even further in favour of the previously dominant classes and groups. Like the coup which overthrew President Allende of Chile in 1973, the Fijian interventions were conservative. But like that coup, they have initiated changes which have made it difficult if not impossible to go back to the *status quo ante*.

Military interventions which have initiated basic structural transformations have been few and far between. Yet they are crucial for our understanding of the relationship between military power and political change. Any list of military revolutions from above would surely have to include the 1965-8 events ushering in the New Order in Indonesia. The military elite which was brought to power by these events transformed the balance of political and social forces by liquidating the social base of the communist and non-communist left, turning around the country's external alliances, and initiating the capitalist restructuring of the economy. Likewise the South Korean coup of 1961 brought to power a military government which dedicated itself to achieving rapid economic growth, promoted by an interventionist state, again within the framework of a capitalist economy.

From a purely ideological point of view, of course, both the Indonesian and the South Korean interventions might be regarded as conservative coups or counter-revolutions, blocking off any prospect of popular revolution or transition to socialism. Yet the transformations they brought about were no less major for being inspired by capitalism rather than socialism, and for consolidating dominant rather than subordinated classes. For what made them distinctive was their unique combination of conservatism and genuine capitalist transformation.

Indeed it is notable that nowhere in Asia or the Pacific have there been radical or socialist military revolutions from above, comparable, say, to those attempted in in Ethiopia or Peru. (Halliday and Molyneux 1981; Trimberger 1978). Myanmar's failed experiment in autarkic state socialism under General Ne Win comes the closest. Nevertheless, the regime's proclamation of socialism and creation of the BSPP party preempted the spread of communism and helped consolidate a military-bureaucratic ruling class.

It may help put military intervention into perspective if we note that there are a number of countries in the Asia-Pacific region where the military has either not attempted coups at all, or has failed in its attempts to stage them. Some of these, like India and Malaysia, have enjoyed considerable political stability and (in varying degrees) representative government under civilian rule. Others, like Singapore, have evolved more authoritarian systems of rule. And others, like the Philippines and arguably PNG, have survived precariously through perpetual regimes of unrest. Yet although the military has remained in the wings in each of these contrasting cases, it has usually been a major actor in the political process by virtue of its proximity to the repressive apparatuses of the state. For military politics neither begin, nor end, with the staging of military coups.

Moreover, by no means all the most crucial political transitions, even those in which military force has been used, have involved coups d'etat. In Malaysia, for instance, the anti-communist Emergency, waged under British military tutelage, shaped the independence settlement, and ensured that Malay-dominated political, bureaucratic and military elites would emerge as the joint guarantors of the post-independence order. The latter in turn established a relatively secure political framework for rapid economic growth. In Singapore the elected post-independence government of Lee Kuan Yew rapidly transformed itself into an authoritarian and extremely effective regime, suppressing all attempts to organise democratic opposition under the ubiquitous Internal Security Acts, without having to stage a coup. Moreover it has used state power to effect a capitalist restructuring from above comparable in scope to that of South Korea, and to build up a well-equipped military machine.

Indonesia underwent three seminal political transitions: the post-1945 independence revolution; the collapse of liberal democracy and the establishment of authoritarian rule (under the political formula of Guided Democracy) in 1957-9; and the installation of the New Order during 1965-7. In each transition the deployment of military force was crucial. Yet only the latter involved a coup, or rather an interlocking sequence of coups and counter-coups. Even then it was the political and social upheavals initiated by the military's seizure of power; and the massive use of force by the security forces to destroy the social base of the PKI and restructure the polity, rather than the coup *per se*, that made the shift to the New Order so decisive.

The revolution which created Bangladesh was sparked by resistance to a coup which had deprived the Bengali-based Awami League of an electoral victory in Pakistan. It took the form of a liberation war, helped on its way by India's invasion of Pakistan. As we have seen none of Bangladesh's three subsequent political transitions, in 1975, 1981-2 and 1990 were straight-forward coups.

The first two involved a complex sequence of public disturbances, assassinations, military revolts, and counter-coups organised by the military hierarchy. Yet despite all the trauma, the new regimes did not differ significantly from their predecessors, either in their social base, or policies, or capacity to manage the economy. The changes of 1981-2 indeed merely ended up by replacing one military government with another, recirculating power within the military elite rather than changing the regime. In contrast the civilian insurrection of 1990 not only brought General Ershad's government to its knees but looks set to restore some form of democracy.

Some of the most seminal political events have not been coups, but rather transitions in the opposite direction, toward more democratic and plural political systems, as in Thailand, South Korea, Pakistan, the Philippines and now Bangladesh. In some cases the armed forces have negotiated reductions in their political role, bringing about a managed (yet seldom completely smooth) transfer of power from military to civilian hands, as in Thailand since 1978, South Korea since 1987, and Pakistan in 1988. In each case considerable civilian pressure was required to extract concessions from the military. In others, military or authoritarian regimes have been literally forced from power by popular insurrections, as in the Philippines in 1986, Bangladesh in 1990 and (very nearly) Myanmar in 1988.

Yet even so, the armed forces' own stance has been crucial, whether in support of the insurrection as in the Philippines, in hesitant neutrality as in Bangladesh, or against it as in Myanmar. The latter is the exception which proves the rule. Economic dislocations and massive anti-government demonstrations brought the regime to the verge of collapse by September 1988, with troops beginning to discuss joining the revolution. However, the leaders of the army, acting on behalf of Ne Win, restructured the government under an all-military State Law and and Order Restoration Council (SLORC), abrogated the constitution and ordered army units to fire on the demonstrators (for an illuminating account of these events see Silverstein 1990:122-8). Although the regime conceded elections in 1990, which the National Unity Party (a reconfigured BSPP) lost humiliatingly, it proceeded to ignore the results and to incarcerate its opponents; being able to do so with impunity largely because of the initial show of force which had demobilised the opposition in 1988.

In contrast the Philippines "People's Power" revolution ran its full course because military units not only refused to turn their guns on the civilians, but actually joined them on the streets. However, it provides a particularly salient illustration of the difficulties of defining political transitions. Was it a popular uprising with military support, or a military coup with civilian support? Did it live up to its billing as a people's power revolution, or even as a change of regime? Or did it in the final analysis merely circulate power within the country's narrow ruling class?

Military withdrawals have sometimes been analysed as if they are in effect interventions in reverse. For it might seem that they can be explained by reversing the signs on all the factors accounting for coups: economic prosperity rather than decline, consolidation of the class structure, a more diverse civil society, stronger civilian institutions, the professionalization and depolitizisation of the military establishment, etc. Nevertheless it cannot be said that enumerations of the benign conditions for military withdrawal bring us any closer to adequate explanation—any more than listing adverse conditions supposedly responsible for coups. Such enumerations are incomplete in that they deal primarily with the conditions for transition from military but not (as in the Philippines under Marcos) civilian autocracy. And they are ahistorical, since the task of reversing the legacy of years of arbitrary rule is bound to differ from the preservation of already functioning representative governments. Indeed such governments have survived against all the odds in countries such as India or PNG—despite the fact that they lack many of the basic "conditions of democracy", and are similar in social structure and levels of development to many countries where the military has seized and held on to political power.

Merely by being in office, military and authoritarian governments have transformed the political, social and economic conditions under which they came to power. For instance during their twenty eight years in office the military rulers of Myanmar, described below by Taylor (chapter 6), have destroyed alternative power bases and delayed the emergence of social forces which might challenge military dominance, despite the build-up of massive popular discontent. In effect the military and security bureaucracies have constituted themselves into the country's major power bloc, directly in control of the economy as well as government. Hence their interests will have to be catered for, or at the very least neutralised, in any post-military order, as the military government's refusal to respect the results of the May 1990 elections clearly illustrates. Their previous maintenance of a command economy remains at the root of the country's economic crisis, which the post-1988 switch to an open economy and uncontrolled sales of timber and other resources to foreign interests will not necessarily solve.

In contrast, the military regimes in South Korea, Thailand, Pakistan and Indonesia, have presided over long periods of market-oriented economic growth, which have brought new interests into being, diversified each regime's social base, and added to the pressures to open up the political system. Yet at the same time the military has established deep roots in the economy, social structure and political system. Even when (as in the first three countries) it has begun to civilianize, it has not permitted this to undermine the structural bases of military power. It is true that in the new political dispensation this power must now be exercised indirectly—although how much difference this makes to political participation, observance of human rights, freedom of expression, or management of the economy, remains very much an open question.

The more general point is that transitions to democracy, like military coups, cannot be properly understood unless they are situated in historical context, and in such a way as to take into a account the variety of ways in which military force can shape transitions, both toward and away from authoritarian governance.

3. Military Rule, Authoritarianism and the State

The topic of military rule and how, if at all, it differs from civilian government is even more fraught with difficulty than explanation of military intervention. As Finer (1982:281) puts it, there is no quick answer to the one simple, brutal and paradoxical question "Who governs in a military government?" Indeed as soon as this question is asked about any military or civilian government the apparently obvious distinctions between the two begin to disintegrate.

Take, for instance, the civilian regimes of the Philippines under Magsaysay and Marcos, or of Indonesia under Sukarno during the period of Guided Democracy. Each of these had leaders who, though not career professional soldiers, claimed legitimacy from their participation in armed anti-colonial struggles, against the Japanese and the Dutch respectively. In each case these governments relied for their survival on their military and security apparatuses. These apparatuses gained representation and influence in the highest decision-making bodies of the state. Such influence was increased by their participation in major counter-insurgency campaigns: against the Huks and later the NPA and Moro rebellions in the Philippines; and against secessionist movements in Indonesia's archipelagic periphery. All three regimes placed their countries under martial law during major crises, Marcos for instance using martial law to prolong his rule beyond the limits laid down in the Constitution. In sum, the concentration of power in the state and its military/security branches was in many respects closer to that prevailing under military rule than to that found in more civilianized polities such as India and (before the late 1970s) Sri Lanka.

Yet even in India, constitution protections were suspended by Mrs Gandhi under the 1975 Emergency. And by the mid-1980s "there were at least 40 million Indians [in Assam, the Punjab, etc.] living under military rule, if not military law, making India one of the world's largest military dominated states—while it was simultaneously the world's largest democracy" (Cohen 1988.:100). After J.R. Jayawardene and the United National Party (UNP) party were swept to power with a large majority at the 1977 election, and even more so with the advent of large-scale ethnic violence in 1983, Sri Lanka has moved step by step toward a presidential authoritarianism every bit as brutal in its reliance on emergency legislation, martial administration, repression by the army and security services, atrocities, and violations of human rights, as any military dictatorship (Moore 1990:344-6 and 357-61). Indeed it is hard to think of any country in Asia and the Pacific where civilian governments have not suspended the normal operation of democratic constitutions, and used the military and police to impose domestic law and order.

Conversely, it is an open question whether it is the armed forces as such which control military governments; or particular fractions of the military elite; or coalitions between the latter and civilian elites; or rather the dominant class bloc as a whole, delegating actual political power to the men in khaki. Certainly the great majority of military governments, including almost all those under consideration here, have based themselves upon shifting coalitions between army officers, police, members of the intelligence services, civilian bureaucrats, and in a few cases civilian politicians, although the precise balance between them has varied.

In some states, like Myanmar or Indonesia under the New Order, a major proportion of the key offices of state as well as management positions in state enterprises have been held by army officers, though with variations from period to period. In some, only members of the ruling junta, or perhaps just the head of state and a scattering of his advisers, have been of military origin. In others, like South Korea and Thailand, the regime has deliberately set about civilianizing government positions, or has obliged officers to resign their commissions before taking up political or administrative posts. Even in civilian regimes, such as that of Malaysia during the post-1969 period, army officers have been brought into "a more direct and institutionalized role in the formulation of development policies" (Soedjati and Cheong 1988: 10), in addition to the role they already play as security managers.

At what point regimes can be considered "military", or cease to be so when they are civilianized, remains a matter for argument. Are governments which are still dominated by former members of the armed forces, yet have been confirmed in power by free or partly-free elections, as is now the case in Thailand and South Korea, to be classified as "civilian"? How much difference does it make when the security services are able to orchestrate parties and elections on behalf of the military elite, as in Indonesia? What of situations where the armed forces no longer officially rule, but are still represented in cabinet positions in the civilian government, and maintain an effective veto over major political and constitutional issues, as in Fiji after 1987. Or where military establishments, whilst remaining behind the scenes, have been able to orchestrate the dismissal of elected governments, such as that of Benazir Bhutto in Pakistan, to replace them with more "acceptable" (to the armed forces) alternatives? Or when all, or large regions of, a civilian-ruled country are ruled under martial law, like the Punjab or the Philippines under Marcos.

In principle it should be possible to analyse military rule in terms of a continuum: ranging from the outright appropriation of the state by a military establishment which proceeds to restructure it in its own image, to more subtle and indirect forms of military control or influence. But whilst this may be useful for classificatory purposes, it still does not help us understand the longer run structural basis of military power, nor its apparent continuity between periods of direct and of indirect military influence (viz Yasmeen's chapter on Pakistan below for a particularly useful discussion of the continuity in effective, as opposed to formal, sources of governmental power). Nor does it tell us what the military does with its power when it is in office: how it governs, on behalf of whom, through which instruments, and with what effects on public policy.

Such questions require a shift in theoretical focus, from the military as such to the military in relation to the state. Since the state was "brought back in" (Evans *et al.* 1985) to political analysis, the literature has grown exponentially. Despite elevating the state, this literature has shown curiously little interest in specific state apparatuses, including the military, police and intelligence bureaucracies. Yet in Asia, as in Latin America, although military power cannot be analysed "without speaking of the state—indeed of a particular form of the state, that of dependent societies, discussions of the state that forget the role of the military bureaucracies are only serving up abstractions" (Rouquié 1987: 35).

All too often "the" state brought back in by political scientists has been an highly aggregated, abstract entity. Or when it has been given any specific content, it has been represented as a pale reflection of social forces, rather than as a palpable power in its own right. Thus according to varying Marxist and neo-Marxist formulations, the state has either acted directly as the instrument of the dominant class; or it has enforced the logic of capital when carrying out its economic functions (not necessarily under the actual direction of the dominant class); or it has acted with relative autonomy because class forces are weak, or stalemated in "ruptural equilibrium". Non-Marxist analyses have concentrated on the capacities of the state and the nature of its interventions in the economy: whether it has been developmental or rent-seeking, weak or strong, effective or ineffective in its implementation of public policy. The common thread which runs through both streams of analysis is a focus on the state's functions, i.e. what it does and on behalf of whom, the policies it "produces" and the class relations it reproduces. Only secondarily has it been upon the structures, practices and capacities which enable it to perform these tasks: i.e. upon the production and reproduction of the state itself, the specific means (including military force) at its disposal and the apparatuses (including the armed forces) upon which it relies.

Yet in certain respects the focus on an overarching state has been a useful corrective to the more simplistic types of institutional analysis. For as we have already seen, distinctions between coups and other regime changes, and between military and non-military governments, are problematic, not least because they are poor predictors of the political behaviour of such governments. Indeed some political analysts have abandoned these distinctions altogether, preferring to differentiate between regimes on the basis of their policies, methods of rule, or support bases, rather than their military or civilian origins as such. Concepts such as "developmental dictatorship" (Gregor 1979), "repressive-developmentalist regime" (Feith 1981) or "bureaucratic-authoritarian state" (O'Donnell 1973 and 1978) have been widely canvassed,[4] since they neatly step around the difficulties of focussing solely on military rule. Military regimes are usually but not invariably authoritarian, and authoritarianism frequently but not always involves rule by soldiers.

The regime in Singapore is a case in point. It is civilian, stable, has never experienced a coup, and is in the process of transferring power to a new leader after the retirement of Lee Kuan Yew. Yet it also maintains a closed, repressive system of government, with high expenditures on defence and security forces, being comparable in a several respects to the regimes of more openly militarized polities, like South Korea. Certainly the regimes in Singapore and South Korea have much more in common with each other than with either the civilian regime of Mrs Aquino in the Philippines, or the military governments of Bangladesh.

Though pitched at a higher level of abstraction than military rule, concepts such as "developmental dictatorship" etc. implicitly recognise the functions of military coercion: in enforcing political stability; in stabilising dominant classes; and in securing the conditions for capital accumulation. Yet they are perhaps too general to be serviceable as instruments for comparative analysis, either of the specifically military functions of the state, or of the state's developmental responsibilities, considered below. They also tend to understate the achievements and potential of "developmental democracy" (Sklar 1987).

4. Military Power and Economic Regulation: Developmental Dictatorship or Developmental Democracy?

From the Meiji restoration in Japan through to the export-oriented industrialisation of the "four little tigers" on the Pacific Rim, Asia provides many illustrations of the proposition that strong states beget strong economies; and that insofar as military coercion is an essential ingredient of state power, it is an economic force in its own right, that can influence both the rate and the direction of accumulation.

During the 1980s the countries of East Asia, followed close behind by South Asia, achieved faster rates of growth in export volume and real GDP than any other group of developing countries and than the advanced industrial countries (World Bank, 1990: 8-20)[5]. In aggregate their incomes per head increased substantially during the decade, despite considerable variations within each region, both in absolute income levels and in growth. They maintained relatively high ratios of investment to GDP, and yet made substantial progress in addressing the problems of poverty. In the process they adjusted more successfully than any other group of developing countries to the external—terms of trade and interest rate—shocks of the 1980s (World Bank 1990: 103-7). In almost all these respects they contrasted sharply with the countries of Latin America and Africa, where the impact of external shocks was greater, investments in productive capacity were postponed or abandoned altogether, per capita incomes stagnated or declined, and immiseration spread.

How much of this success can be attributed to the fact that the developmental states (White 1987) which promoted these changes were for the most part presided over by closed or authoritarian regimes, largely reliant on military force for their security and survival? A number of arguments has been advanced in support of the hypothesis that military power, developmental dictatorship and economic expansion have been mutually supporting.

In the first place, it is argued, nation states desiring to increase their military security, have been strongly motivated to industrialise their economies. Indeed national security has apparently been the natural bedfellow of activist, neo-merchantilist economic policy, especially in countries like South Korea (Hamilton and Tanter 1987; Suk 1990).[6] Moreover, secondly, military spending has had an independent influence on demand, resource-mobilisation, technical change and growth—though this has had negative as well as a positive effects on economic progress. Thirdly, it is alleged that authoritarian (not necessarily military) regimes have provided the political stability and continuity in policy-making required for long term management of the economy. It is, however, worth noting that this assertion depends on a somewhat questionable assumption, that such regimes are in reality more stable than open or democratic governments. Fourthly, military coercion and surveillance have suppressed the political and social discontents which rapid and uneven growth has tended to generate. In particular, they have been used as instruments of labour control: to repress strikes, demonstrations and political radicalization, which could jeopardise the wage restraint on which accumulation and export-oriented industrialization depend. And finally, developmental dictatorships have kept the lid on the short-run political disturbances generated by IMF and World Bank-inspired structural adjustment and market-oriented economic reforms. This in turn has been advanced as part of a more general argument, that economic liberalisation requires a strong state and that democracy is a luxury that developing countries following the path of export-oriented growth cannot afford.

Not all these arguments for development dictatorship seem consistent with each other. In particular, the contention that strong, militarily powerful, states have tended to be economically interventionist is hard to reconcile with the proposition that they have also implemented market-oriented economic reform, unless substantial modifications are made in both hypotheses. Furthermore, there are enormous differences in political institutions, economic structure and development policy between states in the Asia-Pacific region. Arguments concerning developmental dictatorship which appear valid in some countries do not apply equally well in others.

The states which most nearly fit the ideal type of a neo-merchantilist garrison state—combining powerful, well equipped military establishments, repressive regimes, interventionist economic policies, and export-oriented industrialisation—are South Korea, Taiwan, and Singapore. Yet it remains a matter for dispute how far their strong states and national security establishments have been the engines of growth, its preconditions, or merely its by-products.

States like Thailand, Pakistan, Indonesia, and perhaps Malaysia fall into a somewhat different pattern. Political order has been preserved through the frame of a strong, though not in every case highly militarized, state. Regimes have enjoyed less autonomy from social forces than the first group and have been more prone to corruption. Both the repressive and the managerial capacities of the state have been less fully developed. Economic growth and military expansion have both hinged to some extent on external factors, including natural resource rents and foreign economic and military assistance. In a word, they have been as much rentier as industrializing states. Yet they have been able to reinvest at least part of their earnings in industry and agri-business, and to carry through market-oriented economic reforms which permit them to be rated as World Bank and IMF success stories.

There remain some states which have become militarized yet have failed to produce the conditions, either for a strong, autonomous state or for economic growth; these include Bangladesh, Myanmar, the Philippines under Marcos, Sri Lanka since its collapse into inter-communal strife, PNG and potentially Fiji. Such states would appear to be paradigm cases of the relationship between militarization and under-development, not development. Although the state is militarized, it is not necessarily under direct military control. It is repressive yet not powerful, interfering yet not autonomous. Military coercion is used, not to appropriate surpluses for development, but to support corrupt regimes and parasitic ruling classes. Labour and political dissent are repressed not so much in order to promote industry and exports as to preserve a stagnant *status quo*. Military spending creates few spin-offs for the civilian economy. Instead it contributes to the fiscal and foreign exchange crises of the state.

Indeed it seems that neither the hypothesis of developmental dictatorship, nor any alternative hypothesis, stands up to close empirical scrutiny. There have been unstable, as well as stable, military regimes. Developmental democracies (as in India, Sri Lanka before the early 1980s, or more questionably Malaysia) have thrived, as well as developmental dictatorships. Authoritarian underdevelopment (as in Bangladesh, Myanmar, or the Philippines under Marcos) has been as much on the cards as authoritarian development. Military and civilian regimes alike have been undermined by economic failure and crises of ungovernability: as in Myanmar (under military rule since 1962), Bangladesh (under both types of regime), or the Philippines and PNG (both of them under civilian governments). In sum, development failures require explanation as well as development successes.

Nevertheless under all regimes, be they authoritarian or democratic, military or civilian, stable or unstable, capitalist or socialist, development has remained an ideological imperative, the dominant concern of state policy. It is thus not surprising that it has emerged as a powerful theme in military doctrine and ideology. Examples are Thailand's concept of *Yuthasat Pattanta*, or strategic development, and the *Dwi Fungsi* doctrine under which the Indonesian armed forces have laid claim to a role in national development. In military establishments which have grown up in the shadow of the Cold War such military doctrines have almost invariably portrayed development through the prism of security concerns, linking it in particular to anti-communism and counter-insurgency. Moreover, development has usually denoted capitalist development presided over by a strong state, and not socialist development nor participatory development organised from below. Moreover it has not been development for its own sake, but also as an instrument in the struggle for political loyalties. That is, development has often been a sop cast in the direction of those who might otherwise have supported radical challenges to the military and to the state.

Military establishments have not just been enforcers of development doctrine. They have frequently participated directly in economic management. Army officers have taken strategic decisions about economic policy, in their capacities as heads of government, ministers and members of planning authorities. They have directly managed state enterprises placed under military control, as in Thailand, Myanmar, Pakistan and Indonesia. They have intervened in the labour market by crushing strikes and repressing organised labour, as most notably in South Korea. They have joined the boards of private corporations, and set up as entrepreneurs on their own account. Civilian as well as military governments have tried to purchase military loyalty by giving officers the opportunity to advance themselves in public office or enrich themselves in business after (or in some instances even before) retirement as for instance in Malaysia, the Philippines, PNG and Fiji. And military entrepreneurs, together with the managers of military controlled enterprises, have become part of the comprador elite: acting as facilitators for foreign capital and opening up the economy to external investors, as Robison (1985 and 1988) has argued so persuasively in the case of Indonesia.

Overall military management of the economy has sometimes produced striking economic policy successes, as in South Korea after 1961. However, it is worth noting that the Korean career military establishment was for the most part kept out of direct economic and business decision-making. Where the military and the bureaucracy have been directly involved in day to day economic decisions—as in Thailand, Pakistan and Indonesia—contradictions have tended to develop between political patronage and the efficient regulation of the economy. In Indonesia these contradictions dissipated part of the proceeds of the 1970s oil bonanza, and were associated with scandals in military-managed enterprises, including the (subsequently restructured) state oil corporation, Pertamina. Yet sufficient financial discipline was restored to reestablish the economy on the path of capitalist development, and to see it through the economic shocks and IMF/World Bank policy reforms of the 1980s.

In contrast, military-managed dependent capitalist development in Bangladesh, and autarkic socialist development in Myanmar, have helped push the economies of both countries into crisis. In Myanmar, direct military ownership and control of productive enterprises has been so extensive that one might almost talk of a self-contained military sector of the economy. Not only has it contributed to stagnation by supporting inefficient enterprises, it has entrenched it by giving the military a vested interest in preserving existing economic arrangements. Yet it is worth remembering that across the border, in Thailand, a similar network of military-controlled enterprises has enjoyed some commercial success, perhaps because they have had to compete in the context of a more open economy.

Have military and authoritarian regimes spent more on the armed forces than other governments? Cross-national evidence for developing countries suggests that they have (Maizels and Nissanke 1986).[7] Yet there seems to be no such general pattern in Asia and the Pacific. Leaving aside the socialist states (most of which have large military budgets), the countries devoting the highest proportions of their resources to military purposes have been

Pakistan (6.9 per cent of GDP in 1988, the last year of direct military rule), Malaysia (6.3 per cent), Taiwan (6.0 per cent) and Singapore (5.5 per cent), the latter three under civilian governments (SIPRI, 1990: 197-8).[8] South Korea (4.6 per cent) and Thailand (4.0 per cent), both with a legacy of military rule, and now in transition to more open political systems, have spent slightly more on defence than the elected governments of India (3.7 per cent) or Sri Lanka (3.2 per cent). Yet the military governments of Myanmar (3.2 per cent), Indonesia (2.3 per cent), Bangladesh (1.6 per cent) and Fiji (0.7 per cent), have maintained relatively low military burdens, along with Nepal (2.2 per cent), the Philippines (1.3 per cent) and PNG.[9]

Similarly it seems that there have been no consistent relationships between military intervention and changes in military expenditures. Military intervention has been followed by rises in defence spending in some countries (e.g. Pakistan after the 1977 coup, or Fiji after the 1987 coup), and decreases in others (e.g. Indonesia after the military take-over of 1965-8). During the 1980s Pakistan's military rulers increased military spending more rapidly than anywhere else in Asia, more than doubling it in real, inflation-adjusted, terms. Yet there were also substantial increases in India, Sri Lanka, Bangladesh and Nepal, in each country exceeding GDP growth. Singapore raised its military spending almost as fast as Pakistan, nearly doubling it in real terms over the 1980s. There were also rises in South Korea, Taiwan, Malaysia, Thailand and Fiji, though except in Fiji these did not keep up with GDP growth. Only in Myanmar, Indonesia, the Philippines and PNG did inflation-adjusted military spending actually fall during the 1980s.

The rising trend of Asian military spending contrasts with other regions, such as the Middle East, Latin America, and Africa, where depressed commodity prices and debt escalation have forced almost all governments to cut back on defence. Some Asian countries have spent more on their military establishments mainly because they can afford to do so. The states with the highest military spending levels and the largest rises have tended to be those with the most rapid GDP and foreign exchange earnings growth, and with the highest ratios of central government expenditure relative to GDP (Maizels and Nissanke 1986; Ross 1990; Looney and Fredericksen 1990).[10]

In some countries, like Singapore and South Korea, military growth has been supported by export-oriented industrialisation, in others, like India and Sri Lanka, by green revolutions and rises in agricultural productivity, in others like Pakistan, by large inflows of external assistance, in others like Indonesia during the 1970s, by oil or other natural resource rents (Looney and Fredericksen, 1990:

273-3: see also Robison 1988, for discussion of Indonesia as a rentier state), and in others like Thailand, or again Pakistan, by some combination of the above. In contrast, the countries whose national economies have been worst hit by commodity price declines (like Indonesia during the reverse oil shock of the mid-1980s), most encumbered by high debt repayments, or with the least dynamic economic performance, have been obliged to hold their military spending constant or reduce it.

Differences in state structure and international relations have also been crucial. As one might expect, states involved in regional conflict (as in the Korean peninsula and South Asia) have tended to spend heavily on their armed forces. But so too have those with strong, autonomous, interventionist states. Developmental states (some, but by no means all of them "dictatorships" or "authoritarian" in the senses reviewed above) have frequently transformed themselves into national security states, and vice versa. Hence the presence in the ranks of the high military spenders of countries like Singapore and Malaysia, along with countries facing more immediate international threats, like Pakistan, South Korea, Taiwan, and Thailand.

Malaysia is an especially interesting case. For it combines a form of representative government, a good track record in the management of capitalist development, a preoccupation with national and regime security, and well financed and equipped military, police and security apparatuses. In other words a regime does not have to be military in origin or even a dictatorship, to manage a fast growing economy, to maintain a national security state, and to bring in the military and security establishments as partners in both enterprises.

Not only have developmental states promoted accumulation in the civilian economy, increasingly they have also accumulated military hardware. South Korea and Singapore have built up perhaps the most capital-intensive armed forces in all Asia, fully oriented for conventional, as opposed to counter-insurgency warfare. Countries such as Pakistan, India, Malaysia, Thailand, and to an extent Indonesia have also been shifting their procurement from low-technology systems for numerically large military establishments, to cash and credit purchases of state-of-the-art equipment from the international arms market, to equip more professionalized armed forces (Karp 1990). Some of them have been moving into domestic defence production too, though so far India, South Korea and Singapore are the only countries with a capacity to design, develop and export weapons of their own (of these, however, India is the only producer of locally developed major weapons systems).

In contrast, the less prosperous and economically dynamic countries, like Myanmar, Bangladesh or the Philippines, spent proportionately less of their exiguous national resources on defence. Moreover, a relatively small percentage of their spending has been on military capital, most of it being devoted to personnel costs and internal security operations which require relatively little hardware.

The precise nature of the impact of military spending on development remains a matter of controversy (IDS 1985; Luckham 1987; Deger 1986). On the one hand it is contended that defence expenditure is a charge on the economy, diverting funds from investment, and aggravating fiscal and foreign exchange imbalances. On the other hand it is argued that it stimulates industrialization and the transfer of technology to the civilian sector, especially in countries whose industries are already technologically advanced through for defence production. The burden has been greatest in countries facing serious foreign exchange or resource constraints. It has been less in countries with expanding foreign earnings, like the oil producers in the 1970s and the export-oriented NICs, and in countries receiving large-scale foreign military and economic assistance, like South Korea in the 1950s and 1960s, or Pakistan in the 1980s.

However, these effects of military spending are mediated through the differences in state structure, economic organisation, and economic performance already referred to. In the microeconomies of the region, including PNG, Fiji and the other Pacific island states, most military spending can be regarded as simply a tax on development, though some kinds of expenditure, e.g. on fisheries protection vessels, may have tangible economic benefits. Likewise for a number of the more stagnant economies with relatively weak industrial sectors, like Myanmar, Bangladesh or the Philippines; especially as such spending has supported regimes which have failed to implement the policy reforms required that might have transformed the economy. Yet in economically dynamic NICs, such as South Korea, Singapore, Malaysia, Taiwan, Thailand or Pakistan, high defence spending seems to have been compatible with—and perhaps even has stimulated—state-promoted industrialisation within a capitalist framework.

What is less clear, however, is whether the apparent correlation between defence spending and economic growth in the last group of countries results from the stimulus of the former to the economy, or from factors antecedent to both. For it is entirely conceivable that the association arises simply because strong developmental states tend to pursue military strength and industrial growth simultaneously. Indeed some support is lent to this view by cross-national studies which suggest that states with large central government budgets relative to GDP, have tended to spend heavily on defence (Maizels and Nissanke 1986).

Moreover, it makes little sense to assess the military's economic role without also noting the reverse impact of the economy itself on the military and the state structure. Major economic dislocations have often generated regime crises: manifesting themselves not only in the form of coups but also in civilian uprisings against unpopular authoritarian or military regimes, like that of Marcos in the Philippines in 1986, or the military-dominated government of Myanmar, or both civilian and military autocracies in Bangladesh in 1975 and 1990. Such revolts have revealed profound crises not only in development, but also in repressive, yet ineffective, state machines.

Quite different in nature have been the political crises and transitions which have arisen out of long periods of sustained accumulation, as in South Korea, or major shifts in economic strategy, such as the turn toward export-oriented industrialization in Thailand, Pakistan and Indonesia. Indeed what seems to requires explanation in Indonesia is why the regime was able to carry through a major policy shift, from the oil-financed import-substituting industrialization of the 1970s to the fiscal restraint and export-oriented growth of the 1980s, *without* major political unrest or crises at the level of the state.

Broadly-speaking, it may be said that capitalist development has made economies more complex and less amenable to direct state regulation. It has diversified class structures, giving rise to new social groups with their own independent bases of wealth and power, bringing new demands to bear upon the state, including demands for democracy and human rights. And it has reempowered social groups, notably organised labour, on whose exploitation the economies of the region have been built. However, it seems to have been at the moments when accumulation has momentarily faltered that these latent tensions have come to the surface—as for instance in South Korea in 1979-80 when a mismanaged investment plan, an overextension of the financial system and the international oil shock produced a temporary downturn in the economy, and contributed to the political unrest which culminated in General Park's assassination (Chan, 1990: 43).

In sum, these Asian developmental states have been caught in contradictory pressures. On the one hand there has been the institutional momentum arising from powerful state machines, from their neo-mercantile economic policies and from their investment of the proceeds of growth in heavily capitalised national security apparatuses. On the other hand there have been the new social forces and economic dislocations brought into being by economic prosperity itself. In each state the course of the ensuing struggles has varied. It is too early to conclude with any certainty that capitalist development will either bring democracy to the region, or contribute to its demilitarization.

5. The Military as a "Parti Militaire," i.e., an Instrument of Political Representation

The military's importance as a political actor is widely recognised. Yet the idea that it represents political interests is perhaps less familiar. Partly this is because it is assumed that "the" military is an unbroken hierarchy, rather than a fragile unity imposed over contending factions and groups. And partly it is because it is assumed that the hierarchy continues in a one to one relationship with the state—as its servant under models of civilian control; as its master under models of military government—rather than the multiple and contradictory relations between soldiers and civilians which in reality prevail.

Like the state itself, the armed forces *are* both an interest and a site where conflicts between other interests are fought out or resolved. Military regimes not only tend to form their own "partis militaires" (Rouquié 1981 and 1987, chapter 9), the military itself is in some respects a party, and often an amalgam of competing military parties or factions. The latter have sometimes had a largely military basis, like the officers originating from the Eighth and Eleventh classes of the Korean Military Academy. Sometimes they have been in effect armed branches of non-military parties such as the Baathist officers in the Syrian and Iraqi officer corps. Often, however, they have been some combination of the two, such as the factions (the Young Turks, Social Democrats, supporters of General Prem and supporters of General Arthit, etc.) which emerged in the Thai armed forces in the mid-1970s (Muthiah 1988 : 34-6).

Military parties have varied in form and *modus operandi* under different types of rule. Under civilian government they have tended to act more like pressure groups than parties. The channels of influence have run in both directions. Sometimes the military command itself has put pressure on regimes to back corporate or political demands. Sometimes it has been reform groups in the armed forces, like the Reform the Armed Forces Movements (RAM) in the Philippines, which have put pressure on the authorities. But often it has been civilian politicians who have coopted officers into their power and patronage networks: for instance by recruiting them into policy-making positions, and by encouraging them to move from the military into political positions as in PNG.

Military governments have often constituted themselves as fully-fledged ruling parties, so to speak, with their own political support bases, and systems of representation and legitimation. Sometimes this has taken the form of a dominant tendency within the military leadership, such as the loosely organised yet influential "democratic officers" who pressed for Thailand's transition toward representative government during the 1980s. Sometimes military rulers have set up their own parties or front organisations: such as Golkar in Indonesia, the Democratic Justice Party in South Korea, the Burma Socialist Programme Party (BSPP) in Myanmar, or the Jatiya Party in Bangladesh. In other cases they have established de facto coalitions with existing parties or movements, as in the shifting alliances between General Zia-ul-Haq's administration and Islamic parties in Pakistan, or those between the military government, the Alliance Party and the Taukei movement in Fiji (continued after General Rabuka transferred power back to civilian hands in 1987). In Thailand retired officers have continued to be strongly represented in the upper echelons of the main political parties and the government, although serving soldiers have been constitutionally barred from political office since 1983.

Military-sponsored political parties have varied considerably in both structure and relationship to other political forces. Some, like the BSPP, have been formally constituted as direct membership parties, although such parties have rarely developed a genuine mass base. Others, like Golkar, have acted as loose federations of a variety of grass roots organisations. Military intelligence agencies have often funded, organised or indirectly supported parties of both kinds. They have also played a role in orchestrating electoral victories (as in Indonesia), or in coopting or suborning the leadership of non-military parties (as in Bangladesh and Pakistan).

The great majority of military-sponsored parties have functioned as ideological branches of the state apparatus, rather than as truly representative bodies with independent popular support. Only during crises have these parties faced genuine tests of their popularity, as during the elections held in South Korea in 1987 and in Myanmar in 1990. In each of these countries a military-dominated government had disintegrated in the wake of governmental scandals and popular protests. Nevertheless in South Korea the official DJP candidate, Roh Tae-woo, won the election by distancing himself from his predecessor and exploiting divisions among the opposition parties. The 1990 election in Myanmar—held nearly two years after the original protests, after the military had seemingly reconsolidated its grip on power—actually produced a victory for the opposition National League for Democracy. Nevertheless, the caretaker military administration established in 1988 remains in place, rules under martial law, has banned the NLD and imprisoned most of its leadership, and refuses to hand over power to an elected government until there is a new constitution.

Military establishments themselves are often divided into rival fractions, some attempting to influence military or state policy, much like factions in political parties, others seeking advancement through conspiracies and coups or by clinging on to power by repressing or outmanoeuvring opposed political tendencies. Some of these fractions or parties have formed around antecedent social ties of region, ethnicity, religion or class etc. Others have been based on purely military and professional ties, such as graduates of the same academies or military promotions groups, officers with the same foreign training, or members of particular service branches and units.

Peer groups of officers of the same or similar seniority have been a near universal feature of military politics, both in the Asia-Pacific region and elsewhere (Luckham 1971b: chapter 5). Among the most notable examples have been the Eighth and Eleventh classes of the Korean Military Academy. The former class was the main support base for the 1961 South Korean coup, and swept away less well trained senior officers who had lent their support to Syngman Rhee's corrupt and arbitrary government. The Eleventh class was its principal ally during the subsequent period of military rule, and became the dominant faction after General Park's assassination during the events of 1979-80. It included Park's successor, General Chun Doo-hwan, as well as the man who replaced him in 1987, General Roh Tae-woo. In the Philippine armed forces military fraternities have been a major source of factionalism, including among others the RAM based on the 1971 Matatag class at the Philippines Military Academy, the Guardians Brotherhood, a less elite grouping based mainly on reservist officers and enlisted men and the recently formed Young Officers Union (YOU). In Indonesia both armed forces and government have been dominated by the "45 Generation" of nationalist officers who joined the armed forces during or after World War II, and it is only recently that the post-1960 generations, the first to be educated at the Magelang academy, have been moving into the top echelons of the military and state hierarchies.

These military fractions are the elementary forms of political life in the armed forces, structuring both their inner conflicts and how and on behalf of whom they enter politics. Once the military enter politics, they often develop fresh political agendas which carry them beyond their military roots. They become the building blocks of military parties, appealing to new constituencies, both inside the military establishment and in political society. Conversely the entry of politics into the armed forces is mediated through their professional and ideological prisms. Thus microanalysis of factionalism and conflict is as essential for an understanding of the armed forces' political behaviour as macroanalysis of the external forces which sweep them from one political crisis to the next.

6. Professionalism, Power-Knowledge and Intelligence

Much confusion has surrounded the concept of military professionalism, first because so much effort has been devoted to an essentialist quest for universal attributes of professionalism and of the military mind (Soedjati and Cheong 1988 : chapter 1); secondly because it has been taken for granted that military subordination to the civil power, as found in Western parliamentary democracies, is just such a universal—flying in the face of the historical record of countries in Asia and elsewhere. Only recently has an interest developed in "new" and more political forms of professionalism (Muthiah 1988), of the kind which prevails in Latin America (Stepan, 1973 and 1988). The problem with the existing conceptualizations is not simply that they do not fit the evidence. They require reformulation in the light of theoretical advances which have transformed thinking about the professions.

Pertinent is Michel Foucault's (1980) treatment of professionalism as a form of "power-knowledge", which members of the professions exercise through their practice of, and ability to control and reproduce, socially valued professional skills. The particular form of power-knowledge which the military profession controls relates to the production of an "output" of organised force on behalf of the state. The latter, consists partly of outright coercion and partly of symbolically communicated threats. It requires the exercise of complex skills, which are as much political as they are purely technical. Although the military is usually regarded as a repressive apparatus of the state par excellence, it actually *combines* repressive and ideological functions. The importance of the latter is revealed in the emphasis placed on the development and teaching of military doctrine in almost all military establishments, including those considered in this book.

Such a reconceptualization necessarily alters the focus of analysis. Indeed it is precisely the military's professional functions which have made it political. Civilian control does not make it any the less so, even in liberal democratic states. Rather, civilian control has normalised its power simultaneously legitimizing it and establishing rules for its deployment within the context of a differentiated sphere of professional autonomy.

Moreover, military power-knowledge is as much a transnational phenomenon (Luckham 1979)—part of an international organisation of power and knowledge, as an attribute of particular national armies. One aspect of this transnationalization has been the transfer of Western democratic norms of civilian control to Third World military establishments. Another has been the promotion of national security and counter-insurgency doctrines through military assistance programmes. Even the attempts made by some Asian states to produce their own truly "national" security doctrines, such as Indonesia's *Dwi Fungsi* doctrines and Thailand's *Yuthasat Pattanta* referred to earlier, are still grounded in transnational as well as national conceptions of development, of the state, and of military power.

There is not the space to develop these arguments further. However, they can be used to illuminate some important aspects of the relationship between military professionalism and political power in the Asia-Pacific region. In the first place, that relationship has been deeply influenced by the transfer and reproduction of professional models by major foreign powers. Initially this transfer was part of the process of decolonisation. But for much of the post-World War II period it has also been associated with the management of the Cold War.

Military assistance, notably (though not only) from the United States, was, and to an extent still is, used to insert the region's military establishments into an international security system dominated by the superpowers. The stated purpose of such assistance—as put forward in the academic literature and think-tank reports (Pye 1962; Janowitz 1964; Pauker 1973; for a critical view see Klare, 1972) was to mould professional armed forces in a non-political Western image, and to enable them to contribute to modernisation and nation-building. At the same time, however, it was meant to strengthen ties between Asian and Western military elites, and to contain the spread of communism. Hence even if the transferred professional norms emphasised the military's political subservience, the very process of their transfer scripted politics back in.

Thus, for example, US military aid programmes to South Korea after the Korean War not only built up a formidable military machine, they also helped create a sense of mission among the professional elite of middle-ranking officers who staged the 1961 coup. And they reinforced that elite's reluctance to serve under politicians who might weaken the US alliance and reduce the country's military preparedness vis a vis the North. In Indonesia, the United States helped retrain the army during the 1950s and 1960s (but not so much the navy or the air force, largely trained by the Soviet Union), and gave it covert encouragement when it liquidated the PKI and displaced Sukarno (Anderson 1983a). Major military and civilian aid programmes played a major role in consolidating the subsequent military regime and in influencing its ideological direction. In Pakistan, US (and in the 1950s British) military assistance was crucial in establishing the military as the country's most prominent national institution and in creating the basis for its 1958 intervention, as well as in re-consolidating military dominance under General Zia after 1977.

In Thailand, US training of an already highly politicised officer corps has generated contradictory pressures: on the one hand reinforcing its anti-communism and mistrust of politicians; on the other hand encouraging it to disengage from partisan politics and to support democratisation of the political system. In the Philippines, US military aid programmes have had even more mixed consequences. Efforts to professionalise the armed forces and to increase the effectiveness of their counter-insurgency operations have been continually frustrated by the military's politicization and its incorporation in patronage and crony networks, especially under Marcos' Martial Law administration (initially supported by the USA). At the same time it has been precisely the more "professional" middle-ranking officers, whom US military advisers pressed to reform the military establishment, who have plotted most incessantly against both the Marcos and the Aquino governments. And they have conspired disastrously, with little apparent regard for the effects on the military establishment's discipline and ability to carry out its professional tasks.

But it has not just been because it was pressed into the service of the Cold War that the military has been politicized. An etatist politics of national security has been implicit in the professional project itself. It is a depoliticized, non-partisan politics, a politics-of-being-above-politics. It is present even in advanced liberal democracies, where the military and security bureaucracies exercise considerable influence within a relatively autonomous national security domain, to a large extent isolated from partisan political debate.

When transferred to the Third World the professional paradigm has transmuted into quite different structural arrangements, characterized in most cases by one form or another of national security state. In countries where a cohesive civilian elite has taken charge of the latter, as in Singapore, Taiwan or Malaysia, the armed forces, police and security bureaucracies, though under civilian control, have been the pivots of repressive national security systems in which they have enjoyed a certain amount of professional autonomy. In other countries, like South Korea, Indonesia, or Pakistan, the military has established a security state in its own image. In still others, like the Philippines or Bangladesh, both civilian and military governments have ruled coercively, failing to institutionalise either their own rule or the security and autonomy of the state. Yet in all three groups of states, national security politics have tended to dominate the priorities of the state and of the military establishment—even under civilian government.

It has been argued that it has been precisely the shift to national security policies oriented toward internal security rather than external defence that has made politics central to the new military professionalism (Stepan 1973). In the Asia-Pacific region this politicization has been all the more intense because many states have been near the front line of the Cold War, facing real or imagined attempts to subvert them by left-wing and communist insurgents. The theory and practice of counter-insurgency (COIN) and low intensity conflict (LIC) have become the focus of military thinking (Klare and Kornbluh 1988). These doctrines emphasise the need for close coordination between political ("hearts and minds"), economic ("development") and military means of influence, under an effective national security state. Moreover their influence has been inscribed upon the institutional development of the armed forces themselves. A good illustration is the rise of KOSTRAD in Indonesia. This was established by the Sukarno government as a reserve military strike force to deal with internal emergencies; played a major role in the West Irian and *Konfrontasi* campaigns; subsequently spearheaded the military's seizure of power under General Soeharto, and has remained one of the most crucial pillars of the regime since the establishment of the New Order.

Nevertheless in some Asian countries—for instance, South Korea, Thailand, Pakistan and India—external defence has loomed just as large as internal threats. In this the region contrasts with Latin America, the other main testing ground for the new professionalism. Yet it can hardly be said that Asian states are any the less obsessed with internal security. Partly this is because external threats have reinforced internal insecurities, becoming internalised through the dynamics of the Cold War—most notably so in South Korea, where the conflict with the communist North catalysed the restructuring of the entire polity around a garrison state. The latter in turn defined which activities and groups (e.g. trades unions and left wing political parties) were regarded as subversive, both in relation to the state and with regard to the requirements of a labour-repressive economy. It also entrenched the military and security apparatuses at the centre of the political process. In contrast, in India the conflict with Pakistan rather than the Cold War has dominated military planning—and questions of internal and external security, though interconnected, have been explicitly kept separate by the state.

Another aspect of professional power-knowledge has been the influence of intelligence agencies on the military's political involvement. Intelligence has been a major factor in the staging and prevention of coups. It has also been a crucial element in the capacity of military and authoritarian governments to organise efficient repression, without excessive resort to force. Indeed it is precisely because such governments have tended to lack popular support that they have been peculiarly dependent on good political intelligence—lacking any other channels of political representation, through which they might assess the impact of their policies, or broaden their base of political support.

Thus in South Korea one of the most crucial decisions made by the military government after it came to power in 1961 was to establish the Korean Central Intelligence Agency (KCIA). The latter was placed under the command of Kim Jong-pil, one of the prime movers of the 1961 coup from the Eighth KMA graduating class. It consolidated the regime's political support base by funding and organizing the ruling DJP party. Indeed the country's military rulers have relied on it to keep the armed forces themselves in line. Both the KCIA (renamed the Agency for National Security Planning) and the Army Intelligence Command continue to be indispensible (though controversial) parts of the state's control apparatus under "civilian" rule

Under Indonesia's New Order, the military intelligence command orchestrated the liquidation of the PKI, built up an effective political surveillance system, helped form the official Golkar party, and has been deeply involved in its affairs ever since. Likewise, General Ne Win has kept Myanmar in thrall since 1962 through a network of spies and informers, intact until the entire intelligence system began to disintegrate during the popular uprising of 1988. At the same time his military intelligence chiefs have been major players in most of the regime's internal intrigues. The governments of Pakistan and Bangladesh have also built up large and intrusive intelligence bureaucracies. Both under General Zia and under his civilian successors, Pakistan's Inter-Services Intelligence Agency has to all intents and purposes been in control of the country's Afghanistan policy. In the Philippines, President Marcos used the National Intelligence and Security Authority under its former head, General Ver (also the AFP Chief of Staff), as his principle instrument of surveillance over the armed forces themselves. In Malaysia and Singapore domestic surveillance has been equally crucial for political control, though remaining primarily the responsibility of the police and non military intelligence agencies.

In sum, most of the governments under consideration have been as much national security as military or civilian regimes. Nevertheless it is worth stressing that their security systems have had their limits and contradictions. Even the most comprehensive surveillance has not prevented upheavals such as those which arose in South Korea in 1979-80 and 1987, the Philippines in 1986, Myanmar in 1988 or Bangladesh in 1990. Indeed it is arguable that security agencies may have actually contributed to or worsened such crises by stifling criticism and demobilising dissent, making governments less responsive to popular demands, and diverting their attention from the real sources of unrest.

7. Military Power and Social Forces: Social Classes, Nationalism and Ethnicity

Most studies of the military have concentrated on its relations to the state and politics, paying scant attention to its interface with social forces in civil society. Such analysis of the latter as has been available has tended to be reductionist: equally in early studies of "modernising" Third World military elites recruited from the new middle classes, as in Marxist analyses attempting to read off the politics of regimes from their class origins.

The reductionism of both the non-Marxist and the Marxist theoretical traditions has since become more sophisticated. Huntington (1968) and other theorists of "political order" have advanced the hypothesis that the military's class alliances change as class relations are transformed by development. Whilst in the early stages of development soldiers tend to be progressive, during later stages they become more conservative, suppressing lower class protest against the capitalist order.

At the same time Marxist analyses of "bonapartism" and "caesarism" have come up with varying formulations of a similar thesis.[11] Some have suggested that the military takes control of the state in place of national bourgeoisies when they are too weak or divided to rule on their own behalf (a version of the relative autonomy of the state hypothesis); others that it moves in when there is a rupture between more or less evenly balanced rising and declining classes; and others that it seizes power on behalf of external dominant classes (e.g multinational capital), which cannot rule in their own right, and require local allies to act as their local enforcers (viz Luckham 1979, for further discussion of some of these arguments).

These hypotheses have been incorporated piecemeal in individual studies of Asian and Third World military politics. Nevertheless none of them adds up to a wholly convincing analysis. In part this is because they have had little to say about other social forces, like nationalism, religion, ethnicity or clientelism: except as class antagonisms in ideological drag, not dimensions of civil society in their own right. Partly it is because very few studies have presented an historically elaborated picture of the mobilization of class and other social forces, and of the role of military coercion in bringing them to a resolution. And partly it is because much of the writing on Third World states and class structures has been distressingly vague about the social relations of force, i.e. about military establishments themselves, their internal social divisions, and their external social alliances.

A more satisfactory analysis would require detailed empirical scrutiny of the social composition of the armed forces themselves. However, it would also have to be linked to an historical understanding of the broader processes of class-formation and of the social construction of the "imagined communities" of nation, ethnicity and religion etc. (Anderson 1983b). An example is Sanday's analysis below of the ethnic and class recruitment biases which have "feudalised" the Fiji military; entrenching the latter as the armed protector of ethnic Fijian ruling class hegemony and of prevailing neocolonial economic relationships. Another is Yasmeen's portrayal of the way changes in the class base of officer corps recruitment in Pakistan—away from upperclass landlord families, toward officers of more humble petty-bourgeois social origin—have opened it up to conservative fundamentalist Islam.

Another approach would be to consider the military itself as the source of certain forms of class power, and as a corporate initiator of class formation. This is visible in the way army officers in many Asian and Pacific countries have translated positions in the military hierarchy into company directorships, contracts, favours, land, retirement jobs, and positions in political parties: i.e. into both personal and corporate accumulations of power and resources. Moreover such practices have been almost as widespread under civilian as under military government. In Malaysia, as Crouch observes below (chapter 5) the allocation of directorships, retirement jobs and other favour, has served as a safety valve, consolidating the military elite's allegiance to the political establishment. Much the same has been true in PNG, where a number of senior officers who have retired or failed to receive promotion have moved into party politics, facilitated by the fluidity of the party system. In the Philippines the trading of political and economic favours between the political elite and the officer corps has become completely routine, although it has been more a source of political intrigue than of stability. In Thailand and South Korea, political civilianization has been accompanied by major transfusions of officers into politics and business, in effect guaranteeing that the new political order will continue to protect military interests.

These transactions have derived from the military establishment's position as guarantor of the political order and of capital accumulation, thus lubricating its relations with the ruling class. However, its role in structuring class relations has come into focus most sharply during major crises or historical turning points. The establishment of the New Order by General Soeharto in Indonesia, for instance, or the 1961 military revolution in South Korea, were significant not so much because they brought military regimes to power as because these regimes turned their respective economies around, opened them up to foreign capital, and intensified capital accumulation. These economic transformations in turn reconfigured class relations, around a social order which was dominated on the one hand by the requirements of accumulation and on the other hand by the politics of military and national security.

National security has been intimately bound up with the security and interests of ruling classes and military establishments. At the same time it has been manipulated to mediate relations between the state, capital and subordinated classes. Labour-repressive legislation, restrictions on trades union rights, surveillance of unions and left-wing groups by intelligence bureaucracies, use of military and police coercion to break up strikes and demonstrations: all these have tended to come under the umbrella of national security. This has been almost as much a feature of civilian governments (as in Singapore, the Philippines, or Fiji) as of military regimes (as in Indonesia, Pakistan or South Korea). Yet these are aspects of national security and of military politics which have seldom been studied in much detail.

Military establishments typically represent themselves as guardians of imagined national security communities. State security and national identity are almost invariably fused in the military imagination. Nevertheless this fusion is deeply problematic (Enloe 1978 and 1980). For on the one hand, the military regards itself as the unique representative of the nation, almost to the point of obsession in countries like Indonesia or Burma, where it claims to have been at the vanguard of the independence struggle. Yet on the other hand, it often lends its support to more limited conceptions of national identity, by privileging members of certain ethnic, religious, regional or class categories, and penalising members of others.

In effect, most post-colonial states have reconfigured the colonial ideology of "martial races" to match their own political and security requirements. Military recruitment and promotion have been widely used to register and reorder a layered conception of national identity. In countries like Malaysia and Fiji, the post-colonial state has continued the colonial practice of restricting recruitment, so as to entrench indigenous (Malay and ethnic Fijian) nationality groups and ruling classes. In contrast, Sri Lanka reversed colonial recruitment practice after an aborted military/police putsch in 1962. Members of the Buddhist Sinhala majority received preference in recruitment, in line with the government's Sinhala Only language policy. By the 1970s they had largely displaced the members of the urban middle class and of religious and ethnic minorities, who had previously been over-represented in the officer corps (Horowitz 1980: 209-17). In India certain minorities such as the Sikhs have continued to be over-represented, despite official efforts to achieve greater recruitment balance. Yet the emergence of separatism, especially in the Punjab, has transformed these imbalances into perceived threats to national security, aggravated in turn by the government's own heavy handed treatment of minorities both inside the armed forces and in the wider society.

In Indonesia recruitment has tended to over-represent the country's Java heartland. At the same time the military has viewed itself as the chosen instrument of national integration, bringing the outer islands, West Irian and Eastern Timor step by step under the control of the central state. In Myanmar and Thailand the military has taken a similar view of its role as an instrument of the national centre. In the former, the armed forces was originally organized as a federation of ethnically constituted regiments established during the colonial period. However, within a few months of independence in 1948 it was reorganized "with Burman officers and men dominating all units, regardless of their ethnic names" (Silverstein 1990:117)—but not before a number of regiments had defected *en masse* to the Burmese Communist Party and Karen insurrections. Since then the armed forces have been almost permanently at war with the Karen, Shan and other minorities. The failure of the government to incorporate these minorities into the national community—and the rebels' ability to maintain parallel economies, political institutions and armies—have reinforced the stagnation of the economy and the repressiveness of the military regime.

The military and other security bureaucracies typically define their imagined security communities in terms of what Enloe (1980: 12-21) terms "ethnic state security maps" categorizing the groups whom they consider reliable members of the national community and those they consider potential security threats. In some countries, the relevant categorizations have been ethnic, as in Malaysia, Fiji or Sri Lanka. In some like Indonesia, Pakistan or South Korea, the differentiations have been more regional than ethnic. In others, religion has been central to the social construction of the nation and the security community, often alongside region (as in India, Pakistan and Bangladesh), ethnicity (as in Malaysia) or some combination of the two (as in the Philippines and Sri Lanka).

Manipulation of ethnic, regional and religious categories has gone in tandem with, rather than displaced, class categorizations. The latter have perhaps been more sharply defined in some countries (e.g. the Philippines or Fiji) than in others. Yet in almost every country in the region, minorities, dissidents from neglected regions and religious fundamentalists or infidels have found themselves marginalized alongside students, trade unionists, peasant organizations and civil rights activists. They have been marginalized not just by virtue of their social positions, but also through the logic of security itself. National security bureaucracies have tended to apply that logic so as to categorize all forms of dissent as threats to the security of the state, and to their own capacity to defend it.

Yet the enterprise of compressing social forces into the narrow political space allocated by the national security state has been a work of Sisyphus. No sooner have pockets of dissent been eliminated than new ones have arisen. All the states considered in this book have confronted major crises originating in civil society, many of which have compelled changes in government or other major political adjustments. In some countries these crises have arisen from failures of the state itself: to organize development, to stem the immiseration of marginal groups, to integrate minorities, or indeed to organise efficient repression. Cases in point include the popular uprising in Myanmar initiated by student demonstrations in 1988; the 1986 "people's power" uprising which brought down President Marcos in the Philippines; the tumultuous events surrounding the demise of two Pakistani military regimes and the secession of Bangladesh over the period 1969-73; and PNG's almost permanent "crisis of ungovernability", together with its government's troubled relations with secessionists in Bougainville.

In other countries, however, crises have arisen out of the very success of the state in orchestrating capitalist development, class formation and the creation of a more plural political order: as in Thailand, where the urban uprising of 1973 demonstrated the growing power of extra-bureaucratic forces and prepared the ground for the military's step by step disengagement from politics; or South Korea, where large-scale civilian unrest has played a role in all the major political transitions since 1961, most recently in the shift to a democratically elected (yet still partly military based) government following a major legitimacy crisis in 1987.

8. International Dimensions: Security, Dependence and the International Division of Labour.

The strength of Asian and Pacific states varies enormously, whether measured in military power, capacity to manage the economy or ability to control their citizens. Yet even the strongest states, such as South Korea or even Japan, remain internationally vulnerable, "strong in relation to their own economies or peoples, but weak laterally—penetrated by various military, political, economic and intelligence agencies of the hegemonic power" (Cumings 1988:81).

The military sector is where the power of the state has been most visibly concentrated. Yet it is also where its lateral dependence has been most in evidence. Partly this is a result of the process of state-formation considered in section 1, the fact that almost all states of the region emerged to statehood in the context of the Cold War, under the tutelage of major world powers. Partly it follows from the nature of the military as an institution, uniquely identified with the nation-state, yet at the interface between the latter and a conflict-riven international system. Partly it is because the military organisations of Asian states depend upon a modern technology of war largely acquired from a small circle of international arms suppliers. The transfer, along with these weapons, of professionalism, i.e. a social technology which reproduces military power-knowledge, is considered in section 6 above. And partly it is because the economies of the region, which generate surpluses for, or incur debts as a consequence of, military spending, are harnessed to a rapidly changing international division of labour.

This chapter is not the place for an extended discussion of the region's international security dilemmas. However, they are relevant to the extent that they condition the armed forces' political behaviour. A conventional discussion of these dilemmas would start from military threat perceptions, and consider the defence policies, force structures and military spending that correspond to them. But for our purposes it is more fruitful to concentrate upon the hegemonic relationships which create and constitute those threats (Luckham 1987; Tanter 1981) and on the structures and relationships that produce particular national and regional responses to them.

The basic contours of the Cold War system imposed on the region by the major powers might be mapped out in terms of the network of military pacts (the former SEATO, the Manila Pact, the ANZUS treaty etc.) and bilateral agreements between individual great powers and Asian and Pacific states; the bases and facilities scattered through the region (Hayes *et. al.*, 1986); and the flows of weapons and military assistance etc., from the major powers. These hegemonic arrangements have been called in question by the end of the Cold War, though the process of dismantling them is only now beginning. In any case US and Western hegemony over the non-communist states has never been completely watertight,[12] has faced innumerable challenges not only from the socialist countries but also from within, and has become ever more difficult to reconcile with the growing economic strength of many Asian states.

Moreover, there have been major sub-regional variations. Different configurations of state power and national development within individual states, and different histories of conflict and cooperation among neighbouring states, have called forth varying hegemonic arrangements; Buzan (1988) indeed subdivides the region into a number of sub-regional "security complexes".

Among the latter, Northeast Asia has been the second major node (after Europe) of the Cold War, bisected across the China and Japan Seas and the two Koreas. This has produced the heaviest permanent concentrations of great-power and local military forces in all of Asia. It has turned the two Koreas into garrison states. Yet at the same time the Cold War has been complicated by the Sino-Soviet split, the flow of capital into China, and the growing economic rivalry between the United States and Japan.

The non-communist states in Southeast Asia have also formed a single security complex together with their communist neighbours in Indochina, divided, like Northeast Asia, by the Cold War. Yet the partial withdrawal of the United States after 1975, the conflicts among the socialist states, and their economic collapse, have tended to marginalise traditional Cold War concerns. Instead, the non-communist states have turned inwards, being concerned with domestic economic management and regional cooperation under ASEAN. Although the latter has functioned principally as an organisation for economic cooperation, it has taken on political and security functions, most notably in its promotion of a Zone of Peace, Freedom and Neutrality (ZOPFAN). Nevertheless during the 1980s, as we have already seen, the ASEAN states increased their military spending and arms purchases faster than those of any other Third World region. There have been no obvious new external threats which might explain these increases, except conceivably those arising from the insecurities generated by US withdrawal and the expenditures of *other* ASEAN states. A plausible explanation is simply that the proceeds of the sub-region's rapid growth have been reinvested in the instruments of state power and international status, in the manner analysed in section 4 above. Yet if this armament process continues, it could itself create new insecurities, damaging the framework of regional cooperation.

In South Asia, on the other hand, actual conflicts within and between the states of the region have been the driving force behind defence budget increases. The Cold War has also been a factor—though only at the margins, through US efforts to contain the Soviet Union in Afghanistan. Pakistan in particular has benefitted from massive US military and economic assistance. However its military build-up has been driven principally by the confrontation with India, not the crisis in Afghanistan. Meanwhile India has systematically avoided committing itself to either of the major power blocs, has diversified its arms purchases and has built up its own defence industries, much the largest in South and Southeast Asia. At the same time it has actively promoted regional security and cooperation proposals, including the concept of the Indian Ocean as a Zone of Peace, and the South Asian Association for Regional Cooperation (SAARC), formed in 1985. Yet this has not prevented India from playing the regional hegemon. It intervened decisively in the Bangladesh war of independence in 1971, and despatched a "peacekeeping force" to the Tamil north of Sri Lanka in 1987—

eventually withdrawn after supervising a temporary truce which fell apart under the continuing pressure of inter-communal conflict soon after it was imposed. Indeed India's perceived dominance, along with Indo-Pakistan military rivalry, have been the principle reasons why regional cooperation in SAARC has been so limited.

In the South Pacific, security dilemmas have in certain respects been "moderated by water" (Buzan, 1988: 6). Yet in other ways water has made them all the more acute (Hayes *et al.*, 1986). Naval deployments by major powers, especially but not only the United States, foreign fishing fleets, nuclear and missile tests, the direct physical presence of US and French military forces, the activities of sub-regional powers like Australia, New Zealand, or Indonesia—all of these have made the region's micro-states seem vulnerable. A number of these issues are addressed, albeit far from adequately, by common security arrangements under the South Pacific Forum and the South Pacific Nuclear Free Zone treaty (Clements, 1989).

Moreover, all the Pacific states are vulnerable to internal political and developmental crises, as Saffu and Sanday argue in reference to PNG and Fiji in chapters 10 and 11 below. There are few technical barriers to intervention by even the smallest military, police, paramilitary or mercenary forces, as shown by the spate of coups and attempted coups in micro-states in Africa, the Indian Ocean and the Carribean. The internal weakness of Pacific states indeed accentuates their lateral, neo-colonial vulnerability: witness the debates among Australian policy-makers about the advisability of sanctions or some display of military force after the 1987 Fiji coup and about the wisdom of providing the PNG government with arms and security guarantees during the Bougainville secession and other periods of crisis (debated in Fry (ed.) 1991). Proposals have been made for regional security arrangements, including peacekeeping forces, to protect microstates not only against coups but also against separatism, urban and rural disturbances and "rascal" gangs. However, as Fry (1990:20). observes, "in taking the side of the 'legitimate' government ... an intervening force privileges the government's view about what is just and attempts to suppress competing claims".

Indeed, virtually every Asian and Pacific state, however strong internally, and however rapid its economic growth, still perceives itself to be internationally vulnerable. Aside from China, India is almost the only state that can be said to pursue genuinely independent defence and security policies, with minimum great power involvement. Yet its cumbersome state machine remains internally weak, both in terms of its capacity to mobilise resources for development,[13] and relative to the powerful social forces unleashed by inter-communal conflict.

Moreover, the different dimensions of state power, external and internal, military, political and economic, etc., are far from perfectly correlated. Despite their vulnerability, most Asian states assert that their defence policies are autonomous. Yet their autonomy is definitely relative, and dependent in some degree on their regional alliances, relationships with hegemonic powers and place in the international division of labour. Some have attempted to translate economic success into military power by investing heavily in weapons and industrialising their military establishments. In certain respects they have thereby intensified their dependence on major weapons suppliers, though less than previously in the present buyers' market. Furthermore the precarious self-reliance purchased by these investments in military power is costly, especially for the weaker economies of the region, facing fiscal, balance of payments and debt repayment problems.

Asian NICs—notably India, Taiwan, the two Koreas, Singapore and Indonesia—have sought to reduce their dependence by undertaking domestic arms production (Brzoska and Ohlson 1986; Karp 1990). Most of this has been under licence, and has been largely reliant on foreign technology and parts. States like India, which have seriously attempted to develop their own major weapons systems, have been forced to reevaluate this policy because state-of-the-art armaments are usually cheaper to import (Smith 1990). Moreover, defence production has normally involved import-substituting industrialisation, contributing little to export-led growth (though Singapore has enjoyed a degree of success as an exporter of military components and minor weapons systems).

Much of the new investment has been in capital and technology-intensive modes of warfare, primarily oriented toward external defence rather than internal security. It is arguable that this investment will transform the "new professionalism" discussed in section 6 above, in one of two alternative directions. Either military and bureaucratic control over depoliticized states and political processes will be intensified even further. Or the armed forces will begin at last to withdraw from the political arena (as in South Korea and Thailand), moving toward an apolitical professionalism more resembling that of advanced capitalist states. In so doing, they will also be yielding to the demands of more assertive civil societies. Yet as the price of withdrawal they will no doubt insist that defence and security policies be insulated from politics and be retained in the hands of the national security state.

The combination of capitalist development, state strengthening and military professionalization is by no means an assured route to democracy, nor indeed is it the only route. Nor will it necessarily reduce conflict in the Asia-Pacific region. To the contrary, it may well generate new insecurities. These insecurities will be especially severe in the countries that remain peripheralized by economic stagnation (like Myanmar or Bangladesh) or by their small size (like PNG and other Pacific island states). They will be made all the more acute by the acceleration of military spending among their neighbours; by their vulnerability to interventions by the latter, as well as by outside powers; by the difficulty of paying their debts and meeting the conditionality of international agencies like the IMF and the World Bank in a stagnant global economy; by the fallout from the disintegration of the existing Cold War blocs and alliances; and by the pressure from the USA and the Western powers to establish new forms of international hegemony in the guise of post-Cold War regional security arrangements.

Notes

1. Witness the large number of references to 1950s and 1960s authorities such as Pye (1962), Janowitz (1964 and 1977); Huntington (1957 and 1968) and Finer (1962) in recent edited compilations such as Zakaria and Crouch (1985), Soedjati and Cheong (1988), or indeed the present volume.
2. In each of these countries the liberation wars were fought not only against France and the United States, but also against national armies originally established and trained by France and subsequently by the USA.
3. Unfortunately the lack of a chapter on India makes it impossible to adequately explore the reasons for this, and the contrast with Pakistan and Bangladesh.
4. Elision between state and regime in the use of these concepts is common, and is symptomatic of their theoretical difficulties. For seminal discussions of their use in an Asian context see Robison (1988), Feith (1981), Adriano (1984), Im (1987) and Suk (1990). Viz. Collier (1979), for a series of incisive critiques of the bureaucratic-authoritarianism hypothesis in a Latin American context.
5. The World Bank Report does not include Japan, categorised with the industrial countries, in its aggregate figures for East Asia. The basic picture remains the same in both sub-regions when their largest economies, China and India respectively, are subtracted from the statistics.
6. In fairness to these authors, it should be noted that they highlight the contradictions of the South Korean model.
7. This study finds that both military governments and governments which utilized violence against their own citizens tended to maintain high ratios of military spending to GDP and to central government spending

during the time period studied, 1973-80. The regional breakdown for Asia shows a weak, yet not statistically significant, relationship between military government and the two dependent variables.

8. The SIPRI figures for Myanmar and Bangladesh are for 1986 and 1987 respectively, there being no estimates for later years. The small oil-rich state of Brunei has also spent a relatively high proportion of its GDP on defence: 7.7 per cent in 1985, the most recent year for which figures are available.

9. SIPRI provides no estimates for PNG, but see chapter 10 below.

10. Looney and Fredericksen (1990) use a time series analysis to show that although defence budgets increased in line with GNP increases in all six countries studied, there were significant variations between countries in the timing of the increases. In Malaysia, GNP increases translated directly into increased defence budgets; in the Philippines and South Korea there was a more complex lagged increase; in Indonesia oil production was the principal determinant of variations in military spending; and in Singapore and Thailand policy-makers appear to have used defence spending counter-cyclically, increasing or reducing it when GNP fell behind or rose faster than the trend.

11. Alavi (1972), though much criticised, remains the most influential formulation of this thesis in an Asian and Third World context.

12. And likewise with Soviet hegemony in the socialist states, complicated still further by Sino-Soviet rivalry.

13. To be sure, India's economy has performed relatively well since the 1970s. Whether this is because of the policies and activities of an active developmental state is more doubtful.

2

Military-Civilian Relations in Indonesia in the Late Soeharto Era

Harold Crouch

In March 1988 President Soeharto was re-elected as Indonesia's president for his fifth five-year term. Soeharto's military-backed rule has given Indonesia more than twenty years of political stability which stands in sharp contrast to the almost constant political upheaval of the first twenty years after the Proclamation of Independence in 1945. In no less sharp contrast to the first twenty years, military dominance during the last two decades has also been accompanied by unprecedented economic growth and the beginnings of industrial transformation. Many Indonesians, however, are now asking whether the political role of the military will remain unchanged in the years ahead. As a result of the the economic growth since the mid-1960s, the military is facing a society which is significantly different to the one over which it established its political domination a quarter of a century ago. Moreover, the military itself has also been in a process of transformation as the founding generation of anti-colonial "freedom fighters" has given way to academy-trained professionals in the military leadership. The political role of the military in Indonesia might therefore be expected to evolve in new ways in response to new challenges thrown up by a changing society.

In most countries armies perceive themselves, at least formally, as concerned primarily with defence and security while military intervention in government tends to be seen as an aberration which, even when justifiable because of special circumstances, should be temporary. In Indonesia, however, the armed forces have formulated an ideology—*Dwi Fungsi* (Dual Function)—which asserts that the military does not have an exclusively military function but has an additional mission as a socio-political force with the permanent right—even duty—to participate in the political affairs of the nation. The *Dwi Fungsi* doctrine had its origins in the experience of the revolution against Dutch colonialism when guerilla leaders combined military and political roles and the military was for a brief time in effect the government. After an initial period of uncertainty after the revolution the military emerged as a key part of President Sukarno's "Guided Democracy" government and became the dominant force in President Soeharto's "New Order"(see Sundhaussen 1982). Armed with its *Dwi Fungsi* doctrine, the Indonesian military does not envisage an eventual withdrawal to the barracks and the adoption of a purely professional military role. But while it asserts a continuing political role for the military, the *Dwi Fungsi* concept does not prescribe the military's functions in detail and is sufficiently flexible to accommodate varying degrees of military participation in government.

Military domination in Indonesia has been deeply entrenched since General Soeharto took effective power in 1966 and became president in 1968. During the early years of the New Order when the president was still in his prime, the vice presidency was held by civilians but since 1983 that position has been held by generals. The number of military officers in the cabinet has fluctuated. Sometimes it has been quite low-falling to only four out of 27 in the mid-1970s—but the key positions such as the State Secretaryship and the ministries of Home Affairs, and Defence and Security have always been in military hands. In Soeharto's cabinet appointed after his re-election in 1983, 13 out of 32 ministers had military backgrounds, covering such varied fields as Justice, Co-operatives, Agriculture, Manpower, Education and Culture, and Social Welfare, among others, but in the 1988 cabinet the number dropped slightly to 11 out of 38. In addition to military representation in the cabinet, military officers are also strongly represented in the higher echelons of the civil service, often holding the position of secretary-general, especially in ministries where the minister is a civilian. At the level of regional administration, the number of military officers appointed as provincial governors has fallen from 22 out of 26 in the early 1970s to 12 out of 27 at the beginning of 1990 but key provinces such as Jakarta, West Java, Central Java, East Java and North Sumatra are all headed by generals. At a lower level, military officers now make up less than 40 per cent of the *bupati* (district heads). Apart from positions in the government administration, military officers also hold many important economic positions in state corporations such as the rice marketing agency (*Bulog*) although the state oil corporation (*Pertamina*) and the state tin corporation (*P.N. Timah*) are now no longer headed by generals. Further, the Chief Justice of the Supreme Court is a general and 100 military officers sit in the 500-member People's Representative Council as appointed members while retired officers are prominent in the government "party", Golkar.

Military domination, however, is reflected not only in the extent of the military role in government but also in the character of civilian participation. In the early years of the New Order Soeharto co-opted several political party leaders into his cabinet—even though they held only minor portfolios—but in later years civilian members of the cabinet, almost all of whom have been technocrats or bureaucrats, have lacked any organised base of political support of their own. They have held their positions at the military's pleasure and have consequently been in a weak position to push policies which did not have military approval or ran counter to military interests. Similarly at the level of provincial administration, civilian governors have been appointed because they were selected by the military rather than because they had their own independent bases of support. Civilian office-holders in the regime have, on the whole, been instruments of the military rather than real partners.

How has the military maintained its political domination? Clearly direct repression has been very important. The Soeharto regime came to power in a bloodbath in which perhaps half a million supporters of the military's main rival, the Communist Party of Indonesia (PKI), were slaughtered by soldiers and their civilian allies. In addition more than half a million PKI activists and sympathisers were detained in the years after 1965. Although many were released fairly quickly, at least 30,000 were still being held in the mid-1970s and it was only at the end of 1979 that the last of the untried detainees were released while several hundred who had been convicted of "involvement" in the 1965 coup attempt remained in prison or had been executed. Repression, however, was not used only against the PKI. In the years immediately after 1965 many "Sukarnoists" were detained including—apart from Sukarno himself—supporters of the deposed president in the Indonesian National Party (PNI), the bureaucracy and also the armed forces. In later years student activists, journalists, academics and former leaders of the banned Indonesian Socialist Party (PSI) were among those arrested at one time or another but by the 1980s the main target was Muslim opposition. In the early 1980s it was estimated that some 400-500 Muslim opponents of the government were in prison but this number jumped sharply after the Tanjung Priok riot of 1984 (Tapol 1987). During the entire period of military domination, from time to time small numbers of recalcitrant military officers also found themselves in gaol.

The government also moved steadily to limit the scope for organised opposition. Under President Sukarno's "Guided Democracy" the number of legal political parties had already been reduced to ten and two more, including the PKI, were banned by Soeharto after 1965 while one new Muslim party was permitted to come into existence. Under pressure from the parties, the government held elections in 1971 but military, police and bureaucratic backing resulted in an overwhelming victory for a new government-sponsored "party", Golkar. The government then compelled all the parties, except Golkar, to restructure themselves in two new parties which were placed under amenable leaders and depended on government financial support. Although national elections have been held regularly since 1971, they have been managed in such a way as to ensure large Golkar victories, the Golkar share of the vote rising to 73 per cent in the 1987 election. Other potential sources of organised opposition such as business organisations, trade unions, peasant associations and various professional bodies were brought together in corporatist style under single organisations whose leaders were always tied in one way or another to the regime. At the same time tight controls were imposed over the press.

The military's measures to ensure its continued political domination were implemented in the context of a social structure which in some respects facilitated military rule. The Indonesian class structure lacked two important classes—a strong indigenous bourgeoisie and a big-landlord class—which in other countries have provided social bases for political movements which have to some extent been able to balance and limit the power of the central bureaucracy. During the colonial era the indigenous elite was largely co-opted into the Dutch-controlled bureaucracy and an indigenous bourgeoisie was unable to emerge in an economy which was dominated by Dutch enterprises and Chinese traders. After independence nationalised state enterprises replaced the Dutch while the Chinese continued to dominate domestic trade, leaving little scope for the growth of an indigenous trading class which could conceivably have become a base for resistance to, or at least a check on, authoritarian rule by the military. Instead the Chinese commercial class, lacking a political base of its own, quickly tied itself to the military and was in effect integrated with the regime. Indonesia also lacked a big-landlord class, especially in Java, which could mobilise regional opposition to military domination. The social context in which the military came to power in Indonesia was therefore much more favourable than, for example, that of the Philippines where comparisons are sometimes made with the Indonesian experience (Crouch 1985).

It is, however, impossible for any regime to maintain itself in power for more than two decades through repression and tight political control alone. In the long run governments need to serve the interests of sections of society outside the small political, military and bureaucratic elite itself. In the case of the Soeharto regime, an important, although narrow, base of political support was fostered as a result of the government's successful economic development strategy (See Booth and McCawley 1981). From the beginning the Soeharto government gave high priority to creating political conditions which encouraged rapid economic growth. It took strong measures to ensure that political stability was maintained and it opened the economy to Western and Japanese aid and investment. But perhaps the most important factor in stimulating economic growth was the extraordinary rise in the price of oil during the 1970s. For most of the 1970s and early 1980s, oil provided around two-third of both exports and government revenues. During the 1970s the Indonesian economy grew at 7-8 per cent annually and major industrial development took place—including the establishment of heavy industries

While the major beneficiaries of rapid growth were no doubt the members of the military elite and their bureaucratic and business allies, economic development also allowed the government to expand its social base of support as the benefits of growth spread to important non-elite groups. In particular economic growth strengthened the position of the urban middle class and the better-off peasantry. During the 1970s the economic condition of the middle class was transformed as civil service salaries rose rapidly and numerous new employment opportunities opened up in the expanding private sector, especially as a result of the inflow of foreign capital. Although many of its members adopted a very cynical view of the government and the corruption associated with patronage distribution, it could not be denied that materially the small but politically important middle class "had never had it so good". In the rural areas the government's program to increase rice and other food production benefited the rural upper class which in Indonesia, in the absence of a big-landlord class, usually meant peasants owning between one and five hectares. By attracting these groups the regime extended its base of support outside its immediate beneficiaries in the military and bureaucratic elite and to some extent neutralised potential opposition. Regimes which alienate the urban middle class are often faced with constant social disruption while those whose rural support is limited to a small but wealthy landlord class can become vulnerable to rural dissident movements. Nevertheless, the regime's social base of support remained narrow as the urban middle class makes up barely 5-10 per cent of the population while the better-off peasantry amounts to not much more than 10 per cent of the rural population in Java although considerably more in the outer islands (Crouch 1984:77-78).

Apart from these major beneficiaries of growth, the fruits of development appear to have "trickled down" further, especially in the late 1970s and early 1980s, and made it easier for the government to keep mass discontent under control. The huge amount of funds at the government's disposal allowed it to subsidize rice and fuel prices as well as the costs of agricultural inputs such as fertilizers. Government infrastructure projects in the rural areas provided employment for the rural poor to the extent that in some areas agricultural labour shortages were sometimes reported during periods of peak labour demand. In the urban areas industrial growth provided new work opportunities although under-employment remained extremely high. General indicators of welfare such as average calorie intake, participation-in-education rates, and the availability of health care all showed a limited but real improvement in living standards which affected a large part of the population. Of particular importance for political stability was the government's capacity to build up substantial food reserves which enabled it to prevent sudden rises in the price of rice for urban consumers and the political restiveness which often accompanies such price rises.

The longevity of the Soeharto regime also depended on Soeharto's ability to retain the loyalties of the military and bureaucratic elite. While recalcitrant military officers were sometimes arrested, other were tied to the regime through the distribution of material benefits. Indonesian military officers had long been involved in commercial activities. During the revolution against the Dutch, military units were responsible for obtaining their own supplies and some officers became adept in fund-raising activities, often in association with local Chinese traders. In the

1950s the failure of the central government to provide regular and adequate allocations to regional military units resulted in many local commanders reviving earlier fund-raising practices, often involving smuggling and other illegal activities. After the introduction of martial law in 1957 and "Guided Democracy" in 1959 the commercial activities of military officers increased partly to raise funds for military units but also because of the opportunity this gave to individual officers to acquire personal wealth. Thus when the military took full power after 1965, the commercial orientation of much of the new elite was already well established. Military officers continued to involve themselves in commercial undertakings in association with domestic Chinese entrepreneurs and later with foreign investors. Controlling the allocation of licences, contracts., concessions, monopoly rights, credit and so on, as well as all bureaucratic appointments, Soeharto and his colleagues were able to distribute commercial opportunities among the military elite in such a way as to strengthen their own political position. Allies were rewarded, potential dissidents were bought over while recalcitrants were cut off from business opportunities and sometimes arrested (Crouch 1978:ch 11).

Soeharto's patronage network operated in a particularly favourable environment. In the initial years of the regime, the Western nations and Japan launched a rescue operation to rehabilitate the virtually bankrupt Indonesian economy and to tie the new regime to the Western bloc. Substantial economic aid, which was channelled to the government to support the balance of payments and infrastructural development, also placed great resources in the hands of the regime which could be used to fuel the patronage machine. Once the regime had established itself a new source of funds became available in the form of private foreign investment. Foreign businessmen were required to take domestic partners who were usually nominated by the government more on the basis of patronage than technical considerations. And then in the 1970s the series of leaps in the price of Indonesia's main export commodity, oil, gave the government enormously increased funds which provided almost unlimited opportunities for patronage distribution while at the same time financing the expansion of infrastructure, the establishment of many new industries and a significant improvement in popular welfare.

The military-dominated regime headed by President Soeharto has therefore been "successful" according to the usual criteria. It has maintained political stability and promoted rapid economic growth. But can military control continue in the future more or less as it has in the past or will the military be forced to make way for increased civilian participation? One thing that can be predicted with reasonable confidence is that the military will continue to be a major force in the Indonesian government for some time to come. But military participation in government can take different forms. It is possible that the level of military participation in government could decline and that the role of civilians could increase both quantitatively and qualitatively.

There have been signs of rethinking about the role of the military in the government within the armed forces themselves (See Jenkins 1984). Since the late 1970s discussions have been held among military officers about how *Dwi Fungsi* should be implemented in the future. The doctrine of *Dwi Fungsi*, which has been a principal ideological justification for military domination, does not in itself require the military to hold all the major positions in the government. While some officers apparently believe that the present level of military involvement in the government and administration should be maintained or only very gradually reduced, others have argued that the achievements of the regime—in particular the long period of political stability and economic growth—should allow the military to relax its grip and permit civilian participation on a much broader scale than in the past. There is also concern on the part of some military officers that excessive involvement in non-military tasks tends to detract from the military's capacity to carry out the first of its dual functions in the field of defence and security.

Discussion of the possibility of a reduction in the military's political role has coincided with the replacement of the old generation of military leaders who had fought in the revolution against the Dutch in the late 1940s by post-revolutionary officers who have graduated from the military academy at Magelang or equivalent institutions since 1960. The old generation, usually called the "45 Generation" because of their involvement in the revolution which was launched in 1945, rejected a purely military role for the armed forces and claimed, on the basis of their contribution to the success of the anti-colonial struggle, a continuing right to participate in "affairs of state" but it has been suggested that many of the post-revolutionary academy-trained generation might in fact prefer to reduce the military's direct political role and concentrate on the professional duties for which they have been trained as soldiers. It should be remembered, however, that these younger officers did not attend Western military academies which upheld the idea of apolitical professionalism but received their military education in

Indonesia where the *Dwi Fungsi* concept, although at that time less clearly formulated and without that name, was part of the curriculum and that they then served, after they began to graduate in 1960, in an army which was already actively involved in politics and a major component of President Sukarno's "Guided Democracy" government. That there appears to have been some decline in recent years in the number of military officers holding civilian positions in the government may be due less to a lack of interest on the part of the younger generation of professionals than to the fact that there are fewer of them compared to the old generation and they are still needed in their military positions. The oldest of the new generation are now in their early 1950s so it is possible that more will be appointed to posts in the civilian administration when they reach the retiring age of 55.

Meanwhile officers of the academy-trained generation are increasingly being appointed to non-military positions as members of the older generation move on. In contrast to previous practice where the appointment of a military officer to a civilian post normally marked the end of his strictly military career, the two functions now seem to be more closely integrated with officers moving from military to civilian and then back to military positions. It is now not uncommon for an officer to serve a period as a *bupati* or member of the legislature and then be promoted to a military command position such as a regional commander. There appears to be a concern among senior officers that members of the academy-trained generation are not as well-equipped to deal with political matters as the old generation and need to be given experience in civilian positions as a normal part of their military careers in order to prepare them for senior roles in the government later.

A major incentive for members of the old generation to retain their large role in government and administration was of course the economic opportunities that such participation provided them. Corruption was widespread and many military officers holding civilian appointments routinely provided benefits to private companies with which they themselves, their relatives or their colleagues were associated. It is of course difficult to assess the extent to which officers of the younger generation have become involved in similar activities. Compared to the past, serving military officers of the younger generation seem at least to be less blatantly associated with winning favours for particular enterprises but it is not easy to determine whether this change is more apparent than real. Unlike the past when budget allocations were small and military officers were often expected to find extra sources of income for themselves, today's officers receive substantial official incomes and amenities and are therefore in less need of what used to be called "unconventional funds". It has also been suggested that additional income might be channelled to senior officers in ways which are less economically distorting such as, for example, through the issuing of shares in major companies rather than simply giving leeway to officers to find their own sources of income.

That officers of the post-revolutionary generation have their own political preferences was made clear during the 1988 session of the People's Consultative Assembly. Apart from re-electing Soeharto, the assembly also "unanimously" elected Lt. Gen. Sudharmono, the State Secretary and head of Golkar, as vice president. Although Sudharmono was clearly endorsed by the president, he had been a rival of the armed forces commander, Gen. Benny Murdani, and was regarded by many officers as an unsuitable candidate. During the assembly session, many members of the armed forces group in the assembly made clear their dissatisfaction with Sudharmono's nomination. The willingness of military members of the assembly to blatantly display their disagreement with the president's choice for the vice presidency was unprecedented and suggested the possibility that military officers might be less automatically identified with the regime in the future.

The attitude of the younger generation of military officers to continuing military domination is, therefore, still unclear. There is no indication that younger officers are inclined to abandon the military's political role but there appears to be no clearcut consensus on what precisely that role should be.

It is, however, doubtful whether the values and orientations of military officers are the most important factor in determining their political role. Military officers are part of a society which has many components and their behaviour is affected by their interaction with other groups. When civilian political forces are weak, military domination of the government is relatively easy to maintain but military-dominated governments are usually forced to make adjustments as civilian groups grow stronger. In the Indonesian case, it seems that the future role of the military in politics will be determined more by the changes in Indonesian society as a whole than by changes in the outlook of officers themselves or, to put it another way, the outlook of officers will change in response to broader social change.

It could be argued that the modernisation of the economy in itself creates demands for the sharing of political power. While an economy based on traditional agriculture or mining can function reasonably well without sophisticated management and rational administration, a modern economy requires that decisions be taken more on the basis of economic expertise and that policy-makers be responsive to the reactions of key economic groups such as businessmen and managers as well as other social groups. As the economy grows increasingly complex, so the argument runs, military leaders are forced to give greater scope to civilian experts in economic policy-making and to take into account the requirements and expectations of both the private sector and civilian management in the public sector. This argument was strengthened in Indonesia's case by the immediate need to stimulate growth outside the oil sector following the collapse in world oil prices. Indonesia's large income from oil during the 1970s had made it less necessary to create an efficient non-oil sector capable of competing internationally and therefore undermined pressure to give wider powers to civilian experts in the government and to create an environment favourable for spontaneous business development. In the early days of military rule, the role of technocrats in the government was severely limited by the need to avoid policies which might harm politically influential vested interests but the collapse of oil prices in the mid-1980s has forced the government to give more authority to its civilian technocrats as has been seen in a series of reforms and liberalising measures taken since 1983 despite the opposition of vested interests with military connections (See Robison 1987). The modern sector of the economy's need for sophisticated management might therefore be expected to lead to the strengthening of civilian technocratic elements in the government although there is less reason to suppose that it would push the government toward providing more scope for the participation of civilian organisations representing groups outside the regime.

To what extent is economic change likely to bring about social change which gives rise to increased political demands by specific organised groups for greater civilian participation in the government and in politics generally? Among the social classes which usually expand as a result of economic development are two which are especially likely to demand increased opportunities for political participation—the educated middle class and the business class. Modern industrial development also causes an expansion of the urban working class but in an economy plagued by widespread unemployment and under-employment, the bargaining position of Indonesian workers is very weak and their organisational capacity poor as they are preoccupied with the immediate needs of survival rather than broad political issues.

The expansion of the urban middle class—consisting of professionals, white-collar employees, small businessmen and so on—has been an important consequence of Indonesia's economic growth during the past two decades. On the one hand the expansion of the middle class has provided the regime with a growing social base of support but on the other hand members of the educated middle class tend to have higher expectations of government performance than the less educated lower classes and are more aware of their rights and more likely to press for the extension of democratic practices. Although much of the middle class is grateful for its economic progress and not inclined to take the risk of political involvement, some of its members are in the forefront of the struggle for "democratic" representation. In countries where the middle class is small its demands can be safely ignored by governments and organisations representing middle class interests can be repressed but as the middle class grows in size as a result of economic development, military or other authoritarian rulers often find it politic to make concessions to middle class demands. However, unlike the Philippines where the middle class is quite large and middle class discontent played a big part in the overthrow of the Marcos regime, the Indonesian middle class is still small and a large proportion of its members are engaged in government employment. The Indonesian middle class still seems too small to provide an effective base for civilian political movements demanding greater civilian participation in government.

Another class which has become stronger as a result of economic growth and which might be expected to press for greater governmental responsiveness to demands outside itself is the class of businessmen. In many countries it is the business class which provides the most important counterweight to the power of the government and bureaucracy. Continuing economic growth in a capitalist system means that the role and influence of the business community must also expand and a point is eventually reached where governments have no choice but to respond to the needs of commerce and industry in order to induce businessmen to invest. The existence of a strong and independent business community constitutes an important check on the powers of government and provides a kind of umbrella under which other political groups can also organise themselves. A strong business class is likely sooner or later to give its support to political organisations seeking to participate directly in the government.

But Indonesia's business class shows few signs of seeking direct political representation. It has always been very small and drawn largely from a minority community. Because they are mainly of Chinese descent, businessmen have never been able to mobilise popular support in the political arena. Instead of developing into a force that could balance the power of the government, businessmen have usually integrated themselves with the holders of political power through alliances which have brought special favours to well-connected enterprises. In recent years, however, there has been some debate in academic circles over whether enterprises founded with the aid of patronage and whose growth has depended on continued favours from powerful patrons might not eventually develop into strong enterprises no longer dependent on their original connections (See Robison 1986; Crouch 1986). As enterprises move from import-export trade and the exploitation of timber concessions to heavy industry and international finance, it is argued that they will eventually loosen their ties with politico-bureaucratic patrons and finally become more-or-less independent economic forces in their own right. There are signs that this process might be beginning in Indonesia but it has not yet developed far and in any case the Chinese character of much of the business class makes it unlikely that businessmen—at least Chinese businessmen—will seek direct political representation The situation in Indonesia is clearly very different to the Philippines, for example, where the relative independence of much of the business class from the Marcos regime was a very important factor in creating the conditions for the change in government in that country and ensuring that civilian participation remains high under the new government.

It would appear, therefore, that the economic development that Indonesia has experienced during the last fifteen years or so has not yet resulted in the social changes that would make radical change in the nature of the government necessary. The urban middle class and the business class, which have been major counterweights to the power of governments in other countries, have certainly grown in size and strength during the New Order period but they are not yet strong enough to impose their will on the government and force increased popular representation. Social changes caused by economic development have not gone far enough to force the dominant groups in the government to share power with civilian groups with real roots in society so that civilian members of the government are still essentially appointees rather than representatives.

Another possible counterweight to military domination is political Islam. Although Muslim parties and organisations were allied to the military in the struggles against the PKI and President Sukarno, the government gradually reduced the scope for political

Islam in the following years. In 1973 the Muslim parties were forced to merge in the new Development Unity Party (*Partai Persatuan Pembangunan*—PPP) which was placed under amenable leadership and made financially dependent on the government. In the 1980s the government compelled all political and other organisations to accept the national ideology, *Panca Sila* (Five Principles) as their "sole ideological foundation" which further alienated Muslims who believed that there could be no "ideological foundation" apart from Islam. In recent years the military has cultivated the conservative Java-based *Nahdatul Ulama* whose withdrawal of support for the PPP resulted in a drastic fall of votes in the 1987 election. Frustrated Muslim radicals turned to violence—in the form of arson and bombings- after a riot at Jakarta's port, Tanjung Priok, in 1984 but political Islam now seems to lack a strong organisational base.

If representative, as opposed to technocratic, civilian participation is to increase in Indonesia during the next few years it seems to me to be more likely as a consequence of the political dynamics of particular situations rather than fundamental, long-term social change. In present circumstances the political parties do not play a significant role in government. The government "party", Golkar, is essentially an instrument of the regime to win votes in elections rather than a grass-roots organisation conveying popular sentiments to the government while the other two parties, which were formed out of the old parties which did have real claims to mass support, have been largely emasculated. The PPP has been gradually de-Islamified and as a consequence has seen it electoral support drop from nearly 30 per cent to only 18 per cent in the last election while the other party, the Indonesian Democratic Party (PDI), with the old Sukarnoist Indonesian National Party as its core, has consistently come last in each election.

As long as the military remains united and determined to remain in control the possibility that the parties will assert themselves as independent political forces seems remote. At the same time, however, the parties do have organisational structures which could conceivably be reinvigorated in favourable circumstances such as a loosening of military domination. In recent years some younger civilian leaders in Golkar have already shown signs of beginning to prepare for the future when Golkar might have to stand more on its own feet, such as the introduction of direct individual membership in contrast to the old federal structure of affiliated organisations. The PPP, in more favourable circumstances and under different leadership, could presumably once again present itself as the representative of political Islam while the PDI could try to win back some of the constituencies of its original components. The parties, however, are in no position themselves to force the military to loosen its control. The loosening would have to be a result of developments within the military itself.

In this respect the way in which power passes from President Soeharto to his successor will be crucial (see Crouch 1988). President Soeharto has always avoided designating a clearcut successor. His first two vice-presidents were civilians who were never thought of as successors while the third, although a senior general, was regarded as lacking political ambition and the fourth, Sudharmono, does not have a strong personal power base in the military. Like traditional Javanese sultans who kept rival groups of nobles in balance with each other, Soeharto has always distributed key positions in the regime between rival groups of generals. While it is possible that the transition from Soeharto to his successor will be smooth and the successor will inherit Soeharto's powers and authority more or less intact, it seems no less likely that in the absence of a generally accepted heir, the new president will only take power after an intense struggle within the military elite. It is not improbable that the new president will have to establish a new coalition of support including officers belonging to rival groups with the result that he will not enjoy anything like the authority that Soeharto wields now. Moreover, it is likely in the post-oil-boom era that he will lack the patronage resources which Soeharto used so effectively to consolidate his own rule. In contrast to the present situation, a new leader might find himself dealing with brother officers who feel themselves no less qualified for the top position than the incumbent.

Such a development could be quite favourable for civilian political organisations as rival military groups would tend to look beyond the military for additional political support. Some military leaders might have an interest in strengthening Golkar while others might seek alliances with PPP or PDI or even other civilian groups. Developments along these lines seem to have taken place in Thailand after the fall of the military regime in 1973 and especially after the coups of 1976 and 1977 when the military restored itself to its dominant position but factionalism prevented it from returning to the pre-1973 style of government. Since 1977 Thailand's governments have been led by generals but the government itself consists of coalitions of rival parties whose hold on power depends on the retention not only of the approval of the military but also the civilian parties in parliament. In these circumstances the political parties which were formed or revived after 1973 have been able to expand their organisational infrastructure and their popular bases although it is still far from clear that they could stand up to a new onslaught in the apparently unlikely event of the military finally overcoming its disunity and once again asserting its domination over the government.

In conclusion it would appear that the prospects of an immediate expansion of civilian participation, especially the participation of civilians with their own bases of political support outside the regime, are not especially bright. That the new generation of academy-trained military officers will of their own volition change the military's orientation toward civilian participation in the government seems doubtful. Moreover, the important changes in the social structure that have accompanied the rapid economic growth of the last twenty years do not yet appear to have gone far enough to provide a strong social base for new civilian movements demanding "democratic" reforms and strong civilian participation. On the other hand it is quite possible that the increasing complexity of the modern economy and the need to expand the non-oil sector following the fall in oil prices will force the military leaders of the regime to depend more on civilian technocrats. The best prospect for expanding civilian party representation might, however, arise if the coming transition from Soeharto to his successor reveals sharp rifts within the military itself which forces rival factions to look beyond the military for civilian support in order to bolster their positions vis-a-vis their military rivals.

3

The Thai Military and Its Role in Society in the 1990s

Suchit Bunbongkarn

Introduction

The durability of the parliamentary system, the impressive growth of the economy, the expansion of commercialization and industrialization and the increasing pluralism in the last ten years have all led to a change in civil-military relations in Thailand. For more than forty years since the 1932 revolution, the armed forces dominated the political arena without real challenges from the civil bureaucracy, political parties or other societal groups. There were times when the military had to concede to playing a lesser role in society, but its political domination remained unchallenged. However, in the 1980s, Thailand had undergone a significant transformation with politics becoming more open and economic stabilization allowing it to approach the status of a newly industrialized country. This change has affected the military's relations with the state and society.

In his study of the armed forces in modernization in Thailand, Lissak (1976:13) has termed the military's involvement in politics and other civilian affairs as "role expansion". Military role expansion was more evident after the second World War when a number of officers were engaged not only in politics, but also in the economic sphere. Leading members of the armed forces were appointed board members of state enterprises and private firms.

They were needed by Chinese business leaders, most of whom were Chinese or their descendants, to protect Chinese interest to facilitate business dealings with government authorities. In addition, military units were engaged in rural development, mobilization of the rural masses and other mass psychological operations. To legitimize these functions and strengthen the military's role in society, the Prime Minister issued Orders Nos 66/2523 and 65/2525 (Bunbongkarn 1988a). Constraints on its role expansion have recently increased and the military has had to review its involvement in civil affairs. The 1990s will be a decade of re-adjustment of military role expansion, and a new direction for its non-military tasks. It is interesting, therefore, to examine the military's effort to alter its roles, as well as factors influencing the re-adjustment and to project the future trends.

The Military's Political Role: From Ruler to Balancer

The military's involvement in politics can be seen from the fact that in the last fifty years a number of military leaders became prime ministers. Moreover they remained in power much longer than their civilian counterparts. From 1932 to 1984 Thailand had sixteen prime ministers: six were army officers, one was a retired naval officer, and nine were civilians. The six military prime ministers were in office for a total of 44 years, while the ten civilian prime ministers were there for only eight years (Bunbongkarn 1987a: 61-62).

Since 1983, active military officers have been barred by the constitution from taking up political posts unless they quit the armed forces. General Prem Tinasulanoud and his successor General Chatichai Choonhavan were qualified to be prime ministers because they had already retired. This indicates a transformation of the military's role from "rulers" to "stabilizers". Officers have ceased to be leading members of the government, but their influence is still important for stability.

In his comment on Lissak's work, Perlmutter (1980:106) classified the Thai military regime as "market-bureaucratic". He agreed with Lissak that in Thailand after 1932 a bureaucratic-military apparatus became the central focus of the political structure, and as the "heart" of the bureaucracy, it has also become the protector of the executive-administrative center at the expense of a weak legislative branch and unorganized periphery (*ibid.*:107). Perlmutter (*ibid.*) further stated that the Thai military was a market-capitalist military-bureaucratic polity because it sought to "manage the modernization process within the framework of a capitalist market economy".

The analyses of Lissak and Perlmutter were correct for the period between 1932 and 1973. The seizure of power by a group of military officers and civilians in 1932 to supplant the absolute monarchy with a constitutional government was the first direct involvement of the armed forces in politics. Since then the military has been a dominant political force in society dictating the nature of Thailand's political evolution. The regimes, although mostly led by military leaders were not purely military in their composition; rather they were civil-military regimes. In these regimes government authority resided in a coalition of military and civilian bureaucrats; they were oligarchic in nature. The ruling group was split into several factions, each led by a politico-military elite and supported by a faction or factions in the armed forces, the civil bureaucracy and to a lesser extent the national assembly.

This oligarchic rule was supplanted by an autocratic one when Field Marshal Sarit Thanarat took power in 1958. Although most of Sarit's cabinet were civilian bureaucrats; technocrats and intellectuals were drawn in to help develop the country, but the power and authority resided in the military leader. Political parties and elections were prohibited until 1968.

Field Marshal Thanom Kittikachorn who succeeded Sarit in 1963 allowed political parties and civilian politicians to participate in the political process after a new constitution was promulgated in 1968, but the military continued to be a dominant force in Thai politics and coups were an acceptable means of achieving power.

After the October 1973 revolt, the political role of the military changed and Lissak's and Perlmutter's analyses were less relevant. That revolt demonstrated a rise of extra-bureaucratic forces, such as the students, labourers, farmers and the business sector. It also marked the beginning of an end of the bureaucratic military polity.[1] Despite the failure of the civilian representative government to institutionalize itself from 1973 to 1976 and the return of the military to power in October 1976, the bureaucratic polity failed to gain support. The people did not want to go back to dictatorial rule. This desire was expressed through widespread discontent against the rightest authoritarian regime of Thanin Kraivixien which was established after the coup. Discontent was growing so much so that the military hastily dissolved the regime only a year after it took control of the country.

The Military's Redefinition of Its Political Role

Since 1978, Thai politics has been characterized by a new balance between the armed forces and political parties. Throughout the period of General Prem Tinasulanoud's rule from 1980 to 1988, political power was shared by party leaders, who gained legitimacy through elections and military elites whose influence was still recognized. The military, however, did not accept this change easily as during the eight years of Prem administration there were two attempted coups and one attempt to amend the constitution to allow military officers and civil servants to hold political posts (Bunbongkarn 1987b:43).

These attempts demonstrated that at least some factions in the armed forces wanted to regain political power. Additionally, the attempted coups also showed that there were conflicts among military elites on the issue of political involvement. While some wanted to bring back military rule, others agreed that since the political and social environments had changed, the military's political role had to be redefined. The problem was that the redefinition was not widely accepted. In general, military elites agreed that they should participate in the political process to set a course for political development. This was put forward by a group of "democratic soldiers" who dominated the thinking of the military hierarchy during the 1980s. The group's idea was spelled out in Prime Minister's Orders nos. 66/2523 and 65/2525 issued in 1980 and 1982 respectively. In summary: the military should play a leading role in promoting "democratic" development in Thailand since it was the most effective way to fight the communist insurgents (*ibid.*:69-73).

Subsequently, leaders reasserted this opinion on several occasions. General Chavalit Yongchaiyuth, the present army chief, argued that in a country like Thailand where the political system had yet to evolve into a full-fledged democracy, the Army's role was to build it; when finally a permanent and stable democratic system had been achieved, the Army would then assume the role of guardian (*ibid.*: 72-73).

In early 1987, the General raised a controversial issue which could be considered as a sign of the Army's intention to play a leading role in political development. The issue involved the Army's role in staging a "revolution" in Thailand. In February 1987, Chavalit, in distinguishing a coup from a revolution stated that the military would not stage a coup but would not be reluctant to launch a revolution if it had popular approval and if it would lead to an improvement of the people's lives. He insisted that a revolution is something creative not destructive and that the democratic political system with the king as its head would be left intact (*Yongchaiyuth* 1987:29).

The proposed role of the armed forces by General Chavalit was faced with strong criticisms from the press, politicians, and academics who distrusted the military. These groups believed that the military leaders' real intention in getting involved in politics was to protect their corporate and personal interests and not to promote democracy.

Despite these criticisms and distrust, the armed forces continued to use the prime ministerial orders to justify their political role. The political strategy before the 1973 student revolt was "the politics of being above politics". The Army always claimed that it would get involved in politics only to bring order to a chaotic situation, and would transfer power to a civilian government when the country returned to normality. However, when Order No. 66/2523 was issued in April 1980, the Army began to redefine its political role. This redefined role was not simply aimed at justifying a temporary involvement in politics to remedy specific problems, but instead envisaged tasks for the military in the development of the country which implied a more permanent political involvement. According to the order, a dictatorial government is the major precondition for the rise of political offensive operations by the communists. To counter them, the Army believed, all democratic measures must be utilized since economic measures proved insufficient. Moreover, because the military suppression of the communists is the responsibility of the Army, democratic development as a measure to remove this crucial precondition should be the mission of the Army as well.

The Army's move to amend the constitution in January 1983 is the best illustration of the use of the order to justify its role in "democratic development". The proposed amendment was aimed at extending the enforcement period of the provisional clause which would allow military and civilian officers to be cabinet members and maintain the power of the appointed senate. In defending its move the Army stated that the amendment was in accordance with Order No. 66/2523 which emphasized the increase sovereignty of the masses. This, according to the Army's statement, could be achieved by increasing the authority of the senate and making it a democratic one, by the selection of its members to represent all walks of life (The Royal Thai Army 1983).

National Security and Developmental Role

Another task which was closely connected with the political and developmental roles of the armed forces was national security. This role was increasingly emphasized when the communist insurgency became widespread and intensified in the 1970s. The Communist Party of Thailand (CPT) began its subversive activities during Marshal Sarit's period, but the government considered the insurgency similar to banditry and argued that it should be handled by the police force. Indeed a number of army officers admitted that during that period they knew little about communism (Bunbongkarn 1988b:135-136). These officers believed that the increase of communist activities was dictated by the international communist movement which intended to invade Thailand by force. The realization that communism was the product of political, economic and social problems within the country came later when the CPT began to intensify its activities in the late 1960s. After its proclamation of armed insurgency in August 1965, the CPT expanded and intensified terrorist operations in every region. Despite violent suppression the insurgency increased. The frequency of armed contacts between government troops and the CPT grew, and the number of casualties on both sides increased. The failure to suppress the CPT forced military leaders to contemplate means to develop the Army's links with the people and with various specific social groups in urban and rural areas. Several development programs were established by the Army with the intention of influencing the rural people to the government side to weaken the CPT's position and to facilitate the government's armed operations at the final stage.

At the initial stage of the insurgency, the military launched development programs in affected rural areas but they were sporadic, temporary and had no intention of achieving large-scale economic development. They were one-shot projects aimed at achieving a psychological impact. The project, however, did not stop the growth of the insurgency.

During the 1970s, a new concept of development was launched. This concept was called *"yuthasat pattanta"* or strategic development. It was an integrated project of rural development ranging from agricultural development to political education and self-defense training. The project was launched simultaneously in affected areas in order to extend government authority and weaken the CPT's bases (Kullavanij 1986:44-59). The Army was instrumental in bringing people to new settlements around the CPT's stronghold, and due to the integrated development projects the people were able to resist the CPT's threat and willing to work for the government. The settlement encroachment in the insurgents' territory facilitated the government forces attacks on CPT's strongholds.

In addition to this type of development, rural mass organizations such as the National Defense Volunteers, and the Reservists for National Security were established by the military. These mass organizations were mechanisms of mobilization to serve the purpose of the Army. They were intended to rally rural support for the Army against the communist insurgents, but within the process the villagers were expected to become closer to the Army and eventually supporters of its political activities. With its control over programs and structures of these movements, it is not difficult for the military leadership to use them for other political purposes. Although mobilization activities have not often been conducted and the political strength of the mass organizations has not yet been put to the test, the organizations themselves provide a chance for military officers to work closely with rural people to improve the Army's image and to expand support for military leaders.

The Army's Modernization and Its Consequences

The occupation of Kampuchea (Cambodia) by Vietnamese troops and the decline of the communist insurgency in Thailand encouraged Thai military leaders to strengthen the Army's conventional warfare capability. During the insurgency period the Army had to pay more attention to guerilla warfare, leaving the development of conventional warfare and national defense capability to the US Military Assistance Program (MAP). That program terminated in the mid 1970s, when Thai military leaders realized the necessity to become less dependent on the US, though the Americans were still the hope of Thailand in times of crises. Border clashes between Thai and Vietnamese troops, however, showed the ineffectiveness on the Thai side in the area of logistics, with shortage of arms and ammunition. The Thai military leaders then urgently realized the need to modernize and strengthen the armed forces to meet the threat on the eastern border.

In his November 1986 speech at the eleventh Pacific Armies Management seminar in Bangkok, General Chavalit Yongchaiyuth, the army chief, outlined his plan to modernize the Army by emphasizing that the Thai Army would be developed in five major areas: manpower, training, equipment, reserve ratios and force structure. The underlying principle governing the development process was that of a small army of well-trained soldiers who were equipped with modern weapons and backed by reserves prepared for speedy action. As he put it:

> Our standing policy is to emphasize on quality rather than quantity. With effectively trained soldiers, the Army's efficiency as a whole will increase, a large percentage of the Army's manpower can be trimmed down and millions of *baht* would be saved to spend on modernization. A smaller army with well-trained soldiers equipped with modern weapons is what we have in mind (*The Nation* 1986:4).

In modernizing its force structure, the Army is stressing combat readiness, and modern technology. At present, the Army has approximately 15 divisions - combat size and combat support units: 7 infantry divisions, 2 cavalry divisions, 2 special forces divisions, 2 development divisions, one artillery division and one anti-aircraft artillery division. The army chief admitted that the existing forces "are much less in quantity than our potential enemy" (*ibid.*). Therefore, to improve the Army's effectiveness, according to General Chavalit, the combat forces must be modernized. Motorized and mechanized infantry is among the modernization programs. Orders for more sophisticated weapons, tanks and artillery are in the process as part of upgrading combat forces.

Since the end of the second World War, the development and modernization of the Thai armed forces depended on US MAP. From the point of view of the Army the impact of the MAP in the 1950s and 1960s was remarkable. It was recognized that the Army could not have developed without American assistance (The Royal Thai Army 1952). From 1951 to 1975 the regular military assistance to Thailand amounted to a total of US$935 million dollars or approximately an average of US$46 million dollars per annum (Girling 1985:235). This amount was also equivalent to 50 per cent of the total defense budget or 36,463 million *baht* (US$1,824 million). With US assistance, the Thai armed forces were modernized and developed without substantial increase in the national defense budget. From 1960 to 1971, the budget of the Ministry of Defense was kept within the range of between 13 and 17 per cent of total government expenditure.[2]

The Thai armed forces have had to depend on the national budget for development after the end of the MAP in the mid 1970s. But during the latter half of the 1970s, the US continued to be the major supplier of military hardware to Thailand through the foreign military sale programs. Because of the high price of American weapons, in the 1980s Thailand began to look elsewhere and China became a major supplier from which a number of tanks, artillery, anti-aircraft guns, armoured personnel carriers, and frigates have been ordered. Although the Chinese products are far inferior to the West, the prices are, however, more attractive. The Chinese also offer Thailand a friendship price which is only 10 per cent of the market price.

In planning the modernization of the Thai armed forces priority was given to units on the eastern frontiers. This reflected the threat perception of Thai military leaders in the 1980s: Vietnam has been considered as a major and immediate threat since its forces took control of Kampuchea (Cambodia). Although General Chavalit did not name Vietnam as the enemy, he warned that "we must be prepared to be at our best and cannot overlook the threatening fact especially if Vietnam completely gains control over Kampuchea and receives all-out support from her superpower (*The Nation* 1986: 4). Likewise, the New Air Force Chief, Air Marshal Kaset Rojananil continued to perceive Vietnam as a threat. Thus in planning the modernization of the air force, he emphasized that the threat from Vietnam had to be taken into account. Acquiring F16 fighters in 1986 was justified by the threat from Vietnam although some critics believed otherwise (*Matichon Sudsapda* 1989:10). The Navy's plan to build air and coastal defense of the industrialized eastern seaboard costing millions of *baht*, implies that Vietnam is still considered a threat to the eastern border.

What are the consequences of the modernization program? One of the major concerns is whether the acquisition of Chinese weaponry will lead to military dependence on China. Some are worried that this military tie will enhance the Chinese domination over Thai defense and security policies. But Thai military leaders argued, the weapons deal with Peking was based on practical and not ideological factors. Thailand has no intention of establishing a military alliance with China nor does it want to be under Chinese military domination. The Vietnamese threat forced the Thai armed forces to seek a source where large quantities of weaponry could be obtained at the shortest possible notice and at a reasonable price, and China seemed to be the answer. Nevertheless, American weapons still form the core of Thai military hardware and Chinese products are intended only to be supplementary. In comparison, Thailand is perhaps the country which relies more on China for military equipment than any other ASEAN country, but it is to early to conclude that the Bangkok-Peking military axis has become established.

Since American influence is firmly rooted in the Thai military establishment, it is difficult for any country including China to replace it. In addition to military hardware the US continue to provide assistance in the training of Thai military personnel. For more than three decades, promising Thai military cadets have been sent to study at West Point in New York State and officers go to the Command and General Staff School at Fort Leavenworth, Kansas. The curriculum of Thailand's Chulackhomklao Military Academy was revised to replicate West Point's. Training of Thai military personnel, troop deployment, logistics development and defense strategy have therefore been influenced by the Americans. Other American military values and doctrine have also been adopted by the Thai military, except the concept of civilian supremacy.

Another question concerning the consequence of modernization of the Thai armed forces is whether it will lead to an increase of military professionalism and will in turn depoliticize the Army. In general, the armed forces" modernization means an increase of military professionalization. During the late nineteenth century when the Thai armed forces were first modernized, professionalism was also introduced as an integral part of modern armed forces. But since professionalization was not entrenched in the Thai military it did not prevent the armed forces from political intervention, as was evident in the 1932 coup. Its leaders had received advanced military training in Europe. After the second World War, military modernization continued under the MAP. Yet the armed forces involvement in politics prevailed. In the 1980s, the modernization of the armed forces did not lead to political disengagement. Thus, the political involvement of the military cannot be explained by the degree of professionalization, but the political and social environment of Thailand. Uninstitutionalized participant politics, a weak political party system, political apathy by the people and instability of civilian government encouraged the military to seize power. Presently, it is difficult to see a total military withdrawal from politics unless the institutions of democracy are more firmly established in Thailand.

Constraints on the Military's Role Expansion

Several developments in the 1980s have put constraints on the military's role in Thai society. One of them is the stability of the representative government. The system formulated under the 1978 constitution has weathered several political storms. It has survived two attempted coups and elected politicians appear to have had a better opportunity to establish links with the masses, expand their power base and institutionalize their own political parties. The durability of Prem's government from 1981 to 1988 can be attributed to a number of factors. One of them is the leadership of Prem himself. He was able to perform a "delicate balancing act" among three institutions - the Palace, the Armed Forces and the House of Representatives - that supported his administration in general and between the military and the House of Representatives in particular. No single political institution dominated the polity. Power was therefore shared by the three major political institutions. Political compromise among them was achieved by Prem's leadership and political finesse.

In addition, Thai political party leaders were more aware of the weakness of the party system than in the 1960s, and were very careful in exerting their influence. So much so that they tried to avoid confrontation with the military and not jeopardize its corporate interests. Politicians also tried to reach compromise among themselves on various issues. By accepting General Prem's leadership politicians indicated their political maturity and agreed that unless participatory politics were more institutionalized, compromises with other institutions and an acceptance of non-partisan premiership was needed.

The smooth political succession from General Prem to General Chatichai Coonhavan was another significant step in the development in Thai democracy as Chatichai is the first prime minister in more than ten years who is an elected politician and party leader. More important, the ability of his government to respond to the demands of various societal groups and to maintain government stability acts as a major constraint on the military's political intervention. This provides elected politicians with an opportunity to continue to improve their performance and competency and to accommodate divergent views in order to prevent political destabilization. Although the party system needs a lot of improvement, the coalition parties are working together demonstrating a greater ability for compromise.

Another constraint on the armed forces is the prevaling democratic mood among the educated Thais. It appears that people are now more satisfied with the performance of the democratic government. Democracy has in fact been accepted in principle in Thailand as a legitimate system, but never before did the Thais have confidence in a democratic regime until recently. They now want to give representative government a try. Impressive economic growth in recent years has reinforced the belief that a democratic system can be conducive to economic development. The people are more familiar with and tolerant of the effectiveness of the democratic process. Perhaps Thais had been under a dictatorial rule for so long that they did not want a reversion to authoritarian rule once it was over. Thus rumours of coups are heard less frequently and the military is therefore expected to be more professional and less political.

The increasing dominance of the business community in the political process is another constraint on the military. In the long run it is still debatable whether this could lead to political stability. In the short run, however, it is certain that the increasing role of the business community has enhanced the viability of the elected government. Several business elites are financial supporters of parties and some are also elected politicians and cabinet members. Major political parties like the Chat Thai or Social Action Party (SAP) have been strengthened by financial contributions from economic elites.

Local government is also dominated by the business community and local business elites control several local governments. Some have been elected municipal mayors and councilors, and provincial councilors. These local elites and national politicians are linked through interdependent relationships. They are part of the political machine in provinces which work for voters' support in both national and local elections.

Economic domination is another limitation to military role expansion in Thailand. The increasing influence of the business community and the rapid economic growth and expansion have put economic issues to the forefront. Changes in the international and regional environment have led to more complex economic problems while ideological and political tensions have been relaxed. Economic competition between the United States, the European Community, Japan and the newly industrialized countries (NICs) are becoming increasingly tough and Thailand, which is emerging as a NIC, will now be more deeply involved in friction over trade.

The policy of changing Indochina from a battle field to a market place initiated by Prime Minister Chatichai has enhanced the economic priority. He further emphasized that because of geographical and economic advantages, Thailand should serve as the center for the development of mainland Southeast Asia. His policy has prioritized economic over security and political matters and has encouraged interest among the public.

Another trend in Thailand is the increasing pluralism. Thai civil society is now becoming more complex with a proliferation of social action groups. The fastest growing are those concerned with protecting the environment. They have been very effective in campaigning against the misuse of natural resources and the destruction of the natural balance of the ecosystem. Other professional and interest groups and particularly the mass media, students and labor groups will become more vocal and politically potent in the forseeable future. Another interesting development in Thai society is the development of an urban-based middle class comprising professionals, white collar workers, civil servants and medium size business entrepreneurs whose voice is increasingly being heard.

The Military's Role in the 1990s

The characteristics of Thailand's economy, society and politics described above appear to favor the development of participatory politics. Economic prosperity which will continue in the 1990s will enhance the role of the business community and other extra-bureaucratic forces which will in turn strengthen the democratic system. Faced with new political and social developments, the military will have to readjust its role in Thai society. The question is: are these socio-economic and political changes strong enough to force the military to move back to the barracks? Because the Thai armed forces' civilian role has been deeply entrenched, it is difficult to see a complete withdrawal in the near future.

In his speech on the armed forces day on 25 January 1990, General Chavalit reiterated a recently adopted strategy for national security which focuses on the people's economic improvement. He made it clear that if the people become wealthier then the nation will be more secure. In the same speech, the Army chief also declared war on poverty emphasizing that poverty is now the most important enemy of the Thais and it is the Army's mission to get rid of it (*The Nation* 1990). Therefore the armed forces will concentrate more on rural development.

In the 1960s and 1970s the military's development mission was to defeat the communist insurgency. But in the 1990s, it will be different. The mission in the next decade will be fighting poverty which would involve the armed forces in a wider range of development projects. Reduced tension in the international environment and the increasing prospect of peace in Indochina allows the military to expand its developmental tasks. This strategy indicates that there should be no clear-cut boundary between the military and civilians at least in rural development. The military always argues that mobilization of resources, expertise and equipping the armed forces for development purposes will hasten the pace of development and will improve rural life in areas where civilians cannot reach.

The determination of the armed forces to get involved in this area can be seen with the recent establishment of one more development division and one engineering division. These divisions are responsible for developmental tasks in rural areas and the engineering division is assigned to take care of a large scale construction project which is beyond the capability of the development divisions. Several of the military's development projects like the Development of the Northeast, the new hope project for the Muslim dominated areas in the south, established in the late 1980s, will continue into the 1990s. And a number of new programs are being planned and will be launched in the next few years. These show a strong commitment of the Army in this field (Kraprayoon 1990:185-199).

These civic action programs will not be operated without difficulties. One of the problems is concerned with the cooperation of other agencies. It is unlikely that the civil bureaucracy and politicians will be totally happy with this expansion of the military over their constituences. Rural masses are considered major supporters of political parties and parties cannot afford to lose these support bases to the military which they regard as their rival. The Ministry of the Interior also considers rural development as its responsibility and is unprepared to permit other groups to unsurp this project. Civilians may not reject the military's role in rural development outright but their cooperation will not be easily attained.

The 1990s will see no less effort of military leaders to modernize and upgrade the armed foces. Although international tension has been reduced, the military's modernization programs will continue as it insists that it has to remain prepared. Military leaders believed that intra-regional conflicts would persist and thus threats would not actually be reduced. Economic competition, territorial disputes and irredentism may constitute a new form of threat. An economic boom in Thailand will allow the armed forces to press for a large share of the budget for development. The military will seek not only an expansion of its forces but also high-tech development. This will lead to an arms race in the region which could in turn create a demand for further upgrading of the forces.

In the political sphere, military leaders admitted that Thai polity is now shifting from the military dominated to civilian dominated; the role of the military has to be changed in order to facilitate this transition (*Lakthai* 1989). Nevertheless the Army chief did not spell out specific actions to be taken by the military, but his suggestion implied that the Army will not retreat totally from the political arena. In fact the military will be less interested in becoming a ruler. Instead, it will perform a guardian role by focusing on maintaining national security, peace and political stability. The military will also be tolerant of the openess of the political system and the increasing role of political parties. In developing and upholding Thai democracy, the Army's leader has made it clear on several occasions that the armed forces would not like to see the democratic system dominated by economic elites. It is therefore likely that the military will be playing a counter force to business leaders' political domination. The military will encourage business leaders to represent not only the middle class but also the masses.

A military coup or some kind of political intervention cannot be totally ruled out in Thailand. Widespread corruption in the government, a prolonged economic crisis, a deepending conflict in the nation and a serious threat to the throne will encourage the military to step in again to govern. Although military officers are becoming more professionalized, this professionalism does not affect their concern over political social and economic problems. They still consider themselves guardians of the nation and as a result they have to be prepared for any crisis.

With these political, social and economic changes, the market bureaucratic polity model is no longer valid in describing the Thai political system and military role. In fact, a military regime is now a thing of the past in Thailand, but the military's influence will not diminish. Unlike the military in other countries, the Thai armed forces continue to possess several mass mobilization instruments such as rural mass organizations, radio and television stations. Whether these instruments will be utilized to facilitate the role expansion again depends on the success of participatory politics to institutionalize itself.

Notes

1. The October 1973 revolt was organized by students to overthrow Thanom's regime. Two years earlier, due to conflicts among the ruling elites, Thanom decided to launch a coup d'etat to overthrow his own government and set up a dictatorial rule akin to Sarit's. But this autocracy only led to students discontent and revolt which put an end to his regime. For a full account of the revolt and the decline of bureaucratic polity, see Ruth-Inge Heinze, 'Ten Days in October: Students vs Military: An Account of the Student Uprising in Thailand', *Asian Survey* June 1974: 491-508.

2. For the annual defense budget from 1951 to 1959, see *Royal Gazette*, Vol. 68, 3 April 1951; Vol. 69, 16 January 1952; Vol. 10, 19 January 1953; Vol. 19, 9 February 1954; Vol. 72, 22 January 1955; Vol. 73, 27 February 1956; Vol. 74, 5 January 1957; Vol. 75, 23 July 1958; Vol. 76, 26 May 1959; from 1960 to 1971, see Suchit Bunbongkarn, *The Role of the Thai Legislature*, Monograph Series on Political Science No. 3, (Bangkok: Faculty of Political Science, Chulalongkorn University, 1983:. 83) [in Thai].

4

The Armed Forces of the Philippines and Political Instability

Viberto Selochan

Martial law was declared in the Philippines in 1972 and lifted in 1981. During the martial law period, the Armed Forces of the Philippines (AFP) became a dominant force in society and a political instrument for maintaining the corrupt and administratively inefficient regime of President Ferdinand Marcos in power. The AFP played a central role in the overthrow of Marcos in February 1986 and the accession of Corazon Aquino to the presidency. In return, elements in the military expected to be rewarded with a role in her administration. When this did not eventuate these groups made several unsuccessful attempts to seize political power. Although tentative stability has been achieved, the administration still faces many problems which could still see elements in the armed forces continue to try to seize political power in the 1990s.

This chapter will provide a brief historical development of the AFP and then examine the period from 1980, when preparations to lift martial law were being made, to the fall of President Marcos and the accession of Aquino to the presidency in 1986. It will also speculate on what role the military is likely to play in the Philippines in the 1990s.

Philippine Historical Development

After 350 years of Spanish rule the islands of the Philippines were ceded to the United States under the Treaty of Paris on 10 December 1898, after the cessation of the Spanish-American War.

For internal policing of the islands, the US created an Insular Police Force in 1902 modelled on the Canadian Mounted Police. This force later became the Philippine Constabulary (PC), which remains in existence today. In 1935 the Philippines achieved Commonwealth status in preparation for independence in 1946. One of the first steps taken by the administration of President Manuel Quezon was to prepare the country for its defence when American troops departed. The National Defense Act was passed in 1935 and an American Military Mission under General Douglas MacArthur devised the program for the development of the Philippine armed forces. In 1941 the fledgling military was incorporated into the United States Armed Forces in the Far East (USAFFE) to repel the invading Japanese forces. The Philippine military ceased to exist as an automouous body until the islands became independent on 4 July 1946.

After independence the armed forces again depended on the US for training and equipment. This was achieved under the Military Assistance Program (MAP) which was an adjunct of the Military Bases Agreement (MBA) of 1947. The MBA gave the US a 99 year lease on 23 military installations in the islands. The duration of the MBA was reduced from 99 years to 25 in 1966. Thus, the agreement expires in 1991. During the late 1940s and early 1950s the Communist-influenced Hukbalahap (Huk) movement, which had fought the occupying Japanese forces, turned its attention to resisting the Philippine government of Manuel Roxas to achieve improved conditions for the peasants in Central Luzon.

Unable to achieve its aims through negotations, even with its representatives in Congress, the Huks resisted the armed forces which largely protected the landowners. With assistance from Washington, the AFP under Secretary of Defence Ramon Magsaysay defeated the Huks. When he became president in 1953, Magsaysay rewarded the armed forces by appointing active duty officers to positions in government. His untimely death in a plane crash in 1957 forced many of these officers to return to military service.

By the time Ferdinand Marcos achieved the presidency in 1965 most of these officers had been removed from government by his precedessors, Carlos Garcia and Diosdado Macapagal. Marcos, however, saw the potential of holding on to power with the support of the AFP. He nurtured many officers who became loyal to him and appointed loyalists to the position of chief of staff of the armed forces. In the process the military chain of command was subverted. Unwilling to relinquish power after serving two-four year terms as president, Marcos declared martial law in September 1972 under the pretext Communists and Muslim insurgents' threatened society. For its role in maintaining Marcos in office, the AFP became a junior partner in government. Martial law provided the military with power it had never before attained. Unaccustomed to running government departments and private corporations, the latter sequestered from Marcos's opponents, officers became corrupt and abused their new found power with impunity. In fact the AFP was even employed to ensure that Marcos would win elections which he carefully staged managed after 1978, while the country remained under martial law.

Ending Martial Law, Not Military Control

Realizing that it could not defeat President Marcos through the electoral process, as the military and his political network ensured the president's victory at the ballot, some opposition groups decided to destablize the martial law regime by other means. During 1979 the "Light-A-Fire-Movement" started its campaign to destablize the government by setting alight a number of government buildings and hotels (McDougald 1987:166). Between August and September 1980 a number of bombings in Manila informed the president that if martial law continued, urban warfare would ensue (Rodriguez 1985:124-125).

After a bomb had exploded at a travel agents' convention in Manila in October 1980, the president used the opportunity to issue General Order No. 68, which gave the AFP increased police powers in preparation for the termination of martial law. Subsequently he issued Presidential Decree No.1737 [which became a Public Order Act], and Presidential Decree No. 1498 [the National Security Code] which provided the AFP with extraordinary powers of detention and arrest of those considered a threat to national security. Both of these decrees encouraged repression (de Dios 1988:79). Testimony to this was the increase in human rights abuses during the period (Poole and Vanzi 1984:84-108).

President Marcos described the decision to terminate martial law on 17 January 1981 as "an encounter with destiny". But others suggested that the decision was taken to impress the new US President, Ronald Reagan, to improve the atmosphere in preparation for the Pope's visit (*FEER* 23-29 January 1981), and because of the worsening economic situation (Catilo *et al.* 1985:75). Equally important, Marcos realized that he was becoming increasingly dependent on the military to maintain power. Continuing martial law would therefore only further his dependency on the armed forces. Most of the AFP personnel were opposed to the lifting of martial law. Concerned that they could be subjected to trial for their actions during this period, senior officers requested the president to guarantee them immunity from prosecution. They even warned the president that the military might not be able to control the country after the termination of martial law.

To legitimize the regime upon the termination of martial law, President Marcos planned elections for late 1981, but first called a plebiscite to approve constitutional reforms. With an 80 per cent approval, which "virtually exempts the President from public accountability" (ibid.:77), he scheduled presidential elections for 16 June 1981. Victory assured by the AFP, President Marcos ushered in the "New Republic".

For the military, the "New Republic" and the "New Society" differed little. Civilian courts assumed the responsibility for most cases, except those accused of endangering national security and sabotaging the economy (Hernandez 1985a:189). Officers continued performing civilian functions despite repeated requests from civilians for the military to resume its pre-martial law duties. In an interview Colonel R. Ibay, an Assistant Secretary of the Treasury, from 1981 to 1986, told me that officers were more efficient than civilians in performing these functions. Appearing to react to the pressure to remove officers from civil positions, Marcos indicated in October 1983 that officers would revert to performing military functions. But on 4 November the president declared that in the prevailing crisis, civilian-military cooperation was imperative, and officers were to continue in their present positions. To signify the importance of the military in his regime, the president stated that its hierarchy would in future attend cabinet meetings (*Daily Express* 5 November 1983).

Now more confident of the loyalty of all the senior officers, President Marcos retired his long-time loyalist, AFP Chief of Staff, General Romeo Espino on 15 August 1981 and replaced him with his former chauffeur, reservist officer Brigadier General Fabian Ver. A cousin and loyalist, General Ver was determined to maintain Marcos in office. For presidential seurity Ver built the Presidential Guard from a small unit of the AFP to a 15,000 man-strong force during his tenure, which commenced when Marcos achieved office in 1966. Concurrently, Ver was head of the National Intelligence and Security Authority (NISA). By the time he became chief of staff, only he and Marcos could approve officer promotion (*FEER* 13 October 1983). As a reservist, General Ver favoured reservists over regular officers. Appointed to the position of vice chief of staff was another of the president's cousins, General Fidel Ramos, a West Point graduate, who was already chief of the PC.

During the nine years of martial law the military manpower and budget increased markedly. From a force of 54,000 in 1972 the AFP increased to 157,000 in 1981 (The International Institute of Strategic Studies 1975-1976:76-79; 1978-1979:81-91; 1980-1981:112-113). In comparison, Thailand and Malaysia, which unlike the Philippines have external threats, registered only small increases in military manpower and budget (Berry 1986:221-225). Managing a military that had rapidly increased in size in a limited period presented many problems for the regime. Officers disenchanted with the president or the chief of staff easily acquired political support elsewhere. This was easily attained since loyalty to individuals rather than institutions is a feature of Philippine society, and in the AFP, as elsewhere, it assists in gaining promotion.

One politician who was fostering a clique of disgruntled officers and consolidating his power base in the armed forces was Defense Minister, Juan Ponce Enrile. To curtail Enrile's power, Marcos announced in a speech on 31 July 1983 at the Philippine Constabulary-Integrated National Police anniversary celebrations at Camp Crame that the minister of defence was no longer within the AFP chain of command, and that General Ver was now to report directly to the president. From that occasion Enrile became the first defence secretary in approximately thirty years not to be included in the chain of command of the Philippine military.

Concerned that the president was losing control of the armed forces, General Ver created the Regional Unified Commands (RUCs) in 1983 to centralize control of the AFP from the company units to the Genejral Headquarters. Each of the twelve regions was to comprise units from the major services of the AFP, with the commanders reporting directly to the chief of staff instead of to the chief of their service. The new structure allowed General Ver to consolidate his power in the AFP, while effectively destroying the autonomy of the local commanders. More importantly, by limiting the autonomy of most commands Marcos and Ver ensured that the AFP could not easily threaten the regime. For the Constabulary, Regional Commands were incorporated into the new structure and were effectively superseded by them, as was the authority of its chief, General Fidel Ramos. Hernandez (1985b:907) speculates that this new structure could better facilitate "military mobilization for control purposes", and provide "greater efficiency and effectiveness".

But it was apparently "Ver's baby", created for greater centralization so that the president could have direct access to and greater control of each region's command and thus monitor his opponents' activities in the regions. With such powers, the RUCs contributed to commanders achieving unparalleled influence at the regional level (ibid.). To ensure that the unified commands served the functions of the regime, all the commanders were appointed for their loyalty to the president and the AFP chief of staff, to whom they reported. The patron-client relationship that Marcos developed with many officers was institutionalized during the tenure of General Ver. Reservist officers became dominant in the AFP hierarchy, traditionally the domain of Philippine Military Academy graduates (Bauer 1973:28-29). With this restructuring, control over the military by Defence Secretary Enrile and the Vice Chief of Staff, and Chief of the PC, General Ramos, diminished significantly (Santos and Domingo-Robes 1987:33).

The creation of the RUCs and the announcement that officers would attend cabinet meetings further isolated the defence secretary and increased the president's dependency on the AFP. According to one source, the president started to rely on the officers more than the civilians in his cabinet, and officers' suggestions on government policy were frequently accepted in preference to the suggestions of civilian ministers. President Marcos's progressive reliance on the military in government was clearly evident after 1982 when, prior to his state visit to Saudi Arabia, he gave instuctions for the government to General Ver, and not to his civilian ministers. Encouraging senior AFP officers to participate in party politics through the *Kilusang Bagong Lipunan* (KBL - New Society Movement), reflected an attempt to develop stronger links between the armed forces and government, as with the Golkar in Indonesia. Indeed the president's political party was by 1983 developing closer links with the AFP as many officers were active members and some were on the executive committee of the party.

A hiatus developed in the consolidation of power in the AFP when the chief of staff was implicated in the assassination of former Senator Benigno Aquino. Marcos was forced to place Ver on leave of absence while the murder was being investigated. The president reluctantly appointed General Ramos, acting chief of staff. Marcos also decided to retire twenty-one of the extendee generals. Of the ninety-nine in the AFP, about fifty had their tour of duty extended beyond retirement, including the chiefs of all four branches of the AFP. Apparently, there was confusion in the AFP over the transfer of power from General Ver to General Ramos, as the former continued to issue orders despite the public pronouncement that he had been temporarily replaced. During this period, from October 1984 to March 1985, General Ramos allegedly intended to improve morale and discipline in the AFP and increase its effectiveness by restoring the people's confidence in the military. But President Marcos deprived the acting chief of staff of the authority to implement changes. Hampered in his duties, General Ramos developed a close relationship with Enrile, and was sympathetic to the fledgling reform group of junior officers in the AFP which was closely aligned to the secretary.

Cleared by the *Sandiganbayan*, a special anti-corruption court, of all charges, General Ver immediately resumed his position as chief of staff determined to pursue the reorganization which he had directed even during his leave of absence. The US administration, however, wanted General Ver to be retired. He was perceived to be the major obstacle to reforming the AFP. Washington informed Marcos that General Ramos was the best person to institute reforms in the armed forces (*FEER* 27 June 1985). But the president retorted that if the US persisted with the issue of General Ver's retirement then he would also retire General Ramos. Washington relented (Overholt 1986:1160).

The Reagan administration, and especially the Pentagon, advocated reforms in the AFP to make it effective in counterinsurgency operations. The Pentagon argued that these could not be attained without the "restoration of professional, apolitical leadership", which implied the removal of the chief of staff and the overstaying generals. Initially, President Marcos refused to accept such directions from the US. Marcos, however, eventually relented and promised that he would institute reforms in the AFP. They did not eventuate. Marcos realized that relinquishing his control of the armed forces would be tantamount to handing it over to the US (Bello 1987:59,168). What the president failed to realize was that "non-professionalism in the military and widespread corruption alienated the vast majority of soldiers" and would eventually result in his overthrow (*The POOP*, January-February 1987).

Resuming his position as chief of staff, General Ver was determined to prove to the US that he was in control of the military, and decided to eradicate any power base the acting chief of staff had established during his absence. Relegated to the largely ceremonial position of vice chief of staff, General Ramos wanted to resign but the president refused to accept his resignation. Apparently, Ramos wanted to resign because Ver asked the president to appoint his alleged co-conspirator in the Aquino assassination, Major General Prospero Olivas, to Ramos's position of chief of the

Philippine Constabulary and Integrated National Police [PC/INP] (Santos and Domingo-Robes 1987:34). Marcos did not accept Ver's recommendation and also avoided isolating Ramos by appointing Commodore B. Ochoo as navy commander. He also retained loyalists as the chiefs of the army and air force.

The Reform Movements

President Marcos's reluctance to institute reforms in the AFP compelled the Pentagon to court alternative groups, a strategy which in keeping with American foreign policy practices in the Third World. By 1985 the Reagan administration was encouraging opposition to Marcos (Barnds 1986:244).

A number of groups were organized in the AFP in the 1980s espousing various issues such as social and economic needs of the soldiers and professionalizing the military. These groups, called fraternities, emerged as a result of the factionalism that developed in the AFP during the latter years of the Marcos administration. These groups multiplied as resentment against the president increased in society. When the regime finally fell from power in 1986 the number of fraternities was estimated at around sixty (Nemenzo 1986a:18). Many were simply concerned with the welfare of soldiers, which had deteriorated during the conflict with the Muslims in the south. The differences were centred mostly on distinctions between regular officers and reservists, ethno-linguistic divisions and personal loyalties. But as in the Latin American armed forces (Garcia 1978:49-51) factionalism also arose in the AFP as a result of different orientations at military schools at home and abroad.

The most prominent fraternity was the Reform the Armed Forces Movement (RAM), which surfaced at the PMA graduation ceremony in March 1985. The origins of this group are hard to identify. Bonner (1987:442) claims it was "organized and funded" by the US, but he certainly underestimates the role of AFP officers. Athough the RAM received funds from the US it was also assisted by local business groups such as the Benguet corporation. The impetus for its establishment, however, came from the experiences of these officers as cadets of the 1971 *Matatag* [stability] class at the PMA, and later as lieutenants in the conflict in the southern Philippines. The experiences of the younger officers in the Mindanao conflict culminated in the development of the reform group between 1981 and 1982 (Lande 1986:138). Most of the leaders of the reform group were commanders in Mindanao, and were responsible for human rights violations there (Bello 1986:1023).

Officially the RAM was organized on 23 July 1982 by five officers from the PMA class of 1971, with Lieutenant Colonel Gregorio "Gringo" Honasan as its leader (Arillo 1986:166). Without adopting a specific name the group arranged clandestine meetings with other offficers and soon developed a substantial following [but certainly not the 70 per cent of the officer corps which it claimed in 1986]. Testing the attitude of society, and indeed of the AFP, to the disparaging reports circulating in the country about the military, the group sent a letter, signed the "Armed Defenders of Democracy", to a Manila magazine in September 1984 criticizing the leadership of the AFP. PMA graduates from the class of 1978 claimed they and the classes that followed them were integral to the formation of the reform movement. These young officers saw corruption and crimes being committed while they were in the field and reported such infringments to the group at MND [Ministry of National Defense]. The core members of the RAM were working at the ministry. Complaints of this nature provided the impetus for the formation of the movement.

Initially organized under the banner of R.E.F.O.R.M (Restore Ethics, Fairmindedness, Order, Righteousness and Morale) the RAM was perceived to be a result of the "growing idealism" among the young officers (Santos and Domingo-Robes 1987:37). Brigadier General Jose Almonte (1986:81) claimed that "a reservoir of professional integrity prevailed in the young officers since they had not succumbed to Marcos largesse as some of their senior officers". Hernandez (1985b:914) argues that the temporary change in leadership from Ver to Ramos between 1984 and 1985 must have encouraged the formation of the RAM since Ramos was perceived to be a professional soldier. But the movement had its origins before that event.

Hernandez (ibid.:913), however, rightly claims that the RAM could not have been formed without the consent of senior officers. Indeed a number of them, including General Rodolfo Canieso, at the time chief of the army, and many retired officers of the PMA Alumni Association, encouraged the development of the movement because the RAM wanted to restore professionalism to the AFP by improving training and education, acquiring more equipment and achieving more efficient dispersement in the field, and ensuring that promotions were earned meritoriously and not because of political loyalty. Espousing these concepts in February 1985 at a reunion of the PMA Alumni Association, the group issued an unsigned statement declaring:

We have earlier sought to ventilate our grievances and aspirations in conventional fora, but this too has been denied us mainly because of the prevailing military culture that has evolved in the 1980s which rewards bootlicking incompetents and banishes independent-minded professionals and achievers ..... We will no longer tolerate incompetence and indiscipline. We will no longer close our eyes to the graft and corruption happening in our midst (*Crossroads to Reform*, 1985).

At the academy graduating ceremony one month later, the group, identifying itself as "WE BELONG," and issued "The Statement of Common Aspirations". These were to:

1. Maintain a strong and solid AFP that can uphold the sovereignty of the people and the state, support the Constitution and protect the geographical integrity of the country and at the same time extirpate all divisive forces within and outside the organization;

2. Cleanse the AFP of undesirables;

3. Maintain a high standard of discipline;

4. Enforce the merit system. The basis of promotions, assignments, schooling and other related matters must be devoid of favoritism or *bata-bata* [proteges], *padrino* [benefactor] system and other personal considerations.

5. Reorient AFP training and education;

6. Promote the morale and welfare of every man and woman in uniform;

7. Restore camaraderie and *esprit de corps* in the AFP;

8. Rationalize the management of the AFP's limited resources; and

9. Align the concept and practices of leadership with the basic constitutional concepts: "Loyalty must be directed to the constitution, not to any individual or group of persons", and the tasks of the AFP (*Crossroads to Reform*, 1985).

The RAM claimed it was formed "to restore professionalism and eradicate politicization from the AFP", by enhancing the traditional values of loyalty and discipline in the military. In fact Wolpin (1983:214) argues that junior officers are generally professionals as they are "bright and committed to their calling". Such statements prompted analysts of the AFP such as Hernandez (1986:198) to argue that "The reform movement demonstrated that members of these services were capable of asserting their professional values", rather than being "viewed as a monolithic" force for the Marcos regime. Importantly, it wanted "to unify, not divide", and had "no intentions to commit any unlawful acts or undermine the government", according to the movement's spokesman, Colonel Hernani Figueroa. Officers from the middle ranks, majors and lieutenant colonels, where promotion is slow, have generally been the instigators of political activity in the military (Anderson 1964:58).

The Aquino assassination provided an added impetus for the RAM's growth. It gave strength, unity and purpose to the movement (Lyons and Wilson 1987:101). Returning from self exile in the US, former Senator Benigno Aquino, the most popular alternative political leader to President Marcos, was assassinated when he stepped off a plane at Manila airport on 21 August 1983. Allegations that the AFP, and in particular its chief of staff, was personally responsible for Aquino's death led to the movement's increasing animosity towards Ver. This consolidated when RAM members who were security guards at the presidential palace informed me that the night before the assassination "....a lot of activity was going on at Malacañang..... At one point the president, the first lady and General Ver got into a car and drove around the palace grounds.... when they got out they looked angry. The chief of staff must have been the one responsible".

The growth of the movement was facilitated by the general liberalization that occurred in the society after the assassination as the "parliament of the streets,"- a term which gained currency in the Philippines in the 1980s to describe popular demonstrations against the Marcos regime - and the "alternative press" flourished. Colonel Rene Dado told me that "The instability infiltrated the military". Large sections of the AFP lacked respect for the chief of staff. His alleged involvement in the assassination increased the RAM's animosity towards him. Like the Thai Young Turks who staged an unsuccessful coup to restore "respectability to the military" (Bunbongkarn 1987:12), the RAM sought reforms for the AFP.

Additional support was provided to the RAM by US embassy officials in the Philippines who were sympathetic to the group of "reform minded" officers and were prepared to assist them. Informing Congress of this plan, US Assistant Secretary of Defense, Richard Armitage, stated in October 1984 that the AFP needed reforms and said that "the Defense Department was aware of a solid cadre of competent, patriotic officers in the AFP [Armed Forces of the Philippines] who have the determination to institute the necessary reforms" (Schirmer and Shalom 1987:277-278) "and turn the NPA tide" (Bello 1988:168). What Armitage did not disclose, however, was that the US was already funding this group as an alternative to the discredited Marcos regime. In fact, US ambassador to the Philippines, Stephen Bosworth, made contact with the group soon after his arrival in the country in 1981 (Lyons and Wilson 1987:74). Furthermore, a RAM member claimed that US defence attaches were attending the RAM meetings, causing friction among some of its members.

A National Security Council study directive in November 1984 detailed the measures the Reagan administration intended to pursue to pressure President Marcos to institute changes in the Philippines. For the AFP it stated, "Restoration of professional, apolitical leadership ... [and] Improved training" and discipline (Schirmer and Shalom 1987:325; Bello 1988:166). In his testimony to the US Committee on Foreign Relations in October 1985, Richard Armitage again emphasized the need for reforms in the AFP and, referring to the RAM, argued, "Now, more than ever, the AFP must be led by officers of the highest professional standard and of the deepest loyalty to their country". By this stage, the US increased the number of advisers to the AFP. But President Marcos was resistant to any proposals from the US to reform the AFP because he was fearful of increased US control over the armed forces (Schirmer and Shalom 1987:278).

When the RAM, at US instigation, publicly called for reforms to the AFP, Vice Chief of Staff General Ramos claimed he was sympathetic to their cause. General Ver quickly dismissed the movement and ordered it to disband. Meeting President Marcos for the first time on 31 May 1985, the RAM professed it was "pro-government". In fact, its representative, navy captain Rex Robles informed the president that the RAM was using his book, *Towards a Partnership - The Filipino Ideology*, "as its ideological base to serve as the Movement's source of inspiration, guidance, and basic strength" (*We Belong*, 1(3) 1985:12). All it intended to do was change the tarnished image of the military (*National Midweek* 13 November 1985). At that meeting President Marcos offered support for the RAM's ideals.

In July 1985, two months after the meeting with the president, Robles stated that the RAM would not resort to violence "even if the civilian government fails in its efforts to stem the tide of the insurgency". And at the Manila Economic and Political Forum on 6 July 1985 the movement's representative stated that it would not stage a coup or use violence to displace the government. Many officers argued that this attitude among the armed forces had been a major reason why the Marcos regime remained in office despite losing its legitimacy. Quite simply, many officers had a stake in maintaining the government in office since they benefited from the practices the president permitted in the armed forces. Officers from the core group of the RAM were beneficiaries. The movement's rhetoric was deceptive.

The RAM was a "Janus-faced organization"; it planned a coup while professing to institute reforms in the AFP (McCoy 1988:14). Most officers interviewed did not believe that the RAM could institute reforms in the AFP. Firstly, they argued the movement's core members benefited from the status quo, and as a result preferred to retain the system or replace it with a similiar one. Professionalism was therefore used as a ploy. Secondly, the core members had not spent any considerable period in active combat and had not experienced much of the deprivation they referred to; it had mostly been reported to them while they were working in the Ministry of National Defense (MND). "They were in the corridors of power in MND", said Brigadier General Rodolfo Biazon, deputy chief of staff, 'so they could not know what the soldiers were experiencing in the field". Thirdly, the RAM leaders were not professionals; they did not obey the chain of command and they were reportedly guilty of human rights violations. When the RAM leader, Lieutenant Colonel Gregorio Honasan was in Mindanao during the Muslim conflict in the early 1970s he participated in the revenge killing of a Muslim leader, who allegedly killed his classmate. Because he portrayed the image of a professional soldier, members of the military tribunal could not accept that he was guilty. In 1974 Honasan was decorated for bravery in combat against the Mjoro National Liberation Front on Jolo. A few years later, however, it was revealed that he did participate in the assassination, but was able to evade an inquiry. According to a member of the military tribunal, this was because of his links to the defence secretary. Finally, according to a member of the RAM steering committee, the RAM core group "....betrayed us. They planned to overthrow Marcos, but did not call it a coup, and for this they took money from the US, which no longer made us an indigenous group...". "These young Turks were misguided...", according to Brigadier General Honesto Isleta.

Whatever the prevailing view about the RAM it was nevertheless instrumental in the demise of the Marcos regime.

The End of the Road

Marcos's legitimacy after the Aquino assassination in August 1983 was frequently questioned by opposition groups. The parliament of the streets became a common feature in Manila as the economic crisis deepened. Responding to the continuous unrest, President Marcos claimed the demonstrations were orchestrated by the Roman Catholic Church (McDougald 1987:275).

Taunting the political opposition for its disunity, as he frequently did, the president spontaneously announced, during an interview on American television in late 1985, that he would call elections to prove his legitimacy. Elections were scheduled for 7 February 1986. Marcos anticipated using the military to ensure his victory, as had been his practice in previous elections. A Communion on Elections representative stated that the RUCs would supervise the elections in an attempt to avoid terrorism. According to one RUC commander they were ordered to commit fraud and vote rigging, to ensure the president's victory. However, a number of fraternities in the AFP, such as the RAM decided not to support the president. They wanted to ensure that the elections were "clean, honest and fair". For this purpose the RAM organized the *Kamalayan* [Awareness] 86 "to pray for clean and honest elections" (*We Belong*, 1 (5) 1985:1-2). Encouraged by the US State Department which called for the military to play a politically neutral role in the elections, the RAM issued its policy for the election campaign. Its objectives were to:

1. emphasize the non-partisan role of the AFP in the elections, and dispel the suspicion in some quarters that the military would be used to favor certain sectors;

2. develop better appreciation and awareness of the individual and collective roles of the soldiers, as well as the public in general, in the electoral process;

3. enhance the credibility of RAM in particular and the AFP in general vis-a-vis the Filipino people;

4. develop working relationships with civic, business and religious organizations and other government institutions, for

mutual support and the promotion of a heightened civic-consciousness (*ibid.*).

Described as "a perfect cover", this program provided the RAM with the opportunity for working with the people to test their support while monitoring the activities of the president's political party (Almendral 1988:199). Suspicious of this, General Ver met with the RAM representatives on 17 January 1986 and ordered that they cease their activities (*FEER* 6 February 1986), an order they promptly ignored. But the RAM was ineffective in preventing fraud and intimidation during the elections.

The 7 February 1986 presidential elections results were disputed by both the incumbent and Corazon Aquino, each accusing the other of fraud. Marcos was, however, declared the winner by the *Batasang Pambansa* (The National Assembly) - which was created by Marcos in 1976 - and plans were made for his inauguration. Aquino meanwhile disputed the results and organized an "active non-violent civil disobedience campaign" against him. Finally, amid reports of an attempted coup against his regime, Marcos decided to arrest all opposition members and reimpose martial law using the code name "Oplan Everlasting". Events, however, prevented this action as sections of the AFP led by the RAM, supported civilians protesting against the regime on Edsa (Epifanio de los Santos Avenue) - the highway in Manila that runs alongside the AFP headquarters, Camp Aguinaldo and the PC headquarters, Camp Crame.

A Military Coup with Civilian Support

The events of 22-25 February 1986 in the Philippines have defied adequate categorization by analysts. Popularly described as "People's Power" and "The Four Day Revolution", it was instigated by Defense Secretary Juan Ponce Enrile and the RAM, and assisted by General Fidel Ramos, Chief of the PC and the AFP Vice Chief of Staff. Mackenzie (1987:34) prefers to describe it as "a popular uprising with military participation", while Almendral (1988:211) describes it as "a coup d'etat against the Marcos government". Nemenzo (1987) hypothezises "that it was partly a coup and partly an insurrection". Whatever the description it is certain that Corazon Aquino could not have achieved the presidency if sections of the military had not abandoned their commander in chief, President Marcos. As Woddis (1977:22) argues, no uprising against a government can succeed without support from "an important faction" of the armed forces. According to the Philippine Secretary of

Defense, retired General Ramos, without support from civilians the military would not have been successful in removing Marcos from office (*The Manila Chronicle* 28 August 1988).

The events that took place at Edsa were the climax of plans for a coup by the RAM to replace Marcos, with Defense Secretary Enrile at the head of a junta. Commanders in a number of regions had offered support, and plans were formulated by the reform group to displace those who did not cooperate. The economic crisis precipitated by the Aquino assassination also contributed to the loss of confidence in the Marcos regime by business and the middle class. Crouch (1985:292) describes such conditions as typical of coups in a number of Southeast Asian countries. Capitalizing on societal disaffection, the RAM solicited cause oriented groups to stage demonstrations against the regime. The head of the Roman Catholic Church in the Philippines, Jaime Cardinal Sin, appealed to the people to support the military breakaway group against Marcos. Yet even the role of the Church in the demise of Marcos needs to be placed in perspective. Nemenzo (1986:44-46) examines the events and demonstrates that even the Roman Catholic Church was not the primary actor.

What then precipitated the desertion of the commander in chief by elements in the AFP? A loss of control over the military from 1983, when President Marcos effectively removed Secretary of Defense Enrile from the AFP chain of command, had resulted in Enrile's isolation from the center of power.[1] He was disenchanted with the regime in which after 1978 he had supposedly been the heir apparent. Enrile was not interested in returning the Philippines to democracy (Santos and Domingo-Robes 1987:27). Indeed as early as 1982 he discussed with a group of intelligence officers, most of whom were members of the nascent reform movement, the possibility of staging a coup against Marcos (*The New Yorker* September 1986:40).

For General Fidel Ramos, the other principal actor, it was also his personal dissatisfaction with Marcos that turned him against the regime. This dissatisfaction had accumulated since 1981 when the president appointed a reservist, General Ver as AFP Chief of Staff. Immediately upon his appointment, Ver removed the INP from the jurisdiction of Ramos, the PC/INP chief, weakening his control over the AFP. Compounding Ramos's dissatisfaction was the fact that General Ver still exercised power in the AFP while Ramos was acting chief of staff between 1984 and 1985. Additionally, the president prevented Ramos from introducing policies to reform the military during this period. Despite this, President Marcos attributed the development of factionalism in the armed forces to the period when General Ramos was acting chief of staff (*FEER* 6 February 1986). When the president's health deteriorated in 1984 and there was speculation over his successor. Marcos stated that he would install a five-man junta, headed by General Ramos (*FEER* 6 December 1984). But once General Ver resumed the position of chief of staff, Ramos was again relegated to the largely ceremonial position of vice chief of staff. Still expecting to attain the chief of staff's position, General Ramos did not isolate himself from the regime. But his ultimate humiliation came when the president, after a meeting with US representative Philip Habib on 14 February 1986, announced on television that he was appointing Ramos chief of staff, and accepting the retirement of General Ver: confidently, General Ramos went to Malacañang only to discover that he had been deceived (Arillo 1986:147). Ramos's participation in the coup against the president was therefore a culmination of a series of personal disappointments. Both Enrile and Ramos finally withdrew their support from the president when they discovered that he had ordered their arrest along with the RAM core members and opposition leaders.

Essential to the success of the coup were the members of the core group of the RAM who had been working in the Defense Department with Secretary Enrile. He had nurtured these officers sending them to management courses at the prestigious Asian Institute of Management in Manila, and appointing a number as managers in his businesses. Enrile needed to establish a political base of his own and used the officers who worked with him. "Not only were they committed professionals, these PMA regulars were also ambitious careerists who had tied their advancement to Enrile's fortunes" (McCoy 1987:23). The secretary of defence had never denied his desire to be president and publicly announced it in 1984 (Santos and Domingo-Robes 1987:33). Realizing that the RAM provided the best opportunity to attain his ambition after a cleavage developed between himself and other members of the regime, Enrile never flinched from funding the movement and encouraged business groups to follow his example. To overthrow Marcos he employed foreign advisers from Israel and the United Kingdom to train members of his group in special commando tactics. Enrile personally invested in equipment and witnessed "...many of the practise sessions for storming the palace". Bonner (1987:434) demonstrates that Enrile planned with the RAM to overthrow Marcos when the opportunity presented itself. "By mid-1985 Enrile had become involved" (ibid.) "By October 1985 the plans for a coup d'etat were well advanced" (ibid.). Apparently, the RAM had planned to seize power by attacking the presidential palace on 1 January 1986 during the New

Year's celebrations, but Enrile and the RAM aborted the attempted coup when President Marcos announced elections.

Enrile and his cabal believed that a power vacuum existed soon after the elections and decided to re-activate the coup plans. But a few members of the RAM who were officers of the Presidential Guard Command disclosed Enrile's plans to the president because Enrile and the RAM core group wanted to replace one repressive regime with another, according to one of them. This officer also claimed that "Professionalization of the AFP was a camouflage. The RAM had no intention of reforming the military", only to achieve power and bring the AFP under its control. Realizing that his action was treasonable, and that "Marcos was an unforgiving man", Enrile decided to "save himself by implicating others to cover his actions", according to a senior officer. Initially, Enrile invited Aquino to agree to a coup and share power in a junta. When the coup was discovered he sought the support and participation of General Ramos. Mrs. Aquino had, however, already successfully initiated an "active non-violent civil disobedience campaign" against the president and was not interested in participating in a coup.

Although the RAM leaders respected Ramos and realized his assistance was imperative if the revolt was to succeed, they felt he was not forceful enough with President Marcos in pursuing reforms in the AFP when he was acting chief of staff. According to one RAM member, he was not "....macho enough to be the leader". Nevertheless, they enlisted him because as chief of the PC Ramos's assistance was essential in displacing Marcos and policing the country.

The New Armed Forces of the Philippines

On attaining the presidency on 26 February 1986 Corazon Aquino rewarded Juan Ponce Enrile by allowing him to maintain the position of secretary of defence, and appointed General Fidel Ramos the AFP chief of staff.

Eager to eradicate the old image of the AFP as "de-professionalized and politicized", General Ramos stated that the military would start afresh and baptised it the New Armed Forces of the Philippines (NAFP). "Yet it is the same old army, with scores of officers and military units from top to bottom implicated in the fourteen-year repressive rule of Marcos" (Bello 1986:1023). Seeking to sanitize it Ramos instituted a number of changes in the command structure. Of the twenty-three "overstaying" generals in the AFP all except himself were retired. Officers loyal to Marcos who did not resign or retire were replaced with those loyal to the chief of staff and President Aquino. In their place "Ramos named a group of respected military professionals. Since discipline is a function of command, Ramos's appointment of military professionals to key command positions may also be seen as a positive influence on NAFP behaviour" (Wise 1987:439-40). But the RAM noted that most of those appointed formed a new cabal. Other officers claimed that it appeared that political fealty to the president would become the prerequisite for promotion, as it was under Marcos. The president stated that she now had more confidence in the military as the commanders had sworn allegiance to her. On 19 May 1987 the US Deputy Assistant Secretary of Defense, Karl Jackson told the House Foreign Affairs Subcommittee for East Asia and the Pacific that the Philippine military reforms included, "The return to a more professional senior leadership". But, retired Colonel C. Filio argues, professionalism will be affected if President Aquino persists with her present policies. "This starts with Cory's tendency to personalize the military service, as with her usual reference to "my generals: and my soldiers" when they should all be generals and soldiers of the Republic..." (Filio 1986:31). Given the personalistic nature of Philippine society, Aquino was merely reassuring the AFP of her personal trust in the establishment.

General Ramos and the NAFP general staff were determined to eradicate the tarnished image of the armed forces. Special attention was given to military training, which had been neglected during the latter years of the Marcos regime. For this purpose, the military created TRACOM (Training Command) on 10 December 1986 "with the central task of ensuring uniform and standardized quality of training". To further develop professionalism, the armed forces revamped its personnel, logistics and counterinsurgency operations. To improve morale and prevent human rights violations, it instituted the Value Formation Program. In a related restructuring, the para-military Civilian Home Defence Force [CHDF] was to be phased out and replaced by the Citizen Armed Forces Geographical Units (CAFGUs).

Many of these reforms were, however, slow to eventuate. As early as May 1986 the RAM criticized General Ramos for this (*FEER* 29 May 1986). To assist in "the correction of the key deficiencies", the US administration increased the Joint US Military Advisory Group [JUSMAG] personnel in Manila. In a statement to the US Foreign Relations Committee in 1986, retired US Army General R. Stilwell, claimed that JUSMAG had started to play a major role in training the NAFP, to professionalize it. Acknowledging the role of the group in assisting in professionalizing the military, President Aquino awarded the JUSMAG's Commander, General Charles

Teeter, the Philippine Legion of Honor on his retirement on 16 July 1988 (*The Rank and File* September 16-30, 1988).

With US support, General Ramos restructured the NAFP. He did not abolish the RUCs, though he had opposed them when they were established, and the armed forces commanders also opposed the retention of the RUCs. Retired General Ileto, made it clear to me in an interview that the RUCs were an impediment to the military becoming a socially responsive force as they concentrate too much power in the chief of staff. General Ramos has, however, consolidated the fourteen RUCs into five Area Unified Commands (AUCs). In the restructuring of the NAFP he dismantled the National Intelligence and Security Authority (NISA) and the Presidential Security Command. The size of the military, however, has remained unchanged, despite suggestions by the US that a trimmer Philippine armed forces would be more effective in the counterinsurgency campaign.

Another impediment to professionalizing the armed forces is the CHDF. The 1987 constitution called for abolition of the CHDF. General Ramos promised to ensure that this would be undertaken quickly. Reforming this force proved to be difficult. It is entrenched in some regions and apart from augmenting the AFP serves as private security for certain elite families. In 1988, however, Executive Order No. 264 established the CAFGUs to replace the CHDF. Senior officers interviewed argued that these para-military units are essential for local defence and to support the NAFP. The military is supposed to train CAFGU members for approximately forty-five days to make them efficient and respect the community. Critics, however, claim that the CAFGUs will essentially comprise CHDF members and will degenerate into replicas of their predecessors. Others say that CAFGUs are presently being trained for about fifteen days. Former members of the CHDF who join the CAFGUs are not trained.

Addressing personnel matters in the restructuring of the NAFP, General Ramos had to confront the issue of fraternities. They were seen as a hindrance to professionalizing the military because they encouraged allegiance to the leader of the faction who was not necessarily an officer, let alone the commander of the unit. Such practices are anathema to the military which relies on a hierarchical structure to maintain discipline and indeed the command structure. Some officers argue that fraternities contribute to divisiveness in the NAFP. In addition, Simon (1978:xvi) argues that generally there is a positive correlation between factionalism and coups. Because of their adverse effects on the AFP, General Ramos signed an order on 22 February 1987 to disband all fraternities. Incidentally, this order was issued one year after the RAM played a decisive role in the overthrow of Marcos, and also after it and other fraternities were implicated in a number of attempted coups. Since then some AFP commanders have argued that fraternities were contributing to the deterioration of the chain of command in the military. But despite the order to disband, many fraternities continue to exist. Some senior officers claim that it was inevitable that the order would simply force the fraternities underground to the status they had during the Marcos regime.

Aquino and the Military

From Marcos, President Aquino "inherited a corrupt, inept, and factionalized military which took a cynical attitude towards democratic values" (Nemenzo 1988:231). The RAM wanted "reprofessionalization (of the AFP) without depoliticization". Allegedly, one of the movement's members declared to President Aquino, "We toppled one government, and can topple another if reforms are not made. In fact, Cory [the president] didn't give us our jobs; we gave her a job" (ibid.: 232).

When Enrile resumed the position of defence secretary he did not make any specific pronouncements regarding the role of the armed forces, despite the administration's avowed commitment to professionalize the military. The reasons became clear when he was implicated in the July and November 1986 attempted coups against the administration. Realizing that the defence secretary did not intend to accept the government, and would continue to use elements in the NAFP to destablize it, President Aquino replaced Enrile with his assistant, retired General Rafael Ileto. A graduate of West Point, Ileto is described as a "professional soldier" because of a successful combat career during the Huk campaign. Ileto was therefore believed to be capable of reforming the military because of his training and experience.

Soon after his appointment, however, dissension between the secretary and the chief of staff was evident over a range of issues including strategies for dealing with the armed wing of the Communist party, the New People's Army (NPA) and the retention of the RUCs. As these differences became accentuated, General Ramos no longer included the defence secretary in the AFP chain of command, consulting directly with the president, despite promising to eradicate such practices in the NAFP. By the time Ileto attained the defence portfolio, Ramos had dropped the term NAFP and reverted to using AFP. Disappointed with the "Factionalism, poor equipment, politicization and low morale" of the armed forces, Ileto declared in a statement to the press in February 1987, "before I got this job I thought it would take about a year or two to reform the military, unite everybody, and weed out the bad ones. Now I'm convinced it will take 20 years - a generation".

Generally, Ileto was disappointed with the performance of the AFP, especially the incapacity of the command system to develop a coherent approach towards the NPA. He attributed this to General Ramos (*Asian Wall Street Journal* 15 June 1987). Ileto was frustrated in his attempts to introduce changes which would have contributed to professionalizing the military, because the chiefs of the services were loyal to Ramos. This, in addition to the increasing differences between himself and the chief of staff, led to his resignation from the Aquino administration. Said a senior officer: "There goes the chance for the AFP to become professional..." The defence secretary's position was filled by General Ramos, who finally retired after his tour of duty was extended but not before assuring that General Renato de Villa, a man often described as a Ramos "clone", would succeed him. Additionally, Ramos achieved his ambition on 4 November 1988 when Executive Order No. 292 became effective, giving him direct tactical and operational supervision over the AFP. "The code in effect makes the defense secretary the most powerful man in the country" (*The Rank and File* November 1988).

Defense Secretary Ramos supported the appointment of General de Villa because, he argued, de Villa would pursue the policies he had already established. General de Villa was due to retire in April 1988. Since he did not retire with the rest of his PMA class of 1958, the government is arguably in breach of the constitution. (Article xvi General Provisions, Section 5, Subsection 7 of the 1987 Constitution states, "The tour of duty of the Chief of Staff of the armed forces shall not exceed three years. However, in times of war or other national emergency declared by Congress, the President may extend such a tour"). Since Congress has not declared a national emergency, it can only be assumed that the chief of staff is being retained because of his personal fealty to the president and the defence secretary.

Notwithstanding this, the government appears determined to return the military to its role as guardian of the country and people, and remove it from its former political functions. Elucidating the administration's defence policy on 22 March 1986 at the PMA graduation ceremony, the president argued that professionalism and commitment of the NAFP were essential to maintain a stable democracy, which required the military to adhere to civilian supremacy. She said that "a soldier's role is not in politics, but rather to serve as a guarantor of the people's security and protector of the people's government".

The 1987 constitution, which was overwhelmingly approved by voters [except those in the armed forces], includes a number of important clauses defining the role of the AFP in society. It prohibits military personnel from engaging in partisan politics, except to vote; prevents active duty officers from working in civilian jobs; prohibits the extension of officers beyond retirement, and makes provisions for the prosecution of armed forces personnel accused of human rights violations. Above all it emphasizes the concept of civilian supremacy over the military. Article XVI of the General Provisions, Section 5 No. 4 of the Constitution states: "No member of the armed forces in the active service shall, at any time, be appointed or designated in any capacity to a civilian position in Government including government-owned or controlled corporations or any of their subsidiaries". De La Torre (1987:343), speculates that it is the reason why the AFP voted against the constitution. Clearly, the Aquino administration wanted the armed forces to realize that, despite its role in her accession to the presidency, it should not expect to participate in a democratically elected government.

The re-convening of Congress was a major step in reinstituting democratic processes in the Philippines and subjecting the military to civilian control. For the AFP it meant that the Commission on Appointments (CA), which was terminated when Congress was abolished in 1972, would again determine all appointments to full colonelcy. Unaccustomed to this procedure, many officers about to be promoted to the rank of colonel informed me that they were not enthusiastic about being interrogated by members of the CA. A number of them argued that when the commission was functioning it contributed to the politicization of the AFP and to the loss of professionalism, since it was necessary to have a political patron to be promoted. In fact, many officers oppose the system which permits the CA to determine promotions in the armed forces. Other officers and civilian politicians, however, argue that the commission is necessary to ensure the constitutional mandate of civilian supremacy over the military. Without it, they aver, the armed forces will revert to political partisanship. But whether the CA can prevent officers from participating in bi-partisan politics is yet to be determined; it did not prior to 1972.

In the meantime, still wanting to play a more significant role in national politics despite Aquino's assertion that the AFP must revert to its functions, elements in the military, and especially the core members of the RAM, were prepared to achieve this by illegal means. The RAM justifies its rights to govern by the role the movement played in the events of February 1986 (Selochan 1989:8). Yet, the RAM was ostensibly organized "to restore professionalism" in the military, "not to assert a military role in politics" (Lande and Hooley 1986:1095).

Attempted Coups: Testing the System

Denied what they saw as a right to govern or participate in government, elements in the military resorted to the method employed by many Third World armed forces to attain this objective: coups. In the Philippines coups are a new phenomenon (Muego 1987:151; Nemenzo 1987:9).

Between July 1986 and December 1989 six attempted coups were staged by elements in the AFP against the Aquino administration. Not all were expected to be successful. The initial ones were intended to test the government's ability to withstand destabilization, to measure the administration's support in the community, and to reassert the influence which elements in the AFP felt they had lost with the demise of the Marcos regime. A brief examination of most of the attempted coups will draw out some of the issues in relating professionalization and politicization.

The first attempted coup, played out at the Manila Hotel on 6 July 1986, had the hallmarks of a comic opera. It was staged by three Marcos loyalist generals and approximately 300 soldiers who were "members of the Guardians Brotherhood, Inc., a military mutual-aid society" with Lieutenant Colonel Gregorio Honasan as its president (McCoy 1987:25). The intention was for Arturo Tolentino, the vice presidential running mate of former President Marcos in the 1986 presidential elections, to occupy the office of president of the Philippines until Marcos returned. Trying to link the RAM with this coup attempt, elements in the Ramos faction in the AFP declared that Honasan was the leader of the Guardians. But according to a number of leaders of Guardian chapters and some members of the RAM core group, Honasan did indeed want to control the Guardians and bring them under the umbrella of the RAM, but was unable to achieve this because of major differences between the two fraternities. Importantly, the members of the RAM were predominantly PMA graduates and the Guardians were mostly reservist officers and enlisted men. The RAM developed largely as a reaction against the preference reservists received over regular officers during General Ver's tenure as the chief of staff. This attempted coup was also linked to Defense Secretary Juan Ponce Enrile (ibid.). Yet Enrile retained his post as did the RAM officers. And the punishment for soldiers involved in this incident was minimal and did not discourage them from participating in future attempted coups.

Determined to destabilize the Aquino government, Enrile and the RAM made public statements after the attempted coup questioning the legitimacy of the administration. The core group of the movement planned another coup code-named "God Save the Queen", to be executed in November 1986 while President Aquino was on an official visit to Japan. For this purpose, on 3 November 1986, Navy Captain Rex Robles informed Victor Corpus that a letter regarding his defection from the NPA would be used to destablize the government and would "further enhance the scenario for a coup" (Corpus 1987:ix). Robles had recruited Corpus to work with his "study Group" at the Ministry of Defense to devise a new strategy for the AFP's counterinsurgency campaign, prior to Corpus being reinstated in the AFP with the rank of Lieutenant Colonel. Corpus, however, disclosed the plans of the attempted coup, allegedly because he was "rabidly loyal to Ramos and the President" (Nemenzo 1987:15:1988: 264); [simply "pragmatic", was the way Corpus described it to me during an interview on 2 March 1988]. What concerned Corpus about the whole incident was that Robles had told him that he had "reserved a special pistol for Minister Enrile alone if he doesn't go along with [the coup]" (Corpus 1987:xiii), implying that Enrile was not the willing accomplice he may have been in an earlier attempted coup. It is not surprising that Corpus disclosed the plans as he must have felt that if Enrile was dispensible then so was he. To abort the coup, Chief of Staff General Ramos removed the conspirators from the Ministry of Defense and stationed them in regional commands. Again, these officers were not disciplined despite evidence of their role in planning to overthrow the government.

Consequently the RAM was not deterred from planning another coup for 22 November 1986. According to the plan, simultaneous uprisings by soldiers in all military camps were to coinicide with the reconvening of the defunct *Batasang Pambansa* (National Assembly). But again, the AFP chief of staff aborted the attempt, despite efforts to elicit support for the coup by, among others, Vice President Doy Laurel (McCoy 1987:28). Defense Secretary Juan Ponce Enrile was dismissed two days later for his alleged involvement in this coup attempt. No action was taken against the RAM officers implicated in the plan.

After failing to execute its coup plans on two occasions, the RAM core group decided to retreat and reassess its strategies. Members re-read Luttwak's *Coup D'Etat: A Practical Handbook* (1968). Many claimed that they also read *The Thai Young Turks* (1982), which is an account of the failed coup by a reform group in the Thai military in April 1981. Undoubtedly the RAM leaders wished to avoid making similar mistakes in their quest for power.

Although not directly responsible for it, the RAM supported another attempted coup on 27 January 1987, which was led by General Zumel and some members of the Guardians. Executed a few days before the February 1987 constitutional plebiscite, it was intended to reinstate Marcos. But when the US prevented Marcos from leaving Hawaii, and General Ramos ordered the arrest of a number of pro-Marcos generals, the coup fizzled out. The failure of the coup was compounded by the overwhelming support expressed in the plebiscite for the new constitution.The RAM was instrumental in dissuading General Ramos from using force against soldiers commanded by Colonel Oscar Canalas who took control of a television station in Manila. Nemenzo (1988:266) reports that General Ramos was also reluctant to give orders to the troops to attack the rebel soldiers because he feared his orders might not be obeyed. McCoy (1987:28-29) optimistically described this attempted coup as the "final" attempt, and suggested when the constitution was approved, "coup rumours ended and stability returned". Less than a month later, however, and before the scheduled congressional elections, Marcos-loyalist troops again staged a revolt. On 18 April 1987 a small group of soldiers, led by General Reynaldo Cabuatan, released about 108 of their comrades involved in the January 1987 attempted coup from the Army's detention center at Fort Bonifacio in Metro Manila. In the process they seized the Army headquarters. The rebels expected other soldiers to join them. This they believed would allow them to seize government. But officers failed to support the rebel troops since the plans were not properly coordinated. Despite the small size of the rebel force, it took the military approximately nine hours to terminate what the AFP refers to as the "Black Saturday" incident. According to a senior army officer, this incident highlighted the lack of discipline and the disregard of the chain of command within the AFP since the breakout was instigated by enlisted personnel.

On 28 August 1987, just when the institutions of democracy appeared to have been restored and prospects for stability seemed good, the RAM staged yet another attempt to seize political power. More carefully organized, with support from regional commands, the stated plan was to establish a junta and hold presidential elections when stability was ensured (David 1987:6). Officers generally make such statements after seizing political power, but seldom fulfill them. In effect, once in office military regimes try to legitimize their rule through rigged elections and institutionalize military rule. As Finer (1975:24) observed: "the military engage in politics with relative haste but disengage with the greatest reluctance".

Unlike the previous attempts, this coup was characterized by considerable violence which resulted in the death of many civilians. The coup attempt was supported by approximately 2,000 officers and enlisted men and elicited empathy from others in the AFP. Many officers did not immediately support the government but waited until they were certain which side would be victorious before deciding where to pledge their support, earning the tag "the 5 o'clock movers". Despite the severity of this attempted coup, the government again failed to subject the rebels to military tribunals. It was abundantly clear to the AFP general staff, and the Aquino administration, that there was strong support for the coup in the armed forces, even among the cadets at the Philippine Military Academy (PMA). They were in fact ready to augment rebel forces in Manila. The government's response to the attempted coup was to quickly grant a rise in pay and allowance. Also, the AFP's 1988 budget was increased making it "the second biggest recipient and the only institution whose allocation Congress increased despite driving an added 4 per cent in government deficits" (de Dios 1988:314). Commenting on the coup attempt, military personnel claim that without it they would not have acquired the promised remuneration. One influential senior officer boasted to me, "......it showed the president we have the guns. We brought her to her knees". Another said: "It [the coup attempt] was intended to send a message to the politicians". The message appears to be that the military can use force when it considers it necessary to achieve its aims.

Marking the anniversary of the 28 August 1987 attempted coup, the RAM issued a poster which read, "Our dreams shall never die". In 1988 the RAM still hoped to achieve "good government and a complete revamp of the AFP". The leader of the coup, former Lieutenant Colonel Gregorio Honasan, was captured but later escaped and remains a fugitive. Whether the AFP hierarchy really wants to recapture Honasan remains moot. Considering that many of the RAM's expressed grievances persist in the military, resulting in continued support for the movement; it is unlikely that the government seriously wants to recapture Honasan and make him a *cause celebre* of the AFP.

The AFP hierarchy contends that since the attempted coup, the RAM has lost its support and has disbanded. This assertion is difficult to verify, but another "loose network of officers", which shares the grievances of the RAM, has been reported in the AFP (*FEER* 24 November 1988). In March 1989 members of another secret reform group in the AFP, the Young Officers Union for Reform at your Service (YOURS), was apparently "documenting graft and corruption in the Aquino government with the help of the civilian sectors" (*Philippine Situationer* April 1989).

In November 1989 President Aquino made a state visit to the US and Canada. Prior to her departure, rumours of another attempted coup were sweeping Manila. The president returned a few days later with promises of increased aid and investment for the Philippines. The planned coup did not eventuate until 1 December. In the early hours the 4th Marine battalion commanded by Lieutenant Colonel Romelino Gojo seized Villamor Air Force Base in Manila. Other military camps in Manila such as Fort Bonifacio, Camp Aguinaldo and Camp Crame along with the airport on the island of Cebu came under the control of rebel forces. Radio and television stations were also taken. The group aligned itself with the RAM, and Honasan issued a report offering his support for the rebel forces. The *Manila Chronicle* reported on 3 December 1989 that other core members of the movement were "overseeing the entire operations".

This coup attempt which is to date the worst putsch against the Aquino administration lasted until 4 December. In the first two days of fighting forces loyal to the government retook the military camps and communications centers from rebel control. Rebel Scout rangers commanded by Lieutenant Colonel Galvez, a classmate of Honasan, retreated to the central business district of Makati in Manila where they seized a number of buildings housing banks and other financial institutions and hotels with foreign tourists. Eventually the tourists were allowed to leave. Although most of the fighting had subsided by this stage many soldiers and civilians were killed. Brigadier General Arturo Enrile, supertintendent of the PMA, negotiated for the troops to return to barracks, but not before US Air Force flew "persuasion flights" over the rebels forces (*Asia Week* 15 December 1989). The rebel troops finally marched to Army headquarters, Fort Bonifacio, approximately three miles from Makati, from where they had fled. It was reported that the rebel troops marched like heroes, despite Aquino's ultimatum to them "to surrender or die". In response to this coup attempt President Aquino declared a six month state of emergency and revamped her cabinet. Large rewards were offered for the rebel officers who had escaped. By May 1990 at least 10 were captured and about to face court-martial. Revamping the cabinet appears unlikely to satisfy elements in the AFP wanting to play a larger role in government policy-making.

The initial attempted coups against the Aquino administration were clearly staged to test the government's stability, and to ascertain whether the president could rely on "People's Power" for support. But these were aborted or fizzled out and did not require the president to call on the people to show support for the government. The 28 August 1987 coup attempt and in particular the 1 December 1989 putsch demonstrated that elements in the military and some in government and opposition remain opposed to the political organization of the Philippines which they believe is epitomized by the Aquino administration. In 1987 a US National Security Council report stated that the Philippine armed forces have not achieved "the unity, morale, equipment and level of professionalism" necessary to defeat the insurgents (Bello 1988:175). Military theorists argue that if officers devote time to politics they are unlikely to achieve professionalism. Maniruzzaman (1987:215) states that "A professional army may not be apolitical, but an apolitical army must be professional".

To curb the armed forces' political ambitions, advisers of the Aquino administration unanimously agreed after the series of coup attempts in 1986 and 1987 that "the military had to be disciplined and relegated to a subservient role in the new government" (de Dios 1988:306). Concurring in this view, former President Diosdado Macapagal, in a speech at the Makati Rotary Club on 16 October 1987, declared that the military must be restrained from intervening in the formulation of government policy. But, as Retired General Florencio Magsino warned, "The AFP is no longer the pushover it was before martial law" (*The Financial Post* 27 November 1987).

The Communist and Muslim Insurgencies

President Aquino is not only faced with a military that wants to displace her administration but a Communist party that also wants to seize power by 1998 and a Muslim insurgency demanding autonomy for some provinces in the Southern Philippines.

The twin-insurgencies of the Communist Party of the Philippines (CPP) through its military wing the New People's Army (NPA) and the Moro National Liberation Front (MNLF) are rooted in historical social inequities in Philippine society. During the martial law period the size of both groups increased dramatically. For the MNLF martial law presented a threat to the way of life of the Muslim community. To protect it, the Muslim irridentists engaged the AFP in a bloody war which commenced soon after martial law was declared in 1972. Intense fighting only abated after the Tripoli agreement was signed between the Marcos regime and the MNLF in 1975. Under the agreement autonomy was promised to certain Muslim-dominated provinces. Marcos, however, did not adhere to the agreement and sporadic fighting between the AFP and MNLF continued throughout the period his regime was in office.

After achieving office President Aquino offered a peace settlement to rectify some of the Muslim grievances. The talks, which were opposed by the AFP, and in which the government suggested a referendum before autonomy was granted to the Muslim provinces broke down. A plebiscite was eventually held on the autonomy issue. The MNLF called on Muslims to boycott the referendum. A number of provinces voted for autonomy. The results were not acceptable to the MNLF. Since then the MNLF has continued to engage the armed forces in sporadic fighting but this has depended on factors such as internal and external needs and supplies. Taking into consideration the historical roots of Muslim-Christian animosity in the Philippines, it is unlikely that these issues will be easily resolved in the 1990s.

The same can be said for the AFP-NPA conflict. Unlike the Muslims the Communist insurgency pervades the islands with an estimated 63 out of the 73 provinces affected by the insurgents (*FEER* 28 July 1988), with an armed cadre of 16,000.

Like the Muslims, President Aquino also wanted to adopt a different approach with the Communist insurgents. On taking office she freed hundreds of CPP members detained by President Marcos. Aquino also called for a ceasefire and negotiations in December 1988, much to the chagrin of the armed forces. But peace talks broke down in February 1989 as both the AFP and NPA did not adhere to the letter of the ceasefire agreement. Soon after Aquino declared "total war" against the NPA and told the military to "unsheath the sword of war" and achieve a series of "moral victories" (Hawes 1989:13). But according to Shultz (1989:362) the armed forces are incapable of defeating the NPA because of a lack of emphasis on counterinsurgency techniques. Yet Secretary of Defense Ramos set 1991 as the deadline for defeating the Communists (*Jane's Defence Weekly* 1 April 1989:551). This deadline appears overly optimistic as the AFP has not had much effect on the NPA's influence in the intermittent 20-year war. Given these factors it is highly unlikely that the AFP will be capable of suppressing the Communist movement in the 1990s. What appears more probable is a continuation of the conflict but at a low level because of internal problems in both organizations. Factionalism and differences over the role of the military in society and counterinsurgency strategies persist in the AFP, while the CPP continue to be plagued with purgings and arrests. More importantly, changes in Eastern Europe are leading some in the movement to question the relevance of the CPP's present policies in the Philippines of the 1990s.

Prospects for the Future

The Aquino administration realizes that reforms need to be undertaken in the AFP, but relegating the AFP to a subservient role in government is problematic and is among the issues that will continue to confront the Aquino administration. Despite abandoning its civilian commander in chief when Marcos no longer satisfied the interests of certain elements, most commentators on the Philippine military concur that the military had been subservient to civilian control since its inception. What has, however, not been carefully analyzed is the quality of this control, and why the military accepted it.

During its early years the AFP was predominantly occupied with its development, which was undertaken with US assistance. A semblance of autonomy from the US was evident in the military after the country achieved independence in 1946, but the former colonial power largely controlled the AFP as a result of the inability of the Philippines to equip and maintain an independent armed force. Initially oriented towards external defence, the military had to direct its attention to internal conflict when the Hukbalahap movement threatened the incumbent regime. As the campaign against the Huks succeeded, the AFP started to play a more significant role in government policy making and national development. Many officers performed political functions while on active duty, and felt comfortable in this role, in which the US acquiesced. They returned to managing external and internal security of the nation only reluctantly when this period was abruptly terminated with the death of the civilian president, Ramon Magsaysay. But many officers appeared unwilling to accept that the military should not play a role in policy making and consistently made plans to seize power from administrations which curtailed its budget, size and role in government between 1957 and 1965. These coup attempts never eventuated or were quickly disclosed.

The importance of the military as a ally in maintaining political power was realized by President Marcos and he quickly provided it with a prominent role in society. This role increased significantly during martial law and most of the officer corps was agreed that the military should contribute to the development of the society and participate in policy making. From 1972 the AFP's involvement in politics shifted from influence to participation (Hernandez 1985a). In the process, however, "a *misunderstanding* of the constitutional principle of civilian supremacy over the military developed", resulting in the armed forces abandoning the president (Ambalong 1988. Emphasis added).

By 1986 many officers were entrenched in government. It was therefore unrealistic to expect officers accustomed to policy making to return to purely military roles under civilian control, according to most officers interviewed, especially considering the AFP's role in the demise of the Marcos regime and the accession of Aquino to the presidency. Once the AFP had played such a important role in determining national leadership, it felt it could undoubtedly do so again. Moreover, commanders of the AFP appointed in the next decade will be from the group that was socialized into a military accustomed to participating in the formulation of government policy. Aware of this, President Aquino has been trying to redirect officers to the military's function, which, she argued in her speech to the PMA graduating class in March 1988, is fighting the enemies of the government.

Attempts to overthrow the Aquino adminstration through coups clearly demonstrate that elements in the armed forces want to participate in government as they have been accustomed to do for a considerable period of the AFP's existence. They did not want to establish a military-dominated junta, proposing that a civilian would head any future regime. As Professor Nemenzo (1986a:23) rightly asserts, "More likely the purpose was not even to depose Cory but just to pressure her to grant them a share of power commensurate to the role they played in the February Revolution". This point of view is supported by Lande and Hooley (1986:1095). As against this an article in the PMA Alumni Association newsletter states that the military was seeking "good government", while the Aquino administration was busy trying to curtail the armed forces "alleged political ambitions" (*The POOP* January-February 1987). Despite such claims, attempted coups in August 1987 and December 1989 clearly show that elements in the military really want to govern alone or in coalition with civilians.

Civilian supremacy *per se* is therefore not the issue. The military has always been prepared to accept this, but if civilian politicians want soldiers to accept civilian supremacy, they must respect the military's *cordon sanitaire* and not interfere in purely military matters. They must leave the armed forces to determine "counterinsurgency and the defense of the country" (Ambalong 1988). In fact because of the transitional nature of the Aquino administration, and also because of the circumstances under which the administration came to office, civilian supremacy over the military will remain fragile in the Philippines (Hernandez 1987:19-22). Bunbongkarn (1987:25) argued that when politics was in transition in Thailand the military believed it had to play a role until stability was restored in society. Perhaps the AFP also believes democracy in the Philippines is in transition and it therefore still has an important role to play in politics. Therefore when the institutions of democracy are firmly established the possibility exists for the armed forces to accept civilian supremacy. As Huntington (1968:221) said: "As society changes so does the role of the military".

Under the 1987 Constitution active duty officers are prohibited from participating in government. The Aquino administration has, however, tried to satisfy the desire of some military elements to participate in government and divert those elements wanting to seize power, by appointing retired officers to government positions. Among the most significant appointments are the retired generals presently in the departments of Foreign Affairs, Customs, Defense, Immigration, Telecommunications, and Transport (Selochan 1989:2), and especially the elevation to secretary of defence of retired General Fidel Ramos.

Whether such appointments will avert future coup attempts, or satisfy demands that the military play a more prominent role in government, will depend on how significant the military considers its influence to be on the Aquino administration. But the prospects for the military being relegated to an insignificant position in Philippine society in the near future are low while the Muslims demand a separate state and the Communist Party wants to overthrow the government. Moreover, if the Aquino or any future administration is perceived to be incapable of curbing the insurgents, or preventing a serious threat to the nation, then the possibility of the military returning to partnership in government or establishing a civilian-military dominated regime is quite high. A US risk analyst group has already speculated on the possibility of an attempted coup if relations between the two countries deteriorate in the near future (*South*, No.100, February 1989:45). US administrations are not averse to acting against Third World governments by supporting political factions and the military when US national interests are perceived to be at risk. Chile provides a classic example. Judging from previous experiences in the Philippines and elsewhere, once its interests are satisfied, the US is likely to support any government in the Philippines which guarantees American interests.

In this context, the continued presence of the US military installations in the Philippines looms large. The present treaty expires in 1991, and negotiations over its renewal have been rescheduled to start in May 1990. In the meantime, the US is trying to influence various groups to support the retention of the bases. Of all groups, the AFP needs the least persuasion. Dependent on the US for training and equipment, the majority of the officer corps favour the retention of the installations since it means continued US aid. This was clearly evident during the prolonged bases negotiations in Manila in 1987 when a letter, signed by a group of disgruntled officers expressing support for the retention of the bases was published in the *Manila Bulletin* on 27 June. The letter was written after many officers had told American embassy officials in Manila that they supported the retention of the bases. If the decision at the termination of negotiations is for the bases to be dismantled, because of pressure from nationalist groups, the Philippine government will have to give careful attention to the reaction from the AFP. Moreover, if the US perceives it necessary for the installations to remain in the Philippines, then its actions will also warrant careful scrutiny.

Presidential elections are scheduled for 1992. President Aquino has claimed that she will not contest these elections. She might support Defense Secretary Ramos. It is widely known that the president feels indebted to Ramos for saving her government from a number of attempted coups. The retired general claims that he has not made a decision on whether he will contest the presidential elections. In the meantime, realizing the importance of military support, and not generally popular in the AFP, Ramos will ensure that he continues to play an important role in the selection of the next AFP chief of staff and all service chiefs. The tour of duty of the present chief of staff, General de Villa, has already been extended, causing some friction in the armed forces. Ramos is likely to seek to avoid increasing the friction between the military and the government. Given that the officers eligible for promotion have been nurtured by Ramos, he can therefore expect some support from the military if he decides to contest the presidential elections. Considering that Ramos does not have political base, military support is important to him, at least for the short term, although with Aquino's support he may acquire the backing of the *Laban ng Demokratikong Pilipino* [LDP] (*FEER* 9 March 1989).

The possibility of Ramos using the military as his political base depends on the state of the insurgency and developments in society; retired officers, despite shedding their uniforms, retain their allegiance to the armed forces. Ramos's situation is analogous to that of Ramon Magsaysay. Given his avowed commitment to democracy, Ramos may use the AFP to suppress the NPA, accept the credit, and like Magsaysay, use the military as a vehicle to the presidency. It is worth noting, however, that despite his public statements, Magsaysay was not opposed to staging a coup if that was the only method of achieving power. Considering Ramos's preference for the Philippines to maintain close links with the US, and his "qualified support" for the bases to remain in the Philippines (Berry 1989:297), at least until 1998, Washington might support his bid for the presidency. The majority of the AFP officer corps might expect Ramos, if elected, to accommodate their desires to play a more significant role in politics, and Ramos might acquiesce with implicit agreement from the US. Though a May 1990 discussion paper from the US think-tank, the Heritage Foundation questions Ramos's capabilities for the position. In the meantime the list of presidential candidates is growing. Among those already running are Vice President Salvador Laurel and Senator Juan Ponce Enrile. Other likely candidates are Eduardo "Danding" Cojuangco, Speaker of the House Ramon Mitra and Miriam Defensor Santiago.

What future Philippine governments need to recognize is that elements in the officer corps perceive themselves as capable of playing a more important role in government and will continue to try and achieve such a role. Many argue that their education is equivalent to that of the technocrats, and indeed many officers are educated in the same institutions in the Philippines. Some AFP officers are educated in Western military schools, mostly in the US, which encourage them to play a more prominent role in the economic and sociopolitical development of their societies.

Miranda and Ciron (1987) found that in a sample of 500 officers, 96 per cent claimed that the military had an important role to play in national development, defined as an economically and politically secure environment. Sixty-one per cent believed that senior officers were just as capable of performing civilian functions as civilians. Thus, it is difficult to expect officers to concentrate solely on the military mission of defending the nation. According to Brigadier General Loven Abadia, "The AFP can never go back to the barracks". Rather, officers can still be "engaged in certain civilian jobs that would be dangerous to civilians, especially in insurgency-wracked areas" (*The POOP* January-February 1987). Arguments that officers cannot cope with civilian politics because it requires bargaining, compromise and skill in communication (Lissak 1975:49), are no longer valid. In contemporary officership all these skills are well developed. Many AFP officers are well educated and capable of working in government. President Aquino, however, stated in her speech at the PMA in March 1988 that there must be a clear distinction between military and civilian functions: "I want a clear-cut division of labor; civilian department to civilian reconstruction, the military arm to military action". Moreover, she reiterated that the AFP's role should be in combat by declaring: "Your role is to fight and your duty is to fight well".

Despite such pronouncements, it is unlikely that Philippine governments will simply be able to return the AFP to performing a purely military function in the immediate future. Once the military is accustomed to playing a significant role in politics, it is extremely difficult to break the habit. President Aquino had to agree to meet representatives of the RAM in January 1987 to listen to their grievances against the government, and later she agreed to remove members of the administration perceived by the AFP to be sympathetic to the Left. Importantly, in a letter to the chief of staff the RAM reminded the administration that the military is still part of the government (*FEER* 12 February 1987). Elements in the AFP cite examples of other Third World nations, such as South Korea, Indonesia and Thailand, where, they say, the armed forces have been successful participants in government. A US State Department official declared that "The Philippine army has become a Southeast Asian Army in the mode of Thailand and Indonesia. It feels it knows better than the civilians how to run the country" (*FEER* 24 September 1987). It appears therefore more realistic for political leaders to accept the politicization of the military and to encourage the AFP hierarchy to slowly socialize officer cadets not to expect to be involved in national policy making. To curtail their expectations, however, Nemenzo (1986a:25) provides a more terse remedy: "Now that our soldiers have been politicized, we might as well politicize them properly. They should be made aware of the disastrous consequences of military rule in other countries; and how military intervention, far from solving any problem, compounds and makes it worse". But there are also examples of armed forces, such as in South Korea, which have contributed to the development of their country. Even military regimes which have been criticized, such as Chile and Brazil, have achieved economic growth and aspired to attain "social equity" in the society (Horowitz 1981:40).

By not constitutionally mandating the AFP's role in national development, as the armed forces' role is in *dwifungsi* (dual function) in Indonesia,[2] Philippine governments possibly expect that this will discourage the military from seeking a function which is not within its constitutional sphere. But since it started to perform these duties in the 1950s and continues to pursue them under the present administration, national development has been accepted by some as a function of the AFP. Other factors within the armed forces, however, such as factionalism, are likely to ensure that a democratic system persists; factionalism generally hampers the development of professionalism and prevents the military from acting in unison (Garcia 1978:48).

Whether President Aquino's policies of professionalizing and depoliticizing the military are achievable remains to be seen. What appears more likely in the near future is that elements in the AFP, believing themselves capable of playing a more significant role in government, will continue to try and achieve this goal by overt and covert means. The Aquino and future administrations in the Philippines cannot expect to "relegate the AFP to a position of insignificance", as advocated by her advisers. A more pragmatic approach for the government could be a gradual socialization of the armed force to democratic principles, as the institutions of democratic government become more firmly established. These objectives will, however, remain elusive in the foreseeable future.

Notes

1. Arillo (1986:128-146) documents the development of the power struggle in the regime that led to the demise of Enrile.
2. "In Indonesia .....the armed forces have formulated an ideology which asserts that the military does not have an exclusively military function but has an additional mission as a socio-political force with permanent right (even duty) to participate in the political affairs of the nation" (Crouch 1990: 23).

5

The Military in Malaysia

Harold Crouch

In a region where military intervention in politics is commonplace, the armed forces of Malaysia, along with a few other countries, stand out because they have not only never ruled nor played a major role in government but have never even attempted a coup. Since independence the armed forces of Malaysia have always accepted the principle of civilian supremacy and there seems to be little reason to believe that this orientation is likely to change in the 1990s. In this chapter the history of the development of the military in Malaysia is outlined and then the reasons why it has remained an essentially professional force concerned with defence and security are discussed.[1]

Historical Background

The Malaysian army traces its origins back to the formation by the British in 1933 of what was called the Royal Malay Regiment Experimental Company which expanded into two battalions before participating in the unsuccessful defence of Singapore in 1942. During the occupation, the Japanese set up a Malay military unit called Pembela Tanah Ayer (PETA) but this force was very small and, unlike the Indonesian force of the same name which became the backbone of the Indonesian armed forces, disintegrated at the end of the war when the British returned. Although the Royal Malay Regiment (RMR) was revived by the British after the war, it remained small and it was British and Commonwealth forces together with the police which bore the main brunt of operations against the communist insurgency that began in 1948. Two RMR battalions were formed in 1947, another in 1949 and a fourth in the early 1950s (Zakaria 1981: 201) as well as a multi-ethnic reconnaissance corps (Chandran 1980: 4). While the army was used mainly for operations deep in the jungle, the police were largely responsible for the populated areas where the strongest challenge was faced. The police force outnumbered the army, and police casualties during the 1948-60 Emergency period were double the losses suffered by all other security forces combined (Zakaria 1987: 116).

The army was still small when Malaya received its independence from Britain in 1957. British troops retained their bases in Singapore and Malaya and when Indonesia launched its confrontation policy against the newly formed Malaysia in 1963, British and Commonwealth forces played a much larger role in the defence of the new nation than did its own forces which at that stage numbered only about 13,000 men. British officers continued to hold major command positions. The army was headed by a British officer until 1961 and it was only in 1964 that a Malaysian was appointed as Chief of Armed Forces Staff while the navy and the air force, which were not formed until 1958, remained under British chiefs of staff until 1967. Even when the top command posts were taken over by Malaysians, many important positions continued to be occupied by British officers seconded from the British armed forces who were only finally phased out in the 1970s.[2]

The British announcement in 1966 of its intention to withdraw from East of Suez caused the Malaysian government to think more seriously about defence questions and the need to build up its own military forces apart from the police. Although the British withdrawal was delayed until the mid-1970s and the Australian air base remained until 1988, Malaysia identified itself as a non-aligned country and gradually increased the size and capacity of its armed forces. The old Anglo-Malayan Defence Agreement was replaced by the loose Five-Power Defence Arrangements linking Malaysia and Singapore with Britain, Australia and New Zealand but the physical withdrawal of British forces from Malaysia undermined the credibility of the new relationship. The American defeat in Indochina in 1975 and the closing of American bases in Thailand in 1976 further underlined the need for Malaysia to become more self-reliant in security matters.

The big expansion of Malaysia's military forces, especially the army, however, was primarily in response to the racial rioting of

1969 and the declaration of an Emergency which saw power pass from parliament to a National Operations Council on which the military was represented. Although "normalcy" was restored when parliament resumed in 1971, the Malay-dominated government believed that its authority needed to be backed by a larger and stronger military.

During the 1970s the military expanded in size. In 1969 the number of RMR infantry battalions jumped from ten to sixteen, bringing the total, including four multi-ethnic Ranger battalions, to twenty which steadily increased during the decade to 34 in 1980. At the same time the number of battalions in the paramilitary Police Field Force rose from seven in the mid-1970s to 21 in 1980. The emphasis during the expansion was on infantry forces, both in the army and the police, and training and equipment were oriented towards internal security. Although the first Emergency had been lifted in 1960, communist guerilla activities continued sporadically thoughout the 1960s and 1970s and, at a much lower level, until the end of the 1980s when the Communist Party of Malaya (MCP) finally abandoned its armed struggle.[3] At the same time the spectre of a renewed outbreak of racial conflict continued to haunt the leaders of the government.

In the late 1970s a new expansion commenced but this time the emphasis moved from counterinsurgency to conventional defence (Crouch 1983). Following the American defeat in Indochina, Malaysia had adopted a fairly friendly stance towards Vietnam, offering technical assistance to rehabilitate Vietnam's rubber plantations, but the Vietnamese invasion of Cambodia at the end of 1978 and the Vietnam-China war in early 1979 suddenly created a sense of insecurity. It so happened that these external developments coincided with an economic boom in Malaysia, partly caused by the sharp rise in oil prices due to the Iran-Iraq war. The Malaysian military was therefore in a strong position to convince the government to allocate funds to increase the size of the armed forces and to buy conventional hardware. Under the Armed Forces Special Modernization Progam (*Perista*) launched in 1979, the army grew from 52,500 in 1979 to about 100,000 in 1983 while the air force increased from 6,000 to 11,000 and the navy from 6,000 to over 8,000. At the same time the army purchased 450 new armoured personnel carriers, Scorpion light tanks and the controversial Sibmas armoured firing vehicle, the air force brought into service 35 A4 Skyhawk fighter-bombers and the navy aquired two corvettes as well as minehunters and fast-attack craft. Military spokesmen said that 75 per cent of training would now be devoted to conventional warfare (NST 6-4-81).

The implementation of the expansion and modernisation programme, however, was checked by the economic recession that hit the world in the mid-1980s while, with the passing of the years, the threat that Vietnam and China seemed to pose in 1979 had become less worrying. By 1989 the army was planning to reduce its size from its current level of 105,000.[4] According to the Chief of Armed Forces, General Tan Sri Hashim Mohamed Ali, "A force that is not too large yet is highly trained and has a high level of capability in handling modern equipment will be cheaper to maintain in the long run" (NST 12-2-89). As part of the plan to raise the technological sophistication of the armed forces, in 1988 the Malaysia government signed a Memorandum of Understanding with Britain to buy defence equipment worth one billion pounds sterling over a period of 5-10 years. The military hardware included Tornado interdictor-strike aircraft, anti-aircraft missile batteries, a reconditioned Oberon-class submarine and ground-to-air missile launchers. (NST 29-9-88). Reportedly Malaysia also plans to buy more equipment over fifteen years including six new Vickers 1400-tons submarines, short-range Rapier ground-to-air missile systems, off-shore patrol vessels and helicopters (*FEER* 13-10-88).

The decade of the 1980s, therefore, saw the gradual acquisition by the Malaysian military of a conventional capacity. Until the 1970s the Malaysian military forces had been concerned almost exclusively with internal security. The military's two main purposes were to carry out counterinsurgency operations against communist guerillas and to provide the means for the government to restore order in the event of racial conflict running out of hand. In the 1960s responsibility for external defence had been largely left in the hands of the British but British withdrawal, the American failure in Vietnam and finally the Vietnamese invasion of Cambodia and the Chinese attack on Vietnam had spurred the development of a conventional capacity in the 1980s. The emphasis on conventional capacity, however, did not mean that concern for internal security was abandoned. Although communist guerilla activity remained at a very low level and was finally abandoned, the armed forces, in particular the army, as well as the police, remained of political significance as largely Malay instruments which could be used to back up a Malay-dominated government in a crisis.

Why Has the Malaysian Military Not Intervened in Politics?

The factors which explain whether military intervention takes place or not can be discussed at several levels. At the most general level, the broad socio-economic environment can increase or decrease the probability of military intervention. Military intervention tends to occur at low levels of socio-economic development but is less likely at higher levels. Secondly, military intervention usually takes place in the context of a general political crisis which is beyond the capacity of the existing government to control. And thirdly, particular country-specific factors must always be taken into account in explaining particular cases of intervention or non-intervention.

1. Socio-economic Environment

There appears to be a broad correlation between military intervention and various indicators of development and modernisation. Military intervention is more probable in countries in the early stages of industrialisation when per capita income is still low and there are few social classes capable of countervailing against military power. But where economic growth has raised incomes and produced strong business, middle and working classes, authoritarian rule—whether military or civilian—is more difficult, although of course not impossible, to establish and maintain.

From this perspective Malaysian society is not especially conducive to military domination, compared to many other Asia-Pacific countries. At US$2028 in 1989, Malaysia's per capita income was much higher than in any Asia-Pacific state where the military has played a dominant role in national politics except South Korea.[5] As a result of rapid economic growth the Malaysian middle class is larger as a proportion of the population than in any other Southeast Asian country except Singapore. In 1980 some 24 per cent of the work-force was employed in middle-class occupational categories such as professional, administrative, managerial, clerical and sales while 19 per cent of households had cars. On the other hand, in countries like Indonesia and Thailand which had experienced military intervention, the middle class was much smaller and the proportion of car-owning households only 2-3 per cent (See Crouch 1984: 25, 61-2, 77). While Malaysia's socio-economic environment provides no absolute barrier to military intervention, it seems, if the experience of other countries is taken into account, to make such intervention less probable.

2. Political Crisis

Military intervention in the Third World never takes place simply because the military is oriented towards politics and thirsts for power. As Huntington put it, "Military explanations do not explain military intervention" (Huntington 1968:194). On the contrary, the military almost always intervenes in reaction to developments in the political system as a whole. Military intervention usually follows a longish period of declining government legitimacy, often marked by poor economic performance, incompetent administration, apparently interminable faction-fighting within the government, and sometimes endemic regional rebellion. The final coup, however, is often in response to a particular crisis - scandal in the government, rigged elections, student demonstrations, riots, military defeat etc.

Since independence Malaysia has experienced only one political crisis of the sort that might have been expected to trigger a military coup. In the immediate aftermath of the May 1969 election rioting broke out in Kuala Lumpur as Malays reacted to electoral advances made by non-Malay opposition parties. According to the official count, nearly 200 people, mainly Chinese, were killed, but unofficial estimates ran much higher. A state of Emergency was implemented and for almost two years power was in the hands of a ten-member National Operations Council dominated by senior Malay politicians and bureaucrats but also including the Chief of Armed Forces Staff and the Inspector-General of Police with another senior army officer serving as Chief Executive Officer of the council (Funston 1980: 231). But, although military officers in effect joined the government, they did so by invitation of UMNO (United Malays National Organisation), the dominant party in the ruling coalition, and there was never any suggestion that they had any desire to take control of the government themselves. And there was no hint of military resistance to the return to normalcy in February 1971 and the resumption of parliament.

Unlike crises which have led to coups in other countries, the political crisis of May 1969 in Malaysia had not been preceded by an extended period of declining faith in civilian rule among its erstwhile supporters. There had always been substantial non-Malay, especially Chinese, alienation from the government but most of the Malay majority continued to aknowledge the legitimacy of the established Malay elite, whatever reservations some may have held about particular leaders. Rather than further undermining government legitimacy, the racial riots in fact strengthened Malay resolve to entrench the Malay-dominated civilian government which they saw as threatened by non-Malays.

In general, Malaysia's Malay-dominated government has provided stable and effective administration. The dominant party, UMNO, has never been seriously threatened by factional splits (until the party split of 1988) and has always maintained its predominance in the ruling coalition - the Alliance and then the National Front. Although the electoral system favours the ruling coalition, it has generally won something like 60 per cent of the votes in nearly all the elections which have been held regularly since 1959. Despite non-Malay disaffection and some Malay opposition, the government seems broadly acceptable to the majority.

The legitimacy of civilian government, therefore, has hardly been questioned in Malaysia. From the point of view of the Malay community, government policies have brought substantial benefits in such fields as business, employment, education and culture, and there is no presumption that a military-dominated government could perform better. From the point of view of non-Malays, however, whatever sense of alienation is felt from the present government would only be increased if the military took power. The present civilian government is Malay-dominated but at the same time there is significant non-Malay representation. Non-Malay representation in the government is much higher than non-Malay representation in the military.

3. Civilian and Military Elites

It could be argued that military intervention is more likely when the political and bureaucratic elite on one hand and the military elite on the other have different socio-economic origins. In many Third World countries the political and bureaucratic elite is recruited largely from the aristocratic, land-owning or urban professional classes. On the other hand, as Janowitz argued many years ago, it is common in Third-World countries for military leaders to be recruited from the middle- and lower-middle classes, and from the small towns in the provinces rather than the capital city (Janowitz 1964: 49-58). There is therefore considerable potential for the alienation of military officers from the privileged civilian elite.

In Malaysia, however, political, bureaucratic and military leaders have very similar social origins. In fact it seems appropriate to view them all as part of the same elite.

In the first place the military, like the government and the bureaucracy, is a Malay-dominated institution. In its report on the 1969 racial riot, the National Operations Council revealed that in 1969 Malays made up 65.4 per cent of the armed forces officer corps (National Operations Council 1969: p.23, cited by Guyot 1974: 34). As explained above, the army had its origins in the Malay Regiment which is exclusively Malay in composition and remains the core of the army. Of the army's present 38 infantry battalions, 26 are part of the Malay Regiment while the other ten are multiracial Ranger battalions which consisted initially of the First and Second Ranger battalions from Sarawak and Sabah after the formation of Malaysia in 1963 but later grew with recruitment from the Peninsula. The Ranger battalions, however, are also largely Malay in composition. Answering a question in parliament in 1971, the Prime Minister, Tun Razak, said that at that time Malays made up 84 per cent of the other ranks and 50 per cent of the officers in the Ranger battalions. In comparison with the army, the navy and air force were more multi-ethnic. According to Razak, Malays made up only 51 per centof the officers and 74 per cent of other ranks in the navy, and 46 per cent of officers and 59 per cent of other ranks in the air force (Chandran 1980: 66-7).

The racial balance within the armed forces tipped further in favour of the Malays during the next decade. According to a Defence Ministry spokesman in 1981, in the armed forces as a whole 74.6 per cent of officers were Malay and 84.8 per cent of the other ranks. Chinese made up 16.2 per cent of the officer corps and only 6.1 per cent of the other ranks, while Indians constituted 6.2 per cent of officers and 6.4 per cent of other ranks. In addition 2.7 per cent of the other ranks were classified as "other" (NST 18-12-81). That this pattern was likely to continue was indicated by statistics for recruitment to the armed forces. Malays made up 86 per cent of officer recruits in 1979 and and 91 per cent in 1981 while they constituted 92 per cent of rank-and-file recruits in 1979 and 93 per cent in 1981. Of a total of 8,125 rank-and-file recruits in 1981, only 35 were Chinese (NST 20-10-81).

Malay domination is also clearly seen in appointments to key commands. The positions of Chief of Defence Forces (previously Chief of Armed Forces Staff) and Chief of the Army (previously Chief of General Staff) have always been held by Malays as has command of the air force. In the case of the navy, the first Malaysian commander was of Indian descent but all his successors have been Malay. At the beginning of 1990 the Chief of Defence Forces and all service chiefs and their deputies were Malay, as were the army Corps commander and the army Chief of Staff. All five army divisions (including the reserve division) were under Malay commanders but one of the twelve infantry brigades was commanded by a non-Malay. Thus it would not be true to say that divisional and brigade commands are automatically held by Malay officers. Indeed in the early eighties one of the divisions was commanded by an Indian officer and at several times there have been Indian and Chinese brigade commanders. In 1989 a Chinese brigadier was appointed to head the air force's Air Support Command. But there is no question that Malays are in control, particularly of infantry forces which might be needed to back up the government in a domestic political crisis.

Military officers, however, are linked to the civilian elite not only through their Malayness. Although it is difficult to document, it seems that military officers often come from the same sorts of families which produce civil servants and UMNO politicians. Military officers and civilian leaders have generally gone to the same types of school and have often known each other for decades. Moreover, military officers often have brothers or cousins who are civil servants or UMNO activists and it is common for them to marry the sisters of members of the civilian elite while it is not unusual for members of the civilian elite to marry sisters or cousins of military officers. In the 1960s both the military and civilian elites tended to have their origins in the small upper and middle strata of Malay society but as opportunities for higher education extended to the lower levels of Malay society with the implementation of the education policy associated with the New Economic Policy after 1970, Malays of humble background were able to join the elite Administrative and Diplomatic service in the bureaucracy and also to rise in the military.

At the highest levels the links between the civilian and military leadership has been close. The first Malaysian Chief of General Staff (i.e head of the army) and then Chief of Armed Forces Staff, General Tunku Osman Jewa, was a member of the Kedah royal family and nephew of the first Prime Minister, Tunku Abdul Rahman. In 1981, the Prime Minister, Datuk Husseln Onn, promoted his brother-in-law, General Tan Sri Ghazali Seth, as Chief of Armed Forces Staff, and his brother, Lt. Gen. Datuk Jaafar Onn as Deputy Chief of Staff of the army. In 1983 Lt. Gen. Jaafar was replaced by Maj. Gen. Datuk Hashim Mohamed Ali, the brother-in-law of the new Prime Minister, Datuk Seri Dr. Mahathir Mohamad and brother of the governor of the central bank. Dr Mahathir later appointed General Hashim to command the army and then, in 1987, the armed forces. The Deputy Chief of the Army in the late 1980s, Lt. Gen. Datuk Nik Mahmood Fakharuddin Kamil, was the son of the late Tan Sri Nik Ahmad Kamil, an UMNO leader from Kelantan and former speaker of parliament. Another senior officer, Brig. Gen. Raja Rashid Raja Bediozaman, the head of military intelligence, was the brother of Tan Sri Raja Mohar Raja Bediozaman, a former economic advisor to the government who had held many senior civil service positions in the past. Many other examples could be given.

It is therefore difficult to speak of distinct civilian and military elites in Malaysia. As long as the government continues to serve the interests of the Malay elite in general, it is likely to remain acceptable to the military elite which is part of the general Malay elite.

4. *Defence Allocations and Economic Well-being*

Budget allocations for defence can lead to friction between the government and the military in any country but in Malaysia such conflict has never resulted in serious alienation of the military. As the economy grew during the 1970s and 1980s defence expenditure rose steadily from M$437 million in 1970 to a peak of M$3695 in 1982 before declining due to the effects of the world recession (Muthiah 1987). Defence expenditures between 1970 and 1985 averaged 13.18 per cent of the national budget and 4.47 per cent of GNP, ranging between a high of 16.4 per cent of the budget in 1972 down to 9.19 per cent in 1985 (Zakaria 1988: 241). Certainly the Malaysian armed forces have been able periodically to upgrade their armaments and have enjoyed general facilities far better than in most neighbouring countries. It is also worth noting that defence expenditure in Malaysia has often been higher as a proportion of both the national budget and gross national product than in neighbouring countries where the military has dominated the government.

Military salaries are closely related to the general salary structure of the civil service so that military officers have no reason to feel that they are treated poorly in comparison to civilians. Moreover, if officers feel discontented with their lot in the armed forces, they have the option of early retirement and can seek well-paid employment in the private sector. As part of the New Economic Policy the government has applied pressure to private companies to increase the employment of Malays in management positions with the result that retired military officers in their 30s or 40s are easily able to get appointments as personnel officers and similar positions in the private sector. As Chan Heng Chee has put it, describing a similar phenomenon in Singapore, "dissatisfied young officers do not stage coups. They merely resign to join the lucrative private sector with their highly marketable skills" (Chan Heng Chee 1985: 147). Further, the Defence Minister has assured retired officers that companies owned by ex-servicemen will continue to be given priority in the awarding of Defence Ministry contracts (NST 8-7-89)

Senior officers are also well looked after on their retirement. Like retired senior civil servants they are in demand for appointment to the boards of directors of companies which hope to utilise their government contacts. Thus several former Chiefs of Armed Forces Staff or the General Staff in the 1970s were appointed as chairmen of well-known companies after their retirement - General Tan Sri Ibrahim Ismail, for example, became chairman of Petaling Tin, General Tan Sri Ungku Nazaruddin Ungku Mohamed was appointed as chairman of Pahang Consolidated and General Tan Sri Mohamed Sany Abdul Ghaffar joined Island and Peninsula Development Bhd (Crouch 1985). In the 1980s it has also been common for retired senior officers to be appointed as chairmen of companies owned or partly owned by the government or its agencies. Thus General Tan Sri Ghazali Mohamad Seth was appointed as chairman of Malaysia Shipyard Engineering Bhd which is under the control of the Ministry of Public Enterprises (NST 12-4-89) while his successor, General Tan Sri Datuk Mohd Ghazali Che Mat, who retired in 1987, became chairman of Kumpulan Guthrie (Guthrie Group) Bhd as well as chairman of The New Straits Times Press (M) Bhd (NST 30-7-88). General Tan Sri Zain Hashim, who retired as Chief of the Army in 1983, was appointed chairman of Perwira Habib Bank Malaysia Bhd, a bank in which the Armed Forces Welfare Fund (*Lembaga Tabung Angkatan Tentera*) is a major shareholder (NST 27-4-89).

5. *Counterinsurgency Experience*

It is sometimes argued that military forces which have counterinsurgency experience are likely to be more inclined towards political activity than those without such experience. It is suggested that officers engaged in counterinsurgency operations become sensitive to the socio-economic conditions which usually lie behind insurgencies and therefore demand political action to reduce the root causes of dissatisfaction. When governments are unable or unwilling to implement policies to improve the conditions of the rural people from whom the insurgents draw support, military officers can become even more politicized and more willing to take independent political action of their own.

In the Malaysian case, the armed forces faced a communist insurgency from 1948 until 1989, although at a low level after 1960. But there are several reasons why counterinsurgency experience has apparently not politicised the Malaysian officer corps.

First, the peak of the insurgency was reached in the late 1940s and early 1950s when Malaya was still under colonial rule and the armed forces were under British command. At that time, as pointed out above, the role of indigenous army troops was very limited as the main burden was borne by Commonwealth forces and the police. Although the insurgency continued after independence, it declined in intensity with the result that military officers were less affected by the experience and in any case the Police Field Force remained in its central role. Secondly, the social base of the insurgents was among rural Chinese who had "squatted" on government land. While Malay soldiers might well have had some sympathy for poor Malays if the insurgency had had its roots among them, it is reasonable to assume that most were largely indifferent to the fate of Chinese squatters who in any case could hardly communicate their grievances to English - and Malay-speaking military officers. And thirdly, the government has provided formal channels for military officers to participate in policy-making on security issues through the National Security Council and the various State and District Security Committees set up following the return to normalcy in 1971. At the national level the Chief of Defence Forces and the Inspector-General of Police sit on the council which also includes the Prime Minister, the Minister of Home Affairs and various other cabinet members. Similarly the army and police are represented on the state and district councils which often discuss security-related social and economic issues such as the position of illegal squatters, the effects of logging, and development projects. Through these councils the military has been active in promoting its concept of *Kesban (Keselamatan dan Pembangunan* - Security and Development) with its emphasis on the provision of basic amenities to rural communities (see Zakaria 1988: 236-238). In this area there do not appear to be major differences in approach between civilian and military leaders.

6. The Role of the Police

The existence of a separate paramilitary force within the police would be a further complication if the military decided to intervene directly in politics. Unlike some neighbouring countries, in Malaysia the police force is not part of the armed forces but is under the Ministry of Home Affairs. Apart from routine police duties, the police force also maintains its paramilitary Police Field Force (PFF), consisting of twenty-one battalions with about 20,000 personnel. The PFF receives training in jungle warfare and have armour, such as Ferret scout cars and V150 Commando armoured personnel carriers similar to those used by the army. PFF personnel are in fact not recruited directly but are ordinary policemen assigned to the PFF where they are involved in such duties as patrolling crime-prone areas, providing protection for visiting foreign dignitaries or even maintaining order at football matches when they are not posted with the army for jungle operations.[6] In addition the police has the 2,500-strong Federal Reserve Unit trained to meet emergencies such as demonstrations, strikes or riots. And, finally the police Special Branch controls internal political intelligence.

Like the military leadership, the senior police leaders come from the same Malay socio-economic background as the civilian elite although there are more non-Malays among its officers.[7] However, the lower ranks are overwhelmingly Malay, except for certain specialised areas such as criminal investigation. In 1988 the Deputy Home Minister complained that the quota of 800 places for non-Malay police recruits had not been met in 1987 and that the response had been particularly weak among Chinese (NST 22-8-88).

While the separate organisation of the police and especially its paramilitary units would not be an insuperable obstacle if the army decided to take direct political action, it would be necessary for the military leaders to ensure police support first. Given their common socio-economic and communal backgrounds, this could presumably be obtained although not automatically as the Inspector-General of Police is directly responsible to the Minster for Home Affairs.

7. External Influences

It is sometimes suggested that respect for civilian supremacy is part of the British legacy inherited by the Malaysian armed forces —although this legacy does not seem to have been very effective in preventing military intervention in other ex-British colonies. While there is no doubt that the British ethos remained strong in the Malaysian military during the early years after independence when many command positions were still held by British officers, the influence of British values has declined in the military as in society in general. One consequence of the expansion of education after 1970, as mentioned above, was the recruitment of more officers from relatively humble backgrounds where Malay is the normal medium of communication and commitment to conventional Islam is strong. Officers from this type of background are far less subject to the influence of British traditions as can be seen, for example, in the apparent preference of most Malay officers for soft rather than alcoholic drinks in the officers' messes. By 1990 it was doubtful whether British tradition was a significant factor inhibiting military intervention in politics. At the same time there is no indication that the decline in British values has been matched by rising American influence, although an increasing number of Malaysian officers are taking courses in the USA (Muthiah 1986:9).

On the other hand the military relationship between Malaysia and Indonesia has grown extremely close since the end of Konfrontasi in 1966. Malaysian and Indonesian officers attend courses in each others' countries and regular land, sea and air exercises are held - sometimes on a quite large scale. While it would be an exaggeration to say that Malaysia and Indonesia have established an informal military alliance, the co-operation between the two armed forces is greater than that between any other pair of ASEAN countries. This closeness is further reinforced by similarities in language and culture although sometimes close contact results in increased awareness of differences as well as similarities.

But has the close military relationship and the regular contact of Malaysian officers with their Indonesian counterparts led to the adoption of Indonesian concepts about civil-military relations? Hard evidence is lacking but it is my impression from conversations with Malaysian officers who have spent time in Indonesia that they do not usually find the Indonesian system superior to their own and, in some cases at least, it would seem that the experience has strengthened their conviction that military professionalism can be undermined when the military involves itself in non-military activities.

8. Non-Malays and the Military

Although the communal composition of the military elite corresponds with that of the dominant element in the government and the civil service, it certainly does not reflect the communal composition of the population as a whole in which the non-indigenous communities constitute about 40 per cent.

As mentioned above, non-Malays, especially Chinese, have seemed reluctant to join both the military and the police. It is sometimes suggested that there is something in Chinese culture which makes them averse to serving in the armed forces but this does not seem to affect the armed forces of Singapore. It may, however, be the case that many Chinese regard the military and police as agents of a state which does not represent their interests and in fact often takes action in direct conflict with their interests. Moreover, it would appear that non-Malays, in particular Chinese, are unwilling to join the armed forces and police because they doubt that their chances of promotion would be the same as their Malay colleagues, an impression strengthened by the not uncommon resignations of Chinese military officers who have failed to gain promotion beyond the rank of major.

In an attempt to overcome the reluctance of Chinese to join the armed forces, the Chinese political parties - both the Malaysian Chinese Association in the government and the opposition Democratic Action Party - have for many years been calling for the introduction of conscription but these demands have been rejected by the government on the grounds that there is no need to increase the size of the military and in any case it would be too costly. The unstated reason of course is that it would also drastically change the racial make-up of the armed forces.

A military takeover of the government, then, could be expected to be met with dismay by the Chinese and Indian communities. Civilian government at least provides for quite substantial representation of the minority communities in the government while non-Malays are almost totally excluded from the top military leadership and are greatly under-represented at other levels. In these circumstances military intervention could well be counter-productive if its purpose were the restoration or strengthening of political stability. At the very least a military coup could be expected to deter investment and encourage capital flight while at the worst it could even give a new lease of life to the predominantly Chinese communist movement. It therefore seems probable that even if the military did intervene in an emergency, it would very likely hand power back to multi-communal civilian government fairly quickly.

Conclusion

In the Malaysian case it seems reasonable to assume that the factors which have impeded military intervention in the past will continue to make it very unlikely in the 1990s. Civilian rule has been effective and its legitimacy hardly questioned while the military has shown no signs of being interested in taking power. And it would appear that economic and social development has reached a level in Malaysia beyond that which tends to be associated with military intervention in other countries. Of particular importance in the Malaysian context is the communal make-up of society which places the Malay-dominated military on the same side as the Malay-dominated government and bureaucracy.

If military intervention was to take place in Malaysia, it could only be after major changes in the present socio-political environment affecting not just the military but the whole political system. In particular the possibility of the outbreak of communal conflict can never be dismissed although the record since 1969 has been reasonably good. But various other scenarios can also be imagined which might at least raise the possibilty of change in the military-civilian relationship. What, for example, would be the effects of a collapse in the international economy for a country as heavily dependent on international trade and investment as Malaysia? What will be the implications of the current rise in Islamic consciousness (which I personally believe has been greatly exaggerated by many observers[8]) for a predominantly Muslim military? What will be the consequences for political stability of the split in UMNO and possible increased political fragmentation within the Malay community? And how will demographic change affect the entire political system as different rates of population growth result in the precarious balance between ethnic communities at the time of independence shifting to one in which the indigenous bumiputera community is expected to outnumber the non-bumiputera population by more than two-to-one at the end of the century?

While it is not easy to anticipate answers to these very hypothetical questions, it seems reasonably safe to conclude that in the absence of drastic change in the whole political system in response to extraordinary circumstances which are difficult to imagine, the present character of military-civilian relations in Malaysia is likely to endure.

Notes

1. The scholarly literature on the Malaysian military is extremely limited. The most substantial work is Chandran's study of defence policy up to 1973 (1980). Articles include those of Zakaria (1981) (1985) (1987) and (1988), Chandran (1988), Rau (1986), Enloe (1977) and (1988), Guyot (1974) and Muthiah (1987). Several pages are devoted to the military in the general survey of Malaysian politics by Bedlington (1978). There is also my set of articles in the Far Eastern Economic Review (Crouch 1983,:46-52)

2. In 1966 there were 336 British officers and 316 other ranks serving in the Malaysian armed forces (Chandran,1980: 73).

3. According to military sources in 1989 there were still about 1000 communist guerillas in bases across the border in southern Thailand, 200 in the jungles of Peninsular Malaysia and 42 in Sarawak (NS, 25-1-89, 20-3-89). On 2 December 1989, under the auspices of the Government of Thailand, an agreement was signed between the MCP and the Government of Malaysia under which the MCP pledged to end its armed struggle.

4. NST 12-3-89. Estimates of the size of the military establishment are not always consistent. In another report, the Minister of Defence was quoted as saying that the Armed Forces had 114,500 personnel, NST, 4-10-89.

5. Compare for example Thailand ($1194), Philippines ($727), Indonesia ($520), Pakistan ($365), Burma ($200), Bangladesh ($179). The nearest military-influenced country in the Asia-Pacific region to Malaysia was Fiji ($1516). Asiaweek, 2 February 1989, 6.

6. The government's agreement with the MCP in December 1989 ending the MCP's armed struggle raised questions about the PFF's future role. For the time being the force is to be retained although its functions may change. It has been suggested that its new role will include operations against "urban guerillas" and drug- and arms-smugglers., NST 10-1-90.

7. Cursory examination of published lists of police promotions suggests that about 60-70 per cent of officers are Malay. See for example, Utusan Malaysia, 12-11-83; NST,14-3-84. Overall in 1989 Chinese made up only 4.6 per cent of the 75,957 members of the police force. Of these 1808 were officers. NST, 12-10 89. In the 1960s, however, non-Malays were better represented. In 1968, Malays made up only 45.1 per cent of police officers (Gibbons and Zakaria 1971: 341, quoted in Bedlington, 1978: 168) and Enloe reports that Malays only made up some 39 per cent of the total police force then. Enloe, 1978:280.

8. See Crouch 1987.

6

The Military in Myanmar (Burma):[1] What Scope for a New Role?

Robert H. Taylor

Introduction

The role of the armed forces[2] have been central to Myanmar's politics since the 1940s. The nature of that role has changed from period to period, largely as a result of how the leadership of the army has interpreted its proper place in the prevailing conditions (Taylor 1985 and 1987a and Silverstein 1977). There seems to be little reason to expect that the military will adopt a significantly less central role in the 1990s. Nonetheless, the character of the role the military chooses and will be able to play will doubtless be different in the next decade as a result of the economic collapse and consequent political upheavals of 1988, as well as generational changes in the composition of the officer corps. Having been dominated for over 40 years by the generation of officers who entered the military under the auspices of General Ne Win, the pivotal figure in the army's development since the 1940s, the army in the 1990s will come under the control of the generation of officers who entered service in the post-civil war period of the mid-1950s. They will be the first group to command without the dominating presence of Ne Win. Their experiences and expectations were formed in different domestic and international conditions from those of their predecessors and the consequences of this will be seen as their policies and programs emerge through the decade.

The Military's Role in Society

After the introduction of a new constitution in 1974 formally creating a one-party socialist state under the leadership of the Burma Socialist Programe Party (BSPP), the armed forces as an institution was expected to take a less direct role in politics than it had during the previous 12 years. In the period between 1962, when the army under General Ne Win took state power through a coup, and 1974, the military had directly governed through the agency of the central Revolutionary Council and local and regional Security and Administration Committees (SACs). But the leading individuals of the government, and of the militarily-organized and based BSPP, remained without significant changes after 1974. Most of the senior officers resigned their commissions but remained in power through their positions in the BSPP and the state apparatus. Many serving officers also continued to hold leading positions in the cabinet and high administrative and political offices. While the constitutional change provided, at the local and township levels, a greater role for civilians in the management of economic, social and cultural affairs, central political and security policy and control remained in the hands of officers who had begun their careers in the 1940s. Thus their perceptions of politics and society, evolving during and immediately after the anti-colonial, anti-fascist and civil war periods, continued to dominate official thinking.

Consequently, as the one-party constitutional period between 1974 and 1988 progressed, the factors which dominated thinking about the role of the military in Myanmar's politics at the beginning of the period changed only partially. The question of the role of General Ne Win as *eminence grise* is now not dissimilar in essence to the situation nearly a decade ago when he stepped down as state president in 1981 and retained only the formal office of party chairman. The military's continuing involvement in armed conflict with ethnic and other insurgents along the country's borders has not changed and there seems little reason to believe that it will in the near future. The career pattern of officers, from the army into politics, the civil administration and the management of state-owned factories, shops and enterprises, seems unlikely to change much. Despite the post-1988 changes in economic policy away from the socialist autarky of the BSPP period, state created economic organizations staffed by serving and retired officers are also unlikely to undergo any fundamental change.[3] The central role of army veterans in the network of military influence is not apt to change significantly either, following the reorganization of the War Veterans Organization in August, 1989.[4] Had the reformulated

BSPP under the name of the National Unity Party (NUP), under the leadership of ex-military ministers from the previous government, been successful in the May 1990 elections, it might also have provided another conduit for the continuation of military influence in politics and government. However, as it gained only a handful of seats and received only approximately 20 per cent of the total vote, its present utility for the militjary is minimal. What will be most significantly different in the future is both the public's and the military's perceptions of the legitimacy of the army's leading role in politics and government. This stems from several factors One is the generational change alluded to above. The rising generation of officers have none of the personal aura of authority which came from involvement in the independence struggle and post-independence civil war which Ne Win created and the lead generation possessed.[5] The training many of the second generation officers received in the 1950s, during the last period of ostensibly multi-party elections and civilian government included some, even if minimal, indoctrination in the concept of civilian control of the military. More importantly, the consequences of the armed forces" role in putting down the pro-democracy demonstrations in Yangon and other cities in 1988 and the army's continuing limitations on the organizational activities of its most vocal civilian critics,[6] even after the May election, has placed doubts in the minds of a significant proportion of the public as to the altruistic purposes of the military. The growing corruption of the military and the civil service in the 1980s as the economy collapsed and the apparent unwillingness of the Ne Win generation to abandon power in the face of urban protests and the May 1990 election,[7] caused many to question the national purpose of the armed forces.[8] The armed forces will have to regain public respect if they are to retain any legitimacy for an obvious and explicit governing role in the future. This will require the military to develop a different position within the state and in so doing establish a new relationship between the state and civil society.

Related to this development will probably be some reorientation of military thinking about external influences and economic development.[9] Though clearly still nationalist in outlook, the second generation of officers have experienced the economic and social stagnation which accompanied socialist autarky. The model of Thai and Indonesian officers, with their private sector business interests and their links with foreign capital, as well as the significant military perquisites which can be derived from foreign investment leading to more rapid economic growth and an expanded resource base for the state, has not been lost upon the armed forces of

Myanmar. What is the sense of having a politically dominant military which presides over a poverty stricken government which cannot provide sufficient resources to fund a modern, well equipped and well paid army, is a question many officers have been asking themselves

The continuing constraints on defense expenditure caused by slow economic growth are apparent from a cursory examination of recent available statistics. According to estimates made by the Stockholm International Peace Research Institute (SIPRI), in constant price United States dollar terms, Myanmar's defense expenditure grew slowly from US$ 247 million in 1978 to peak at US$ 295 million in 1981 before declining and then returning in 1985 to near the peak figure. In 1986, however, the last year for which estimates are available, expenditure returned to just US$ 253 million, not far from the figure a decade previous (SIPRI 1988:164). This pattern fits that established in Myanmar from 1962 onwards (Taylor 1987b:254-276). Defense expenditure, being almost entirely dependent upon internally available funds, and receiving no significant foreign assistance, has been severely constrained by prevailing economic conditions. The decline in 1986 shadowed the crisis of the economy as revealed in gross domestic product (GDP) figures for the period. Real GDP growth was negative both in 1986, -1.1 per cent, and in 1987, -4.2 per cent (Burma 1989:23). However, only in part the result of higher GDP growth rates in the early 1980s, military expenditure as a percentage of GDP fell from 4.0 per cent in 1978 to an estimated 3.2 per cent in 1986 (SIPRI 1988:169). During the same period, the size of the armed forces grew from 153,000 troops to 186,000 but with no additional major equipment. The growth was entirely in terms of additional manpower to which 60 per cent or more of defense expenditure is directed.[10]

The collapse of the military-backed BSPP order in 1988 was the consequence of a series of economic and political factors, both systemic and immediate (Steinberg 1989a and 1989b; Yitri 1989; IISS 1989; Guyot 1989). The immediate economic and political factors are not of central concern in trying to fathom the nature of the military's political role and future. However, the catastrophic economic decisions of August/September 1987, including the demonetization of 25, 35 and 75 *kyat* notes, 60 per cent or more of money in circulation, without compensation, and the government's inability to cope with initially minor student protests in March/April 1988, revealed the systemic nature of the crisis. At root was the inability of the armed forces and its founder, General Ne Win, to allow for the BSPP to develop as a viable governing party in its own right. Born from the armed forces, the party was never able to move away from its military character. Thus, it lacked the independence and flexibility to come to terms with changing social, economic and political conditions. As the leadership aged and became more remote from current reality, the party mechanisms lacked the autonomy to inform and correct government policy decisions.

The inability of the BSPP to develop was a consequence of the unwillingness, perhaps as a result of the requirements of regime and personal survival, of the army's leadership, and especially General Ne Win, to allow autonomous institutions to develop.[11] Initially, as a consequence of the economic advice of the army's ex-communist and socialist advisers in the period between 1962 and 1966, but increasingly as it became necessary to undermine independent centers of economic power in the society, the military kept a firm grip on all large and most small scale economic enterprises. Rather than allow state enterprises to be run efficiently by trained personnel who through their knowledge and expertise could develop independent authority, trusted but untrained military and ex-military personnel were sent to run all nationalized enterprises. After the nationalization in 1963 and 1964 of the property of Indian and other foreign entrepreneurs who had dominated domestic and foreign trade since the colonial period, no legal class of indigenous traders was allowed to develop as an alternative center of class power to the military ruling group. The consequence was the development of the extensive but tolerated black market which became increasingly essential as a source of consumer goods but whose operators remained politically powerless and insecure because of their illegal status. In the end, the black market became a part of the system as military officers and government and party officials used their special access to privileged and subsidized goods to increase their salaries through illegal trading. Also as a consequence of the military's autarkic and strongly nationalist posture, foreign governments and multinational corporations could develop no influence over government policies.[12]

At the same time as the military/BSPP government ensured that no independent sources of economic power might develop, it also worked to emasculate and control other institutions in the state and society. All previously legal opposition political parties were disbanded in 1964 when the BSPP became the sole party. The marginal independence of the civil service surviving from the 1950s was eliminated as military officers took over leading positions. Private schools and hospitals were nationalized in the 1960s. The universities and all other institutions of higher learning were placed under effective government control, losing what residual autonomy they had had from the colonial period. The last autonomous institution to come under government control was the

Buddhist monkhood or *sangha* in 1980 (Tin Maung 1988b). When the Revolutionary Council took power in 1962, it assumed all executive, legislative and judicial authority and despite attempts at power sharing in subsequent years through the formation of the *Pyithu Hluttaw* (People's Assembly) and the People's Courts and related institutions, the military remained in control. As in the party's central committee, though civilians were gradually increasing in the proportion of members of central political and administrative institutions by the mid-1980s, the majority of key positions were still held by military and ex-military personnel (Taylor 1987a:315-33). At the local level also, because of the leading role that state economic and administrative agencies played in people's lives, ex-military personnel often served in leading positions [13]

Having eliminated all legal centers of economic and political power to balance the army and the party, the regime became increasingly isolated. As government ministers themselves eventually admitted, officials were falsifying data and paying little attention to their duties but the government had lost the economic and political incentives to control such behaviour. Unlike one-party systems in countries such as Viet Nam and North Korea, and rather more like the Communist Party of Poland, the BSPP and its military cadres had little faith in their ideological and programatic pronouncements. Socialist images and rhetoric were affixed to the party, not part of its formative experience, and this was reflected in government behaviour.

While much of the population either accepted or acquiesced in the one-party system created by the military because of its nationalist and socialist credentials, increasingly many became frustrated at the lack of opportunities which developed for social mobility outside the army. The party provided too few opportunities and the absence of economic growth and independent institutions meant that the growing numbers of university educated were unemployed or under-employed. By 1988, 26 years after the formation of the system, and two years after severe economic crisis brought on, ironically, by a mounting foreign debt burden,[14] increasing price inflation and an inability to keep government plants and factories operating, the frustration of the urban population poured out on the streets in the demonstrations of July-August-September, 1988.

Even before then, the regime's policies had inadvertently helped maintain the military's most powerful post-independence civil war armed opponents, further weakening the self-confidence and capacities of the state. The black market provided the means for the maintenance of the Karen National Union (KNU) insurgents, the Karen National Liberation Army, which financed its operations largely through control over the smuggling routes into Thailand. Other armed ethnic separatist opponents of the regime lived off opium and other smuggling in the north as did eventually the Burma Communist Party (BCP) after a decline in support from the Chinese Communist Party in the late 1970s. Because it was unable to adequately fund armed forces to take and control the peripheral areas of the country, the government was unable to undertake the exploitation of minerals and other raw materials in these areas and in turn use the foreign exchange revenues which would have resulted to finance industrial and agricultural development in the central regions. By the end of the BSPP period, a web of interrelated dilemmas,.apparently inherent in the nature of the economic and political system installed in the 1960s, had compounded to create the regime's final crisis.

The internal politics of the military and the party leadership increasingly came to occupy the time and efforts of the senior leadership of the government. Rumours of rivalry between the party and army organizations were mooted from time to time as were alleged splits between those officers serving in the anti-insurgency campaigns in the border areas and the party/administrative officers in Yangon.[15] Structurally more important were the rivalries which developed within the government and military between the intelligence services and other sectors. Military intelligence had served as a means of social control throughout the existence of independent Burma. From the 1950s to the present, the military maintained an intelligence network separate from the civilian government and the party. The head of military intelligence was always close to General Ne Win but often became so powerful as to be seen as a threat to his position.[16]

Future Prospects

Given the history of the role of the military in Myanmar's politics and assuming that this analysis of it and the nature of the armed forces is reasonably correct, what role can the second generation officer corps adopt for themselves and their successors to the end of the century? Can the relationship between the armed forces and the state and civil society be altered and, if so, how? History has provided two models which have both been tried and failed, at least in the eyes of the army or of the politically active civilian population. One was the model of military-civil relations which existed between 1948 and 1962. The other was that of the BSPP rule to 1988.

Could the 1948-62 model be resurrected? The pattern of military-civilian relations during the first 14 years of independence was one which doctrinally and constitutionally recognized that the military was the servant of the civilian controlled state. Over time, however, the reality of this relationship began to undermine the norms of civilian control for in actual practice, the military held a great deal of independent power and authority during this period. During the post-independence civil war, the army assumed the role of guardian of the civilian government and the party which led it. While from 1948 to 1958 this function was little seen behind the facade of elections and largely civilian cabinet government, in 1958 it became explicit with the establishment of the military "Caretaker Government". The Caretaker Government saw itself as playing a role similar to that of the old British colonial administration, "holding the ring" while the civilians played the game of party politics. When the civilian politicians could no longer control their ambitions and the demands of their supporters, and violence threatened, the army intervened. Otherwise, the army stood apart from "politics".[17] Though severely tested, this norm remained sufficiently strong to permit the holding of elections in 1960 and the formation of another civilian government led by U Nu and other individuals out of favour with key military officers. The 1962 coup, however, demonstrated how weak the norms of civilian control had become as well as how strong were the incentives for direct military intervention.[18]

Is the "holding the ring" option viable now? After the September 18, 1988, coup, the army presented its role as comparable to that of the 1958-60 Caretaker Government. It had intervened temporarily to rectify the errors of the previous BSPP regime and to prepare conditions for the holding of multiparty elections. Much of the behaviour of the army in the first months after the coup echoed its actions at the end of the 1950s. Squatters were relocated, cities were cleaned up, efforts were made to control prices through the operation of low price shops for the poor, and economic rationality was given preference to ideological incentives. But the conditions in which the army took power in 1988 were fundamentally different from those of 1958. The economy was in a much more serious state of decline with popular demonstrations of massive disaffection with the old order undermining administrative effectiveness. Moreover, the army was much more deeply entrenched in economic and administrative roles beyond merely national security and defense. Though defining its role as supererogatory to those of the civilian politicians clambering for an interim government and the holding of elections, the military had also to defend itself and the record of the previous administration of which it had been a central part. The army's deep involvement in the management of the state for the past 26 years created too many personal and institutional commitments to allow it to merely "hold the ring". In holding the ring, it also had to ensure that individuals and organizations opposed to its interests were placed outside the ring of legitimate authority.[19] It has too much to lose if, in holding the ring, the result is a government which denies the military the right to maintain its special prerogatives and autonomy. It is this set of conditions that has made it impossible for the army to allow the most severe critics of the BSPP period and its leadership to participate in defining the future role of the military in politics.

The second option provided by history, for the military to attempt the BSPP experiment again, is also unavailable. Even if the army were to promise to pass effective power over to a new party sometime in the future, few in Myanmar would actually believe this would happen. More importantly, the vested interests of the military, as well as the requirements of rule, would almost certainly make it impossible to achieve. The military is attempting now to establish a new position for itself within the state, and for the state to develop a new relationship with civil society, through a program laid down by the SLORC in the latter part of 1988. "Free and fair elections" are held in May, 1989. The machinery to carry out these elections, from a civilian Election Commission through to the formation of village and township electoral organizations and the establishment of electoral rolls, was established. Rules were announced denying either military or civilian government employees a direct role in either the conduct of the election or in the activities of political parties. General Saw Maung, as the Chairman of SLORC as well as the Prime Minister and Minister of Defense, promised that freedom of speech and the opportunities for political campaigning would be granted three months before the elections take place.[20]

Despite these policies which formally place the army back to the position of "holding the ring" as in 1958-60, the military government has carried out actions which serve to indicate that it is not willing to relinquish power to any civilian government which might be elected. Indications of this are apparent in the placing under arrest the central leaders of the electorally popular National League for Democracy (NLD), and the arrest of other organizers from the NLD and related parties. These arrests have been justified with the accusation that the party leaders have violated the conditions of martial law including a ban on the holding of political rallies and criticism of the army and the present administration. Similarly, freedom of speech and the speech was not restored during or after the May elections. Parties were given only limited opportunities to express their views and since then individuals have been arrested for expression of criticisms of the army or for allegedly attempting to undermine the unity of the military or the nation.

The establishment of the SLORC government and the continuation of martial law government has been justified in terms of the necessity to establish law and order in the country so that democracy can be established.[21] The popularity of the NLD was based upon their strong criticism of the record of the armed forces and their involvement in the former BSPP regime. Having stated that such criticism is likely to cause public unrest, the logical action was to suppress such activities. "Holding the ring" inevitably must include defining what legitimately can take place within it.

There is nothing unusual in this condition. Politics in most countries are constrained by legal and hegemonic restraints on the political activities of groups which are defined as outside the legal community.[22] In the view of the armed forces, the greatest danger to the future of the state stems from the possibility of fissure within itself. Since 1948, when the army split at the beginning of the civil war and significant numbers of units joined with the Communist Party or the KNU, the danger of division for the sovereignty of the state has been a preoccupation. Similarly, the discord and debate of the period of civilian government in the 1950s has been held up as evidence of the danger to state sovereignty posed by the possibility of foreign involvement in politics through multiparty politics. Even if these conclusions are correct, and the repeated statements by ministers that they will hand over power to an elected legislature after a new constitution is drafted are sincere,[23] the vested interests of the military in the existing order make it extremely difficult for it to abandon a leading role in the governance of Myanmar.

Notes

1. Myanmar Naing Nan was made the official English name of Burma by the armed forces State Law and Order Restoration Council (SLORC) government in 1989. It is the literal translation of the Burmese language name of the country. Official spellings in English of other geographical terms have also been changed from those familiar since the colonial period. Thus Rangoon has now become Yangon and Pegu has become Bago. The new official terms have been accepted by major international agencies such as the United Nations, the World Bank, and the International Monetary Fund. Myanmar will be used in this chapter

except when referring to organizations and institutions in existence before 1989.

2. The armed forces in Burmese are referred to as the *tatmadaw*. Largely composed of the army, the air force (*tatmadaw lei*) and the navy (*tatmadaw yei*) are relatively small and politically unimportant. Throughout this paper the terms armed forces, military and army will be used as synonymous with *tatmadaw*.

3. It is noteworthy that the first two foreign joint venture firms established in August 1989, Myanmar-Singapore and Myanmar-Malaysxsia, were formed with state trading companies under the Ministry of Trade.

4. The legislation reorganizing the War Veterans Organization (WVO), issued by SLORC on 10 August 1989, ensured that it could be the sole war veterans body in the country. It is ostensibly non-political. The new legislation was necessary following the disbandment in 1988 of the BSSP to which the previous WVO had been an affiliate organization along with women's, youth, peasants', and workers' organizations.

5. However, as almost every officer in the army has at some time in his career seen combat against the country's ethnic and communist led insurgent groups, the military's claim to be national saviours will persist longer in Myanmar than in Southeast Asian countries where the military has been less active in fighting "externally linked" political opponents in the post-colonial period.

6. The placing under house arrest of the leaders of the National League for Democracy (NLD), U (a former General), Tin U and Daw Aung San Suu Kyi (the daughter of the nationalist hero General Aung San) on 20 July 1989, along with the arrest of other NLD leaders, placed the the NLD in a disadvantaged position. Further arrests of NLD leaders, after its overwhelming electoral success, plus a continuing campaign of anti-NLD statements, is apparently directed toward placing the League outside the legally permitted range of political activists.

7. The major demand of the leaders of the demonstrations in Yangon and other cities in mid-1988 was for the BSPP/military government to step down and be replaced by an interim government composed of individuals who emerged during the demonstrations. Quite who these peole would be, other than for the four or five most prominent figures from the past, was never clear and the military refused to consider such a possibility. Nor, after the establishment of a government in August under the presidency of the civilian Dr Maung Maung did the military seem willing to expand the base of the government to include civilian figures popular with the demonstrators. However, in the two years following the elections organizations were created which could form a government.

8. The leaders of the NLD accuse the military of being a "pocket army" of Ne Win rather than a national institution. This argument is perceived by the army leadership as an attempt to divide the army and could lead to civil war. This is a major justification for the detention of Daw Aung San Suu Kyi and other NLD leaders.

9. Within two and a half months of taking office the SLORC issued an investment law providing extremely liberal terms and conditions to foreign investors. However, under the continuing political uncertainty and without clearer guarantees of financial security and adequate infrastructure, no significant foreign investment had been received at the time of writing.

10. Compare the estimates in IISS 1979 and 1985. Between 1972 and 1987, defense expenditure fell from 31.6 per cent to 18.8 per cent (World Bank 1898:184). However, given that a significant proportion of military personnel actually serve in non-defense agencies, the actual proportion is doubtless higher. Also, between 1972 and 1987 budget details were altered to place pensions and other gratuities under a separate budget. The military is now estimated to be approximately 230,000 strong. There are an additional 85,000 para-military forces, though many believe the number of People's Militia is greater than the 35,000 estimated by the IISS. (See IISS 1990:158-159). The most complete discussion of the structure of the military is found in Tin Maung 1989:40-60.

11. An excellent discussion, but only partially applicable to Myanmar, of these dilemmas is found in Migdal 1988 chapter 6. The initial Revolutionary Council government had a program of reform not dissimilar to comparable regimes in Egypt, Indonesia and elsewhere in Asia, Africa and Latin Ameica. But, as Migdal writes, these regimes "........have faced the structural dilemma in power......the danger of fostering the growth of powerful state agencies in the absence of adequate capabilities for political mobilization; this has caused a critical shift in priorities. No agenda is worth anything if its sponsor has not lasted through the hazards of politics. Political survival, the central issue occupying the attention of state leaders, is the prerequisite for achieving any significant long term social change. Programs for social change may still have been the basis for public rhetoric and even for policy statements and legislation, but at the apex of the state the politics of survival have denuded state agencies of capabilities to see those programs through" Migdal 1988: 226).

12. In the end, however, this proved illusory for one of the factors which led to the economic collapse of 1988 was the pressure applied by the Japanese government, Myanmar's largest aid donor, for a change in economic policies. Japanese aid declined precipitously in the years prior to the 1988 collapse from US $266.1M in 1986 to US $ 192.4M in 1987, though this latter figure was still higher than the Japanese aid provided in either 1984 or 1985, according to OECD data. However, total bilateral aid fell to below the 1985 level in 1987 though a small increase in multilateral aid ensured that the total aid received in 1987 (US $406.1M) was higher than that received in 1985 (US $382. 8M) but lower than that of 1986 (US $452.9M).

13. The esmaculation of all alternative institutions to those of the central state complex, the BSPP and the army, is a primary reason why when the political upheveals of 1988 occurred, individuals representing other classes and groups in society were unable to provide the unified

leadership and basis of continuous support to effectively challenge army dominance.

14. Myanmar's foreign debt had reached US $4,457M by 1987 compared with a minuscule US $106M in 1970. The debt service ratio (total long-term debt service as a percentage of the export of goods and services) had reached 59.3 per cent by 1987 (World Bank 1989:208). The most recent OECD data suggests that Myanmar's total foreign debt had reached US $5,980M at the end of 1987 (OECD 1989).

15. I never found these rumours convinvcng for several reasons. First, almost all officers served at one time or another in their careers in command positions in the anti-insurgency campaigns. Second, in as much as the party remained dominated by serving and retired military personnel, a party-army rivalry seemed unlikely. The institutions shared a symbiotic relationship, not one of institutional conflict. Careers and personal advantages were linked with both the army and the party and with both combat and administrative functions.

16. The most internal regime crises of the 1970s and 1980s ended with the sacking of the head of military intelligence and his closest cohorts. Both, just to confuse matters, were named Tin U. The General Tin U who lost his position as chief of the defense forces in 1976 is now the chairman of the NLD referred to above. The other, who had risen from Director General of the National Intelligence Bureau to become General Secretary of the party, was removed from office along with the Home Minister and many others in 1983. Subsequently, the intelligence services were reorganized under a committee of three composed of the Prime Minister, the Defense Minister and the Home Minister, apparently to ensure that no one person became too powerful. (For details see Taylor 1987a:369-371). The role of military intelligence was highlighted by the apparent collapse of its effectiveness during 1988. It has since been resurrected under the leadership of Brigadier General Khin Nyunt, the First Secretary of the ruling SLORC and allegedly close to U Ne Win. For an interesting and relevant discussion of the role of the military intelligence services in regime maintenance and change see Stepan 1988, chapter 2, 'The Brazilian Intelligence System in Comparative Perspective', (pp.13-29).

17. Reflecting on the role of the military in politics in 1959, General Ne Win made this parallel explicit: 'It was the country's bad fortune that unity had been so transient. One consolation, however, was that the factional struggles did not end up in violence and bloodshed. The British Government could afford to stay neutral, the entire administration kept aloof. Hence the fight was contained in a narrow arena' (Maung Maung 1969:24-25). By implication, Ne Win was saying, that the army could not stand aside given the severe conflict which existed within the independent state.

18. Though the 1962 coup was justified in terms of preserving the unity of the state in the face of pressure for greater autonomy by the "traditional" leaders of the peripheral areas, the declining capacity of the military to

defend its economic interests in the face of civilian criticisms was probably also a factor.

19. The army has thus created for itself the same delemma that faced the British administration in the 1930s. Party politics were to be permitted but on terms which were acceptable to the colonial authorities. Groups which rejected those terms were declared illegitimate and forced into violent political action.

20. Since the 1988 coup, all radio, television and newspapers have remained under government control despite announcements before September that nationalized newspapers would be returned to their previous owners.

21. "Our government is one which with a view to establishing a Multi-party democratic State has systematically formed the Election Commission and is making efforts for the general election to be held successfully. At such a time the enforcement of rule of law and order is a dire need in the State. At this time, activities such as agitative work to bring instability to the country, creating disturbances; opposing and trying to discredit the Government by spreading malicious rumours; causing the people to suspect the *Tatmadaw;* sowing discord within *Tatmadaw* and acts tending to disintegrate the *Tatmadaw,* should be brought to a standstill and this we have explained from time to time" WPD 29 July 1989.

22. Accusations by the SLORC Secretary and other government spokesmen and media in August 1989, that both the illegal Myanmar Communist Party and foreign, mainly Western, governments and agencies have either infiltrated or influenced the NLD and other critical organizations, some armed and some unarmed, is part of the process of defining such groups as outside the ring. See Brigadier General Khin Nyunt's statements: *Burma Communist Party's Conspiracy to Takeover State Power* and *The Conspiracy of Treasonous Minions within the Myanmar Naing-Ngan and Traitorous Cohorts Without.*

23. Ministers reiterate that the reason they all have several portfolios is to demonstrate that they are in office only temporarily and that the policies they are introducing are merely those immediately necessary to create positive conditions for a future civilian government to inherit.

7

The Military in Pakistan Politics: Direct or Indirect Participation?*

Samina Yasmeen

On 5 July 1977, the Pakistan military intervened in politics for the third time in its thirty year existence. General Zia-ul-Haq explained this intervention in terms of preventing Pakistan from facing an impending civil war and economic ruin. He also promised to hand over power to democratically-elected representatives within 90 days. It was, however, not until March 1985 that a semblance of democracy was restored to Pakistani politics with the election of a Parliament on a non-party basis. It was another three and half years before elections were held on a party basis and power handed over to the Pakistan People's Party (PPP) in December 1988. Effectively, therefore, the 1977 coup enabled the Pakistan armed forces to play an active and open role in Pakistan's politics for more than eleven years. This raises a number of questions:

i) What general factors have accounted for the military's involvement in Pakistan's politics since 1947?
ii) What were the immediate causes of the 1977 coup?
iii) How did the military succeed in retaining its control over power for more than eleven years? What ideological outlook did the regime have? What forces, both internal and external, did it align itself with?
iv) Why did the military hand over power to the PPP in December 1988?

v) What role is the military likely to play in Pakistan's politics in the 1990s?

This chapter attempts to answer these questions by putting the military's role in Pakistan in a historical and institutional context. Accordingly, it is divided into four sections. The first section describes and analyzes the historical and structural trends that enabled the military to regularly intervene in Pakistan's politics. It also focuses on the immediate developments that provided the military with a rationale to impose a third period of martial law in July 1977. The second part deals with various domestic and international strategies adopted by the military regime to legitimize and perpetuate its rule. The third part focuses on the transitional period which finally culminated in Benazir Bhutto's ascent to power in December 1988. The last part analyzes the strategies presently employed by the armed forces and discusses the possibility of them intervening in the country's politics in the future.

The Pakistan Military: A Gradual Redefining of Roles

The origins of the 1977 military coup can be traced back to a multitude of structural/institutional factors operating in Pakistan since its inception in 1947. At the time of independence, the nascent state of Pakistan inherited relatively weak political institutions. This weakness stemmed from the lack of political experience of the leaders who had successfully convinced the British Government of the need to carve a muslim state out of the united India. The Muslim League, which took power in 1947, for example, had only "seven to ten years of experience" at the mass level. Most of its leaders had joined the party during the last two years of the independence struggle, a time when the creation of Pakistan seemed imminent. Therefore, they were ill-equipped to work together, resolve intra-party conflicts and devise common strategies for the new state within the framework of a political party. Nor did they have sufficient experience in negotiating and/or resolving conflicts with other political groups and organizations in Pakistan (Rizvi 1988:413). The situation at the provincial level was not very different either. With the exception of East Pakistan, which had a long experience in parliamentary democracy, leaders of the other areas that came to constitute Pakistan had little or no experience of participating in political institutions.

Instead of being ameliorated, this weakness was reinforced in an independent Pakistan. While the country continued to be ruled under the Government of India Acts of 1919 and 1935, a Constituent Assembly was set up in 1947. This Assembly was allocated the responsibility of identifying and elaborating the operational meaning of the "Two Nation Theory" which had been used as the basis of the Muslim League's demand for Pakistan. It was also entrusted the responsibility of resolving "the federal issue", i.e. the division of powers between the center and the constituent provinces. Unfortunately, personal interests and ambitions of individual political leaders as well as the conflict between the "centralists" (those who favoured a strong federal government) and the "provincialists" (those who advocated the principle of provincial autonomy) prevented the Constituent Assembly from meeting its responsibilities quickly (Jackson 1975:13-20). It took almost ten years to deliberate and negotiate for a constitution. Even when the constitution was drafted and promulgated in 1956, the political scene in Pakistan continued to be marred by frequent squabbling among politicians which led to changes of governments.

In marked contrast to the weak political institutions, Pakistan had also inherited two well-disciplined and well-organized institutions: the civilian and military bureaucracies. Of these, the civilian bureaucracy was the successor of the British Indian Civil Service (ICS) which had been organized by the British Government as the "steel frame" of the empire (Rizvi 1988:413). By virtue of its past experience, the civilian bureaucracy was more capable of and adept at running the government than the political leaders who took over in 1947. Hence, while the politicians argued and deliberated on the nature of Pakistan's constitution, the civilian bureaucracy gradually acquired control over the effective running of the government. By the mid-1950s, the higher echelons of the civilian bureaucracy were effectively running the country.

Even more remarkable was the rise in the strength of the military in Pakistan. At the time of partition, the core of Pakistan's armed forces consisted of more British officers than Pakistanis. As opposed to about 500 British army officers the Pakistani component ranged "between 100 and 200 well trained ... officers" (Hashmi 1983:148-156). These Pakistani officers primarily came from rural landowning backgrounds though not strictly the landowning aristocratic class. They inherited and accepted the role traditionally assigned to the British (Indian) Army, the role of being the "custodian of law and order" (ibid.). However, as members of a rather weak and ill-equipped military establishment, initially these officers were not capable of playing this role in Pakistan. The situation was soon to change.

In 1951, the first Pakistani general, Mohammed Ayub Khan, took over as the Commander-in-Chief of the armed forces. Soon afterwards, against the background of differences over the division of assets, the sharing of water resources, the Kashmir dispute and the first Indo-Pakistan war, the Pakistan Government began expressing an interest in receiving military assistance from the United States. Such indications were accompanied with an expressed willingness to join Washington in its crusade against the Soviet Union. The US Government responded to these overtures in 1953 by announcing its decision to re-equip the Pakistan Army at the cost of at least US$250 million. In 1954, Pakistan concluded its first defence agreement with the United States. This was followed by Pakistan's membership of the South East Asia Treaty Organization (SEATO) in 1954 and the Baghdad Pact renamed the Central Treaty Organization (CENTO) in 1955. Within the framework of these and the subsequent agreements, Pakistan became one of the major recipients of American military assistance. This assistance, the total value of which was estimated to be around US$522 million by 1959, took the form of major weapons as well as training for "hundreds of Pakistani military officers and other ranks" under the Military Assistance Program [MAP] (Hashmi 1983:156-164). On the one hand, this enabled the Pakistan Army to counter Indian military superiority. On the other hand, it strengthened the military's position domestically to such an extent that by the late 1950s the military had emerged as the strongest institution in Pakistan.

Throughout the period of its meteoric rise, the Pakistan armed forces maintained a close alliance with the civilian bureaucracy. This alliance provided the framework within which the military intervened in Pakistan's politics for the first time in 1958.

Martial law was imposed in 1958 against the background of two years of political squabbling and changes of governments and was legitimized in terms of the military's inherited role as the custodian of law and order. The martial law regime, under General Ayub Khan, identified its immediate objective as the rehabilitation of the civil and constitutional organs of the State which had become "ineffective and oppressive through misuse and exploitation" (Khan 1967:77). The *direct* military participation, therefore, was apparently to last only until the "rehabilitation" was completed. However, Ayub Khan's decision to abrogate the 1956 Constitution signified that the martial law regime intended to determine the manner in which such a rehabilitation was to proceed. It was a clear indication that, within eleven years of its establishment, the Pakistan military had redefined its role in society; instead of merely *maintaining* law and order in Pakistan, it also intended to *define* the structure and nature of such an order.

The subsequent constitutional developments in Pakistan added another dimension to the military's role in the country. The 1962 Constitution, which was drafted during General Ayub's reign as the Chief Martial Law Administrator, replaced the parliamentary system with a Presidential one. It also introduced the concept of *Basic Democracies* which was ostensibly aimed at "inculcating a spirit of self help in people" and providing a "meaningful electoral system for the election of the President and the members of the Assemblies" (Khan 1967:207). Within the framework of this constitution, elections were held in 1962 for the National Assembly and the Provincial Assemblies. Soon afterwards, General Ayub relinquished control of the armed forces to General Musa and took over as the first elected President of Pakistan. It was obvious that the military did not intend going back to the barracks; it wanted to continue playing at least an *indirect* role in Pakistan's politics. For the next seven years this arrangement enabled the military to receive a disproportionately high share of national resources. It also ensured that most of the senior military officials could move directly into choice positions in the civilian bureaucracy upon their retirement from the army—a mechanism that indirectly reinforced the military's supremacy in the country's political structure.

On 25 March 1969, the military intervened directly in Pakistan's politics for the second time. In the wake of growing dissatisfaction in East Pakistan with the Center, disillusionment among the middle class in West Pakistan and the formation of the Democratic Action Committee resulted in widespread demonstrations in West Pakistan against the Ayub Government. Ayub Khan stepped down and invited the then army chief, General Yahya Khan, to take over. This transfer of power was once again justified in terms of the military's inherited role as the custodian of law and order. Ayub Khan wrote to General Yahya that he was left with "no option but to step aside and leave it to the Defence Forces of Pakistan which ...represent the only effective and legal instrument to take over full control of the affairs of [Pakistan]" (Feldman 1972:271).

From the outset, the new martial law regime, like its predecessor, indicated that it not only intended restoring and maintaining order in Pakistan in the aftermath of the protest marches and demonstrations against the Ayub government but also defining the structure of such an order. The 1962 Constitution was abrogated. The "One Unit", the formula by which all the four provinces in the western wing of the country had been amalgamated into one province, West Pakistan, was dissolved. A year later, on 30 March 1970, General Yahya issued the Legal Framework Order which presented a blueprint for the future political structure of Pakistan. The country was to have a Parliamentary, and not a Presidential, system of Government. The members to the National Assembly were to be elected on the basis of universal suffrage in December 1970. Members were to draft a constitution within a short period of 120 days or face the dissolution of the Assembly. Elections were also to be held for the new Provincial Assemblies in December 1970, and the constitution was to ensure "maximum political autonomy" for all five provinces (Ziring 1980:100).

The results of the December 1970 elections, however, proved unpalatable to the military. The Awami League, which had a strong hold in East Pakistan and was led by Sheikh Mujib, won 167 out of 313 seats and emerged as the majority party in the Constituent Assembly (Akhtar 1989:255). The League had traditionally favoured maximum political autonomy for constituent provinces and a reduction in defence expenditures for the country. Its rise to power, therefore, entailed the possibility of seriously undermining the military's institutional strength and its future participation in Pakistan's politics. Hence, senior military leaders were reluctant to handover power to the Awami League. Zulfiquar Ali Bhutto, leader of the Pakistan People's Party (PPP), capitalized on this fear. Having emerged as the leader of the second largest political party, he began demanding the right to negotiate on the nature of the draft constitution prior to the first meeting of the Constituent Assembly. The demand was supported by the military which soon came to establish a *de facto* alliance with Bhutto. The Awami League, supported by Bengalis in East Pakistan, threatened to secede. The subsequent military crackdown in East Pakistan, the civil war, and India's interference led to the third Indo-Pakistan war in December 1971.

Soon after the war, which resulted in the secession of East Pakistan as Bangladesh, the imprisonment of 90,000 Pakistani soldiers and the loss of territory on the Western front, General Yahya asked Zulfiquar Ali Bhutto to take over as the Chief Martial Law Administrator. In his capacity as the first civilian martial law administrator (until April 1972) and President (until August 1973) and then as the Prime Minister of Pakistan, Bhutto embarked on a process of arms acquisition. Within two and a half years, the Pakistan military received approximately 495 T-59 tanks, 101 MiG-19s and 8 naval vessels from China (Yasmeen

1985:259-261). The Bhutto regime also reorganized the Atomic Energy Commission and initiated its own nuclear program. On the one hand, these steps narrowed the margin of "regional military imbalance" between India and Pakistan (Yasmeen 1985:263). On the other hand, they indicated Bhutto's desire to sustain a close alliance with what was still a strong institution in Pakistan, the military.

Meanwhile, however, Bhutto also took steps to undermine the military's preeminent position in the Pakistani system. Within a few months of taking over, he forcibly retired some 20 to 22 senior military officials. Notable among these were General Gul Hasan and Air Marshal Rahim Khan, two prominent officers who played important roles in bringing Bhutto into power. Later on, with a view to minimizing the chance of another military intervention, the 1973 Constitution identified any attempt to overthrow the legally constituted government as treason, with those involved in it subject to capital punishment (Burki 1988:1085).

The command structure of Pakistan's armed forces was reorganized. A new office, the Joint Chiefs of Staff Headquarters, was established and was to be headed by a four-star general. The Chief of Joint Staff (CJS) was directly responsible to the President who assumed the position of the commander-in-chief. The day-to-day running of the three branches—the army, airforce and the navy—was retained by the three relevant chiefs of staff. Of these three, the office of the Chief of Army Staff (COAS) received Bhutto's special attention. Since traditionally the army, and not the airforce or the navy, had intervened in Pakistani politics, he ensured to appoint a COAS with the least likelihood of toppling the civilian regime. Initially the post was given to General Tikka Khan (a close confidant of Bhutto), despite his blemished record during the military crackdown in East Pakistan. When General Tikka's four-year term finished in March 1976, Bhutto passed over a number of senior military generals to appoint General Zia-ul-Haq as the new COAS. This decision, which was made in consultation with General Sahibzada Yaqub Khan, was apparently based on General Zia's emphasis on military professionalism and a total lack of interest in politics. Bhutto believed that coming from a middle-class *Arian* family with extremely conservative muslim ideas and lacking any charisma, Zia was unlikely to form an alliance with the dominant group of *Pathan* and *Rajput* generals in the army and topple the PPP government (Burki 1988:1086-1087). Soon Zia was to prove Bhutto and his advisors wrong.

The Third Period of Martial Law: Immediate Causes

In early 1977, Bhutto announced that elections for the National Assembly and the four Provincial Assemblies would be held on the 7 and 10 of March 1977 respectively. Within a few days of this announcement, nine political parties formed a coalition, the Pakistan National Alliance (PNA)[1]. While from the outset, the PNA was considered unlikely to replace the Bhutto regime, its strategy of nominating one joint candidate for each constituency was expected to reduce Bhutto's overwhelming majority in the National Assembly. The results of the elections to the National Assembly negated these expectations; the PPP won 155 of the 200 seats, conceding the PNA only 36. Quite interestingly, the PNA won only 8 out of 116 seats in the Punjab with none in Lahore or Rawalpindi—two cities where meetings held by the PNA had attracted huge crowds. It was obvious that the government machinery had been used to rig the elections and that the PPP had won the elections by a far wider margin than even Bhutto himself envisaged.[2] The PNA decided to boycott the elections to the provincial assemblies and launched a protest movement against the Bhutto regime. During the next four months, the PNA continuously demanded Bhutto's resignation and called for new elections, to be supervised by the judiciary and the army (Syed 1978:119).

Despite the PNA's open encouragement and approval of the military's political role in the post election period, the army initially sided with Bhutto's regime. General Zia-ul-Haq imposed "mini-martial law" in Lahore to curb the growing protest movement led by the PNA. He also reportedly reprimanded some senior officials who refused to side with the government against the people in Lahore (inteview February 1990). Soon, however, the military began to veer away from this position. After being contacted by a number of PNA leaders, senior officials in the army began to seriously consider the possibility of intervening in the country's politics. Ironically, the actual move was made as the PPP and the PNA had almost concluded an accord that would have paved the way for new elections. On the eve of 5 July 1977, in what he described as the "Operation Fair Play", General Zia-ul-Haq took control of the government and imposed martial law. Leaders of both the PNA and the PPP were put under house arrest. The military was once again playing a direct and active role in Pakistan's politics.

Consolidation of Power: Domestic and International Alliances

Intervening against the background of the Constitution of 1973 which had equated a military takeover with treason, the Zia regime initially claimed to have limited objectives. It identified its aim as that of restoring the law and order situation in Pakistan without any intention of redefining the structure of this order. Hence, unlike the two previous military regimes, General Zia did not abrogate the Constitution; it was merely suspended. He was also cautious to stress that, unlike his two military predecessors, he did not intend prolonging the task of restoration of order over a period of two to four years. He assured the public that he had no political ambitions, that he intended to hold elections within 90 days and that he neither favoured the PPP nor the PNA (*Dawn* 6 July 1977).

The subsequent events led to a redefining of these objectives (Rizvi 1984:538-540). On 2 August 1977, having framed new election rules and having appointed a new election commission, General Zia announced that elections would be held on 18 October. Leaders of both the PNA and the PPP, who had been released from detention a few days earlier, were allowed to hold party meetings, make statements and choose candidates for the elections. These steps, according to a number of observers, were taken on the assumption that the PNA, and not the PPP, would win a future election. The public's response raised doubts about these assumption. During his visit to various cities especially Lahore, Bhutto attracted large crowds. Emboldened by this reception, Bhutto began hinting at the possibility of "teaching the generals a lesson" after the new elections. These references, the prospects of the PPP's return to power and the possibility of Bhutto further undermining the military's strength, prompted the regime to reconsider its priorities.

Instead of handing over power to elected representatives, the Zia regime was to now engage in "Operation Clean Up". The stated objective of this new operation—the "process of accountability" as it was popularly known—was to remove all traces of corruption in Pakistani politics and to make politicians accountable. In reality it meant that although the military was prepared to acknowledge the relevance of the political order established in 1973, it wanted to determine the political outcome of any election held under such an order. To put it differently, it wanted to deny the PPP any future chance of taking over the government. This became clear as General Zia ordered Bhutto's arrest in September 1977 for complicity in a murder, and began referring to him as the "evil genius". A few days later, on 1 October 1977, General Zia postponed elections indefinitely.

The military regime's policy of attempting to exclude the PPP from any future participation in Pakistan's politics continued even after Bhutto's execution in April 1979. In fact, during this period General Zia also began toying with the idea of redefining the structure of a future order (interviews in Pakistan:February 1990). Two weeks before the execution, for example, General Zia announced that elections would be held in November 1979 under revised rules. Soon afterwards he also announced the decision to hold elections for local bodies on a non-party basis. This decision, which was taken with a view to discredit political parties and exclude them from playing a role in politics, backfired. Despite various tactics used by the regime, a number of people with affiliations to various political parties, especially the PPP, were elected to the local bodies. Fearing that the outcome would be repeated in national elections, Zia postponed the elections on the pretext that Pakistan did not need "elections for the sake of elections" (*Dawn* 18 October 1979).

The decision to postpone elections for a second time intensified the crisis of legitimacy already faced by General Zia-ul-Haq. Hence, the Zia regime resorted to the use of a variety of means to acquire the required legitimacy and perpetuate its rule.

Firstly, it established an alliance with conservative elements in the country. Seeds of this alliance were sown during the 1978-1979 period when, following the High Court's verdict against Bhutto in the murder case, General Zia began to woo the PNA leaders by offering them posts in Federal cabinet. Some of the constituent parties of the PNA, including *Tehrik-i-Istiqlal*, the *Jamiat-ul-Ulema-e-Pakistan*, and the National Democratic Party shunned these offers. Others including the Pakistan Muslim League (PML), the *Jamaat-i-Islami*, and the Pakistan Democratic Party responded favorably to Zia's overtures and joined his "civilian cabinet". While causing a split in the PNA, this decision initially provided Zia's regime with the necessary legitimacy to rule the country. This military-PNA alliance abruptly came to an end after Bhutto's execution in April 1979 when the political leaders resigned from the "civilian cabinet" in an attempt to distance themselves from the regime. The shock was absorbed by the military regime within the next few months as it began to reestablish an alliance with the PML (Pagara Group) and the *Jamaat-i-Islami*. Of these, the former group acted as a sounding board for the General's ideas regarding a desirable future political structure for Pakistan. The *Jamaat*, with its excellent organization at the grass root level provided the medium through which the military regime justified its policies and perpetuated its rule in the country. These alliances were given some credibility in 1981 when Zia promulgated the Provisional

Constitutional Order (PCO) and began ruling the country with the help of *Majlis-e-Shura* (a body of advisors). The Majlis, which consisted primarily of people supported by the PML (Pagara Group) and conservative elements in the country, did not have powers to enforce their decisions, but by virtue of its cooperation with the military regime the PML provided the armed forces with much needed legitimacy.

Secondly, unlike the previous military regimes that stood for "modernization" and "progressive ideas", the Zia regime espoused a conservative ideology. "Islamization" of the polity was identified as its main objective. The process began with the suggestion of separate electorates for muslim and non-muslim voters, and the promulgation of *Hudood* Ordinance dealing with sex related crimes (*Zina*) and theft, in February 1979. The next year, judicial reforms were introduced and a separate Federal Shariat Court (FSC) established to deal with the cases under the Hudood Ordinance. Interest free banking was introduced, and *Zakat* and *Ushur* (taxes levied on savings and farm produce respectively) were imposed.

To some extent this emphasis on Islamization was a function of General Zia-ul-Haq's orthodox muslim upbringing. It also reflected the changed class structure of the Pakistan armed forces as the majority of officers no longer came from upper-class landlord families. Neither were they educated at Sandhurst or the *Dheradun* military academy. Instead, the Pakistan armed forces drew most of its officers corps from middle-class families based in the central Punjab who joined the army for economic rather than prestige reasons. These officers accepted and identified more with the traditional Islamic concepts than with "modern ideas" propagated by their predecessors and by the Bhutto regime. Hence, despite some dissatisfaction with the emphasis on Islamization among senior military officials, the military was prepared to explore an Islamic solution to Pakistan's political problems.

Most importantly, Zia's emphasis on Islamization was politically motivated. Interest in retaining an alliance with the conservative groups within Pakistan necessitated at least some cosmetic changes in the legal and economic systems of Pakistan. These steps did not always pay off. On occasions they caused dissension among the populace. The Shiite muslims, for example, objected to being forced to pay *Zakat* forcing the administration to exempt them from paying the tax. The administration was also occasionally criticized by the *Jamaat-i-Islami* for not accelerating the pace of Islamization. Nevertheless, the minimal steps towards Islamization were sufficient to win the Zia administration enough support from the conservative elements in the country to legitimize military rule.

While wooing domestic groups, the Zia regime also built up a web of external relations that provided it with the necessary support to hold on to power. To begin with, the administration established close links with some Middle Eastern states, especially Saudi Arabia. Foundations of this relationship had been laid by Bhutto who had consistently highlighted Pakistan's geostrategic significance for its Arab and Iranian neighbors. Pakistan had already begun receiving substantial economic assistance from the Middle Eastern states. The Zia regime further strengthened this relationship. It closely identified itself with the Saudi Arabian government, stationed troops in Saudi Arabia, provided military training to officers from various muslim countries and even offered to mediate between Iran and Iraq in their conflict. In return, the Saudi government financed some of the arms acquisition programs initiated by Islamabad. Some Middle Eastern states also responded by stepping up their economic assistance to Pakistan.

The most significant external support, however, was provided by the United States. Following the Soviet invasion of Afghanistan in December 1979, a perceived threat to oil supplies from the Persian Gulf to the Western world prompted the Carter Administration to enlist Pakistan's support against the Soviet Union. With a view to building Pakistan's strength so that the Soviet Union could not exploit its economic and military weakness to further move southwards in the direction of the Persian Gulf, Pakistan was offered military and economic assistance worth US$400 million. The offer was rejected by the Zia regime as "peanuts". The Reagan Administration was, however, prepared to improve on this offer. In mid-1981 it concluded an agreement to provide Pakistan with a US$3.2 billion aid package. Half of the assistance was used for supporting the economy, whereas the other half was utilized for purchasing state-of-the art military equipment. The United States also provided training to a number of Pakistani officers under the International Military Education and Training Program (IMET). The first aid package was followed by another agreement worth $US4.02 billion for American military and economic assistance to Pakistan. The terms for this aid package were softer than those of the first aid agreement; instead of charging treasury rates, the new loan was provided on concessional terms thus markedly increasing the grant component of the aid-package.

On the one hand, the US assistance enabled the Zia regime to prevent the country from facing a total economic collapse since Pakistan was able to sustain a GNP growth rate of over 6 per cent annually. It also corrected the military imbalance between Pakistan and India which was acquiring modern weapons from the Soviet Union and West European states. On the other hand the aid package enabled the military to further strengthen its position and retain its dominance in the domestic political structure. Significantly, the Soviet invasion of Afghanistan and the US assistance provided General Zia with justification for prolonging his rule and not holding elections. This, in turn, often led to criticisms within Pakistan that the Reagan Administration was supporting a dictatorial regime.

An Experiment in "Controlled Democracy"

The US policy towards Pakistan was criticized from various quarters in Washington. Senators John Glenn and Clairborne Pell, and Congressman Stephen Solarz, for example, questioned the logic of continuing aid to a dictatorial regime. They also asked the US Administration to urge the Pakistan Government to return power to democratically elected representatives. This pressure coincided with increasing domestic disillusionment with the continued military rule. In 1981 a number of political parties organized themselves as the Movement for Restoration of Democracy (MRD). By mid-1983 they decided to launch a civil disobedience campaign against the Zia regime with the idea of forcing it to hold elections.

Faced with the mounting domestic and US pressure, General Zia announced a new plan on 12 August 1983. Made public only two days before the MRD was to launch its movement, the 12 August Plan (as it came to be known) contained the blue-print for a future constitutional structure for Pakistan. The plan provided for the holding of elections to the National and Provincial Assemblies by March 1985. But the elections were not to lead to a complete *transfer* of power from the military to civil administration. Instead, the 1973 Constitution was to be amended to enable the military to *share* power with political leaders (*FEER* 25 August 1983:25). The exact manner in which this power-sharing was to occur was unfolded by General Zia gradually during the next two years.

To begin with, as before, elections to local bodies were held on a non-party basis in 1983. This was followed by General Zia's indication on 4 August 1984 that, despite his previous denials of any political ambitions,[3] he was willing to continue as President if requested to do so. Immediately, a number of members of local bodies, who owed their position to the military regime, and cabinet ministers issued statements requesting Zia to continue as president after the restoration of democracy. As if bowing to "public demand", General Zia announced on 1 December 1984, that a national referendum would be held within three weeks to assess public opinion on the military regime's policy of Islamization. Interestingly, an affirmative vote was also to serve as a vote of confidence in General Zia by electing him President for the next five years (*Muslim* 2 December 1984). This "linkage" meant that the people of Pakistan had to chose between voting for Islam and General Zia or against Islam! In a muslim majority country, it was highly unlikely that those participating in the referendum would opt for the second choice. The MRD, therefore, boycotted the referendum. Nevertheless, the military regime claimed that voter turnout exceeded 60 per cent and that, of these, 97.7 per cent favoured the policy of Islamization. This "overwhelming support" was claimed to have provided General Zia with a mandate to rule as President until 1990.

The next stage in the gradual unfolding of the constitutional order prescribed by the military began on 12 January 1985. General Zia announced that parliamentary and provincial elections would be held on 25 and 28 February 1985. Consistent with Zia's previous indications that Islam did not approve of the concept of political parties, these elections were to be held on a non-party basis with separate electorates for muslims and non-muslims and special seats for women. To ensure that the armed forces could control the outcome of these elections, candidates were to be cleared by the military or by persons specially appointed by it for the purpose. Candidates were not permitted to hold public meetings, organise processions or use public address systems. These strict rules for electioneering encouraged two separate trends in Pakistan's politics; on the one hand they increased the candidates' tendency to rely heavily on the print media and spend exorbitant amounts of money to conduct a "deaf and dumb" election campaign (Rizvi 1986:1069). On the other hand they changed the agenda for the elections. The non-partisan nature of the elections left little room for discussion of national issues; important foreign policy issues like the situation in Afghanistan received little or no attention during the campaign. Instead emphasis was placed on local issues including the building of bridges, roads and hospitals. This, directly and indirectly, contributed to the election of candidates on the basis of their *biradaries* (clans), tribal loyalties, religious influence and the amount of money they could spend to buy votes in their respective electorates. The elections also enabled a number of proteges of the military regime to join the National Assembly (interview February 1990).

General elections were followed by elections to the Senate. In addition to each of the four provinces electing fourteen senators, the upper house included twenty special seats reserved for scholars, technocrats, and professionals. Two senators represented the Federal Capital Territory and five were appointed for the Federally Administered Tribal Areas (Akhtar 1989:261). By "indicating its preferences", the military regime ensured that most of the 83 Senators were either pro-military or did not harbor very strong anti-military feelings (interview December 1985).

Having filled the upper and the lower houses of Parliament with members sympathetic to military rule, General Zia called the first joint session of Parliament on 23 March 1985. This session marked the beginning of "controlled democracy" in Pakistan. General Zia took the presidential oath and, upon advice from Pir Pagara, appointed a Sindhi veteran politician, Mohammed Khan Junejo, as Prime Minister. The next day Junejo obtained a vote of confidence from the National Assembly and within a few days appointed his own cabinet ministers. In line with Zia's preference for "continuity" as opposed to a complete "change", the new cabinet included some who had already served as ministers during the last few years. The process was paralleled in the provinces with the installment of provincial governments. Martial law, however, was not lifted until 30 December 1985 when Junejo formally took over the civilian administration.

Neither the elections nor the lifting of martial law in 1985 brought the military's direct participation in politics to an end. Rather, even before holding the first joint session of parliament, the military regime had taken steps to ensure that power was *shared* with, and *not transferred* to, political leaders. The Revival of Constitution Order (RCO) issued by General Zia on 2 March 1985 introduced amendments to the 1973 Constitution. By revising 67 of the 280 articles of the constitution, these amendments changed the balance of power between the president and the prime minister (Rizvi 1986:1070). While the Constitution in its original form tilted in favour of a strong Prime Minister, the RCO concentrated more powers in the hands of the President and provided for a relatively weaker Prime Minister and a submissive judiciary. The President acquired powers to appoint the Prime Minister, Provincial Governors, Judges of the Supreme Court and the High Courts and other high army and civilian officials. He was also given powers to dissolve the National Assembly and/or dismiss the prime minister if convinced that the prime minister did not command the support of the legislature. The president exercised powers over provincial governments as well; provincial governors had the power to appoint the provincial chief ministers with the approval of the president. These wide-ranging discretionary powers carried relatively no checks; the RCO stipulated that the president retained the sole authority to interpret these powers.

Soon after the parliament held its first session, the military regime moved to "legitimize" the RCO in the form of the Eighth Amendment to the 1973 Constitution. Junejo and his advisors, knowing that without such an amendment martial law would not be lifted, assisted the military regime in the process. The Amendment, known as the Indemnity Law, was passed in October 1985 validating all the decisions taken by the military regime during the past eight years. Some of the provisions of the RCO were also amended in the process, thus redressing some of the imbalance in the powers between the executive and the legislature. However, those entrusted with the job of examining and interpreting the draft of the Amendment neither questioned nor amended the clause authorizing the president to continue as the COAS. Acceptance of this anomaly was apparently part of a calculated attempt to prevent a new COAS from reimposing martial law once it was lifted at the end of 1985 (interview February 1990). Nonetheless, it provided legitimacy to the military's continued *direct* participation in Pakistan's politics.

Immediately after the Eighth Amendment had been passed, the Zia regime acquiesced to revive political parties. Moves in this direction had already been made in the parliament with the formation of the Official Parliamentary Group (OPG) under Junejo's leadership and the smaller Independent Parliamentary Group (IPG) that assumed the role of opposition. The Political Parties Act, passed in December 1985, paved the way for these groups to openly coalesce on platforms of various political parties. However, with the approval of the parliament, the Act was worded so as to ensure that the military could continue to determine the type and nature of actors (parties) permitted to participate in the country's political system. The Election Commission, a federal body appointed by the President, was to screen all the political parties for registration. These parties were required to submit their manifestos, list of office bearers, full-paid members, and a copy of their constitution (Rizvi 1986:1072). Yet they could not be sure of being registered under the name of their choice as the Commission could register only one political party under one name. This posed a dilemma for various splinter groups that either had to rush to register themselves, and therefore organize along the lines preferred by the Commission, or find a new name for their party thus losing its previous identity. Once registered, the parties still ran the risk of being "deregistered" by the Election Commission and being denied the right to participate in the political system.

These "safety mechanisms" instituted by the military regime did not prove foolproof. The events following the lifting of martial law in December 1985 gradually exposed the limits to the military's ability to totally control the future directions of political developments in Pakistan. In January 1986, for example, the Pakistan Muslim League [PML] (Pagara Group) was reorganized; the Pir of Pagara, who had been the main force behind Junejo's nomination as prime minister, relinquished his position as the president of the party in Junejo's favour. Immediately, the newly reconstituted PML began enlisting the support of a number of parliamentary members and senators. By July 1986, it had been registered as a political party with an eleven point manifesto highlighting social and economic programs for the rural and urban masses. Also relying on its role as the party that had won Pakistan's independence, it was presented to the masses as an alternative to the PPP. While the possibility of the PML undermining the position of the PPP, which by then was being led by Benazir Bhutto appealed to General Zia, Junejo's record as the new civilian administrator did not.

Soon after martial law was lifted, Junejo began asserting his independence and testing the limits of presidential power by appointing and/or transferring various officials to top positions. Soon, the prime minister's secretariat began emerging as another source of power in Pakistan. General Zia, who expected Junejo to play a subservient role, was reportedly annoyed by this assertion of civilian supremacy. Within a few years, signs of friction began emerging between the president and the prime minister. The rift deepened in early 1988 with Junejo's decision to convene an All Party Conference to discuss the Afghanistan situation and sign the Geneva Accord. General Zia, who until then had controlled Pakistan's Afghanistan policy with the help of the Inter-Services Intelligence (ISI), considered the initiative as directly diminishing his status in the system and began indicating his intention of replacing Junejo with a new prime minister (interview February 1990).

Had Zia gone ahead with this decision, it would have reflected his desire to fully explore various possibilities of ensuring the military's superiority within the framework of the newly established political structure. But the developments in the next few months presented a different picture; instead of "perfecting" the system, General Zia decided to replace it with yet another system. On 29 May 1988, in the aftermath of the *Ojri* Camp disaster of April 1988, and the rumors that Junejo might insist on removing the head of

ISI, General Hameed Gul, and the Joint Chief of General Staff, General Akhter Abdur Rehman, Zia dismissed Junejo as Prime Minister and abruptly dissolved the National Assembly. During the next ten weeks, various prescriptions for a new political order were suggested. The idea of a parliament with half of its members elected through adult franchise and the other half *appointed* by the president was mooted indicating the military's interest in restraining any future prime minister from questioning its supremacy.

Meanwhile, General Zia tried to quieten the growing dissatisfaction with his policies by promising to hold elections on 16 November 1988. However, in order to pave the way for prescribing another structure, political parties were denied the right to participate in these elections. This was despite the fact that Zia himself had only recently supported the Political Parties Act. Interestingly, at this juncture a number of political parties, including the PPP, began seriously entertaining the idea of operating within the confines of the structure defined by the military and thus participating in the non-party elections. This change of policy probably stemmed from the confidence that they could emulate Junejo and try changing the political structure from within rather than remaining outside the system.

The End of "Controlled Democracy"

General Zia's sudden death in a plane crash on 17 August 1988 changed the picture. Immediately following the crash, which claimed the lives of the American ambassador and 29 senior Pakistani military officials, General Aslam Beg took over as the COAS. According to some reports he initially considered imposing martial law but was dissuaded by the Chiefs of Air and Naval Staff. Faced with their opposition, he asked the Chairman of the Senate, Ghulam Ishaq Khan to take over as Acting President. However, instead of forming an interim cabinet and appointing a caretaker prime minister, Ghulam Ishaq announced the formation of an Emergency Council. The Council comprised the four chief ministers, senior ministers from Zia's cabinet and the Chiefs of Army, Air Force and Navy (*Nation* 18 August 1988). Since the four chief ministers and the cabinet ministers owed their continued participation in the government to the backing of the army, the Emergency Council essentially provided for continued military rule under the name of a civilian administration. The armed forces retained the position as the major center of power in Pakistan.

The Emergency Council oversaw the elections on 16 November 1988 as announced by General Zia. Contrary to Zia's plans, however, the elections were held on a party and not on a non-party basis (Baxter 1989:24). The main contest occurred between the PPP, led by Benazir Bhutto, and the *Islami Jamhuri Ittehad* (IJI)[4] led by Mian Nawaz Shariff. The army preferred Shariff to Bhutto; he had risen to prominence during the Zia regime, had worked as the Chief Minister of the Punjab and, to the chagrin of a number of veteran Muslim Leaguers, had successfully retained the position even after the dissolution of national and provincial assemblies in May 1988. Hence, he was more aware of, and willing to protect the military's interests. This stood in marked contrast to the position taken by Benazir Bhutto during the preceding years; consistently promising to avenge her father's death, accusing the military regime of oppression, and underscoring her interest in "teaching the military a lesson" she was perceived as a threat by the military (*FEER* 10 November 1988:36).

The results of the November 1988 elections, however, favoured the PPP. While unable to win a clear majority, the PPP succeeded in securing 92 of the 205 contested seats in the parliament. The IJI, on the other hand, won 54 seats, emerging as the second largest political group in the Assembly (*FEER* 8 December 1988:13). Despite the election results, the military initially resisted handing over power to the PPP. Benazir had to hold lengthy discussions with the COAS, Aslam Beg, and President Ishaq Khan to assuage the military's fears. It was only after these discussions that the military accepted her claim that she could form a government with the help of the Muhajir Qaumi Movement (MQM) which had emerged as the third largest political party in the Assembly.

The United States Government played a significant role in facilitating the transfer of power. It managed to receive assurances from Benazir Bhutto through ambassador Robert Oakley that she would not change Pakistan's Afghanistan policy, not cut defense spending, and would retain Ishaq Khan as President and Sahibzada Yaqub as Foreign Minister (*The Economist* 3 December 1988:25). Only afterwards, on 2 December 1988 did President Ishaq Khan nominate Benazir Bhutto as the Prime Minister. The announcement ended the *direct* and *active* participation of the military in Pakistan's politics which had lasted for eleven years.

Experiment in Controlled Democracy: Phase I & II

Phase I

The formal transfer of power to Benazir Bhutto ushered Pakistan's politics into another era. The military began claiming that it had transferred power to political leaders. The COAS, General Aslam Beg, frequently claimed a total lack of any political ambitions, underscored the military's emphasis on professionalism and insisted that it wished the political processes to take their own direction. Yet his claims do not correspond to reality; while the *direct* participation by the military in Pakistan's politics came to an end, the military continued to play an *indirect* and *active* role in Pakistan's political system. Motivated by its interest in retaining its preeminent position in the political system, the military resorted to three different strategies.

Firstly, it relied on the Bhutto regime itself to protect its interests. Fully cognizant of the fact that undermining the military's position could affect her own position as the Prime Minister; Benazir Bhutto avoided shaking this confidence. Pakistan's defense budget was not reduced after December 1988. Rather, in the wake of the increase in India's defense for 1990-91, Islamabad began considering an increase in its own defense budget (*Nation*: 15 April 1990). The new administration also continued the arms acquisition program initiated during the Zia regime; not only did it continue receiving ships ordered in view of India's naval build-up, but it has also placed an order for an additional 60 F-16 aircraft. Moreover, the military and the airforce conducted the biggest military exercise in Pakistan's history, *Zarb-e-Momin*, in 1989. Significantly, contrary to the fears expressed by the military before Bhutto's ascent to power, the new regime did not wind down the nuclear program (*Defense and Foreign Affairs Weekly* 15-21 May 1989).

Benazir Bhutto's conciliatory approach vis-a-vis the military did not command unanimous support from the PPP. Unlike the groups that accepted a policy of accommodation with the armed forces, certain circles in the party favoured "taking the army head-on". This, in turn, prompted the military to rely on another avenue as well to ensure that its interests were protected; it maintained a close alliance with President Ghulam Ishaq Khan. As a career bureaucrat during the Zia regime, he restrained Benazir from undermining the interests of the armed forces. This was most obvious in the "Sirohey affair": Benazir's announcement that the Joint Chief of Staff (CJS) was due for retirement was interpreted by some circles in the army as a case of her testing the limits of the president's interest in siding with the military and as a prelude to strengthening her position vis-a-vis the COAS, Aslam Beg. Therefore, instead of agreeing with the Prime Minister, the President refused to retire the CJS thus indicating that he was not prepared to be instrumental in changing the balance of power between the PPP and the armed forces.

Finally, to protect their interests, the armed forces relied on the opposition as a counterweight to the PPP. They supported, at least tacitly and indirectly, the IJI and especially Nawaz Shariff who gave up his seat in the National Assembly to become the chief minister of Punjab. This avenue provided them with the option of putting pressure on the Benazir government if it acted contrary to the interests of the military. Also, as demonstrated during the no-confidence motion of 1989, contacts with the IJI provided the armed forces with an option of toppling Benazir's government and replacing it with a pro-military group.

Essentially, therefore, Benazir's ascent to power in December 1988 ushered the military into a new era; instead of playing a *direct and active* role, it began playing an *indirect and active* role in Pakistan's politics. It basically relied on "constitutional means" to ensure that its interests were not undermined by the PPP with the hidden proviso that any such threat would mark the end of Benazir Bhutto's administration.

This recourse to indirect and constituional means became more obvious as ethnic violence in Bhutto's home province, Sindh, acquired serious dimensions in early 1990. Tensions between the Urdu-speaking Muhajirs and local Sindhis had been high even prior to Bhutto's rise to power in December 1988. By establishing an alliance with the MQM the PPP had managed to keep the level of violence to a minimum. Once the alliance broke down in late 1989, and the MQM joined hands with other opposition parties to form the Combined Opposition Parties (COP), the law and order situation worsened in the province. Faced with frequent clashes between the two communities and mass scale murders in the province, the Bhutto government was forced to call the military in to control the law and order situation in Sindh. Instead of bringing the PPP Government and the military closer, the decision proved divisive. From the start, the armed forces expressed dissatisfaction with the limited powers accorded to them by the civil government; the military captured terrorists and the civilian courts released them, especially if they happened to be pro-PPP. This resulted in the fear that the military could be identified as being partisan in its attempts to control the problem in Sindh. Hence, the military began demanding greater powers to control the situation in Sindh. Bhutto consented to these demands but only grudgingly. At the same time she resisted the military's suggestion that the Sindhi issue required negotiations between all the political parties. Instead, eager to retain her power base in the Sindh province, she insisted that it was a provincial and not a national issue (Yasmeen 1990a).

Added to this "irritant" was the military's quiet disapproval of the manner in which the Bhutto Government had initially handled the unfolding crisis in Kashmir. Instead of quickly capitalizing on the situation, the Bhutto Government had initially taken a 'softer' line on the developments in the Indian part of Kashmir. Only, when faced with the possibility of being "upstaged" by the opposition did the the Pakistan Government call a joint session of the Parliament and express its concern over the situation in Jammu and Kashmir. Given that Pakistan military has traditionally identified itself closely with the goal of "liberating" Kashmir, the relutance on Bhutto's part was not looked upon favourably by some senior military officials.

Phase II

On 6 August 1990, therefore, the military decided to use "constitutional means" to remove the Bhutto government. President Ghulam Ishaq Khan, using his power stemming from the Eighth Amendment to the 1973 Constitution, summarily dismissed the Bhutto regime without even the courtesy of informing her in advance. The Bhutto administration was replaced by a caretaker government headed by the leader of the COP, Ghulam Mustafa Jatoi, and new elections were scheduled for 24 October 1990.

The results of the October elections proved more appealing to the military than those of 1988. Contrary to all the predictions, the PPP failed to even retain the number of seats won in the 1988 elections, and the IJI won a landslide victory. The results paved the way for Nawaz Shariff's rise to power as the new Prime Minister of Pakistan (Yasmeen: 1990B). As someone who had risen to power during the 11 years of martial law, Shariff is openly acknowledged as a more "reliable" ally for the Pakistan military. However, interestingly enough, the military is still pursuing a "dual-track policy": while being sympathetic to the Shariff Government, it still relies on the President, Ghulam Ishaq Khan, as its main ally in the system. (So strong is this reliance that the PPP is openly urging the Shariff government to join hands with the opposition to repeal the Eighth Amendment and curtail the presidential powers vis-a-vis those of the prime minister).

What about the future prospects? Given that the dissolution of the National and Provincial Assemblies in August 1990 brought a pro-military government to power in Pakistan, the military's interest in reverting to a direct role in the country's politics has been temporarily checked. For the forseeable future, Pakistan military, therefore, is likely to rely on constitutional and indirect means to protect its interests. This, however, does not mean the military is unlikely to revert to direct and active participation in politics in the future. If the Shariff government begins to question the president's powers in running the country, if it accepts the PPP's suggestions that the Eighth Amendment be repealed, and/or if law and order problems in Pakistan acquire serious dimensions, the military might once again intervene in its capacity as the custodian of law and order.

Conclusion

Within a few years of its existence, the Pakistan army had redefined its role as one of not only *restoring* law and order but also *defining* the structure of a desireable political order in Pakistan. Also, against the background of relatively weaker political institutions and arms supplies that strengthened the military's position vis-a-vis other institutions, the armed forces managed to play an *active* role in Pakistan's politics that varied from being one of direct to an indirect participation at various stages in the country's history (Appendix 1). The 1977 coup, therefore, was a continuation of a historical and structural trend that enabled the military to intervene in Pakistan's politics in the aftermath of the March 1977 elections. The military regime legitimized and perpetuated its rule through a combination of alliances established both domestically and internationally with conservative elements, and by espousing a conservative ideology of Islamization. When forced by domestic and international forces to return power to politcal leaders, the military initially relied on a new prescription that provided for a sharing and not transfer of power, and led to an experiment in "controlled democracy". Only after Zia's death and Benazir Bhutto's ascent to power in December 1988 did the military move from a direct to an indirect participation in Pakistan's politics. Currently, the armed forces have opted for a "triple track strategy" with primary reliance on "constitutional means" to ensure that their interests are not jeopardized. This trend is likely to continue in the 1990s. However, as in the past, the possibility of the military reverting to direct participation cannot be totally ruled out. If the military perceives its institutional interests being threatened by political leaders and/or if the present climate of uncertainty continues to prevail, the military may intervene and prescribe yet another structure of political order for Pakistan.

Appendix 1

The Military and Pakistan's Politics 1947-90

Years	Form of participation
1947-58	Political rule: Military got stronger.
1958-62	Martial Law: Direct and active participation.
1962-69	Presidential rule under Field Marshal Ayub Khan.
	Indirect and active participation
1969-72	Martial Law: Direct and active participation.
1971-77	Bhutto in charge: First as the civilian martial law administrator, and then as the prime minister.
1977-85	Martial Law: Direct and active participation.
1985-88	Controlled Democracy: Direct and active participation.
1988-	Return to democracy: Indirect and active participation.

Notes

* The author wishes to thank Malik and Sarfraz Iqbal, Ghalib Iqbal, Jeff Malone and Ravi Tomar for assisting in researching of this paper.

1. The PNA included Pakistan Muslim League, *Jamaat-i-Islami, Jamiat-ul-Ulmae Islam, Jamiat-ul-Ulemae* Pakistan, *Khaksars, Tehrik-i-Istiqlal,* National Democratic Party, PDP and All Jammu and Kashmir Muslim Conference.

2. In all fairness to Bhutto, it must be pointed out that, although keen to win the elections by enlisting the support of public servants like District Commissioners, he did not favour rigging on a massive scale!

3. In an interview with Hussain Haqqani in October 1983, for example, General Zia said: "My eyes are fixed on having a peaceful transfer of power as well as seeing that at the end of the transfer of power there is stability in the country. I personally do not have any political ambitions" (*FEER* 27 October 1983: 46).

4. The IJI is also referred to as the Islamic Democratic Alliance (IDA). For purpose of consistency, this chapter will use the name commonly used in Pakistan, IJI.

8

The Military in Bangladesh

*Chowdhury R. Abrar**

Of its two decades of existence, Bangladesh has been ruled by the armed forces for approximately one and a half. Although successive military rulers have attempted to civilianize their rule by holding referendums and elections, the country continues to be ruled by the military as democratic institutions and processes fail to become entrenched.

This chapter argues that the seizure of state power by the armed forces can neither be adequately explained as the actions of ambitious or disgruntled sections of the officer corps, nor on the premise that in the military's view it was their prerogative to assert a historic role in modernizing the society. Although such factors have undoubtedly contributed at times, they cannot of themselves explicate the recurrent cycle of military rule/parliamentary form, nor covert collusion in the continuance of military control on the part of civilian politicians and parties. Instead, it will be argued that the primary objective of the military regimes has been to protect and promote the interests of the ruling petty bourgeoisie, and that therefore the continued military dominance over Bangladesh political processes can be better explained in terms of a crisis in the ruling class control of the state. In that sense, military intervention in Bangladesh is to be seen as the logical outcome of a crisis ridden peripheral state. Such an approach helps establish causal links between economic and political processes and facilitates a better understanding of actions of political agents with reference to broader socio-economic conditions.

The chapter is divided into three main parts: the first part deals with the development of the military and its role in Bangladesh, the second concentrates on the armed forces relation with the evolving petty bourgeois order, while the last focuses on the more crucial aspects of the military in the 1970s and 1980s and concludes with some speculative notes about the 1990s.

The Origins of the Bangladesh Armed Forces

Like most of the institutions of Bangladesh, the military has its origins in the colonial period. As a hallmark of its post-colonial peripheral order, the colonial legacy of the Bangladesh military remains strong, and not necessarily restricted to the ranks and regalia but appears in the military's ethos and *modus operandi*. This is not to suggest, however, that the colonial legacy is an irreversible phenomenon. The disorientation of a conventional military establishment from colonial influence can perhaps only take place through participation in a national liberation movement led by class forces which have an alternative hegemonic mission. Therefore, accepting the political leadership of such class forces and interaction with the masses in the process of a national liberation struggle are necessary preconditions for the transformation of a colonial nurtured army to a patriotic people's force. Yet this was not the case with the Bangladesh armed forces.

Pre-Independence Legacy

The origins of the Bangladesh army, like its counterparts in India and Pakistan, can be traced from the military establishment of the East India Company. The main task of this establishment was to coerce the indigenous population, which was necessary to facilitate the expropriation of native resources by the Company. Lindquist[1] (1977) observes that such forces played an important role in the penetration of British capital in the region. The establishment of direct rule by the Crown over India brought about an enhanced role for the British India army. Described as the "largest and most effective colonial army in the world" it was called to perform a host of tasks, ranging from extending British control over the rest of India and other areas. This included the suppression of local uprisings and containment of the nationalist movements of the twientieth century to challenging other imperial armies in the first and second World Wars. The success of the British in raising the Indian army was mainly due to careful recruitment, training and organization of Indian soldiers (ibid.:10). Ironically, while the British Indian army was initially constituted by troops from Bengal, Bombay and Madras (the regions that first came under British domination), recruitment from Bengal was discontinued after the Sepoy Mutiny of 1857,[2] in which Bengali forces played an important role, and was not reconstituted until 1910. Lindquist (1977) further argues that it was after the mutiny that the myth of the "martial races" was developed by the British, promoting the notion of racial superiority of the Punjabis, Dogras, Jats and Gurkhas as racial groups more adept to military skill and discipline.

Although there have been instances of naval mutiny immediately before the British withdrawal, on the main the British had been successful in staving off any involvement of the armed forces in the nationalist struggle. Needless to say, on the attainment of independence it was "this conservative and "anti-national" military establishment inherited from the Empire [which] became the armed protector of the post-colonial state" (ibid.:10).

The military's role in thwarting national integration and the democratic political process in Pakistan has been well documented (Ali 1970). Suffice to say that the collusion of the civil-military bureaucracy with the feudal-trading oligarchy and American support was vital for the continued domination of the military over the state. The civil-military bureaucracy's dominance was formally demonstrated in the declaration of martial law and the abrogation of the parliamentary process by General Ayub in 1958. More than a decade of military rule contributed to the strengthening of the armed forces and the development of the Punjab (a region which was identified by the British as the producer of one of the "martial races"), but at the cost of the underdevelopment of other regions, including Bangladesh (formerly East Pakistan), and overall national integration.

As a result of growing mass movements in both East and West Pakistan, General Ayub was forced to resign in 1970 and hand over power to the chief of the armed forces General Yahya Khan. The new army chief promised to hold general elections and accordingly in late 1970 elections were held with the Awami League (AL) winning a majority of the seats in parliament. The refusal of the Pakistani military junta to hand over power to the Bengali leader Sheikh

Mujib, and Yahya Khan's subsequent resort to a military solution of a political problem, forced the Bengalis to take up arms. The result of this conflict was the creation of Bangladesh as an independent state in December 1971, after a short but a decisive armed conflict in which India played an important role.

Experiences of the 1971 War

An immediate response to the Pakistani army's crack-down on Bengalis was the emergence of three main resistance forces. The first one consisted of the military, para-military and police personnel then serving in the Pakistan forces and later constituted the core of the Bangladesh army. The other two were the disparate groups that spontaneously arose in different parts of the country, and those organized by the left wing parties. The first group remained divided in terms of strategic planning. The main stream led by General Osmany and other army commanders chose the military tradition and opted for conventional warfare. This group liaised closely with the provisional AL government based in Calcutta and coordinated its activities with the Indian army commanders. Their approach, Lindquist (1977:11) argues:

> was to organize all trained Bengali military personnel into conventional units which would operate from bases in India. And their political goal was to bring an Awami League government to power in Bangladesh as soon as possible by whatever means including direct Indian intervention.

Following this strategic concept, emphasis was given to conventional military tactics and formations. India was relied upon to train and supply arms and ammunition. As opposed to this approach the alternative stream led by Majors Taher and Ziauddin preferred to wage guerilla warfare and had strong reservations about the provisional government's dependence on India. Their view was that all available military personnel should be dispersed throughout the countryside to train and raise peasant guerila units, and rely mainly on weapons captured from the enemy.

The basic difference between these groups was their perception of what constitutes "national liberation". Osmany's goal had been to put the AL into power in an independent Bangladesh in the shortest possible time and with all available means. Taher and Ziauddin's group opted for a strategy which was geared, not only to attain national independence but also the transformation of society in the process of the struggle. It appears that they were not in a hurry to put a specific party in power. In contrast to the mainstream strategic thinking and arguments favouring dependence on India, Taher and Ziauddin's group wanted to base their hopes and reliance on grassroots participation, since they were perceived as the supplier of manpower, resources, shelter and intelligence. That is, a resort to classic guerilla warfare tactics. The mass character of the struggle appears to have convinced Taher and Ziauddin of the ultimate success of such a strategy. They were aware of the resistance being organized in various areas of the country, some spontaneously and others under the auspices of the leftist forces. And envisaged linking these disparate elements under a broad alliance. The petty bourgeois leadership of the AL and their external patron, India, were aware of the wider ramifications if such a strategy was to succeed. And it is this factor which largely contributed to the Indian government's decision to intervene in the ninth month of the struggle, aborting the potential development of a national liberation movement in Bangladesh. The Indian move circumvented the growing influence of the alternative strategists such as Taher and Ziauddin and thus thwarted the prospective transformation process of the regular forces into a "people's army" with cross sectoral participation. Within weeks of direct Indian involvement, the Pakistani occupation forces surrendered to the Indian commander[3] and the state of Bangladesh was created.

The Bangladesh Phase

The new state of Bangladesh was bequeathed with an army, already showing fissiparous signs. There was the conservative section groomed in colonial tradition with the task of maintaining the status quo on behalf of the propertied classes. This group consisted of Bengali officers who were repatriated from Pakistan after the creation of Bangladesh, and other armed forces personnel who along with para-military and police forces deserted the Pakistani military and joined the resistance.[4] The Indian intervention and the subsequent setting up of the AL government in Dhaka denied the Bengalis a potentially successful national liberation movement. In December 1972, a regime dominated by petty bourgeois elements was established with the active support of the Indian bourgeoisie. The character of the state apparatus largely remained unaltered due to the incomplete nature of Bangladesh's national liberation movement. The laws governing the state were essentially a continuation from Pakistan's rule and, as such, had roots to the Raj. In spite of the factors inhibiting successful national liberation[5] the nine month experience of the armed resistance had an important bearing on shaping the military establishment and military thinking in particular in independent Bangladesh.

In the changed circumstances the newly installed petty bourgeois rulers were wary of armed civilian resistance forces and quickly disarmed them. The Awami League leadership also initiated policies of reorganizing various state institutions. It is not surprising that they opted to build a conventional army emphasizing traditional military professionalism. In spite of the claims made by army commanders and defence planners of having a professional force, in its nineteen year existence the Bangladesh army has developed into anything but a professional force.[6]

Professionalism in any particular sector of the state apparatus in a peripheral state such as Bangladesh is not a feasible proposition.[7] The notion of professionalism in a state bureaucracy presupposes a certain degree of maturity of the capitalist state itself, which is contingent upon the the existence of a hegemonic bourgeoisie. In other words, it is only those social formations which have experienced a successful transition to capitalism, with accompanying bourgeois democracy in the political realm, normally provide conditions for the development of professionalism of state functionaries. In such cases the professionalism of the military bureaucracy entails upholding the constitution of the state and restricting its activities within the parameters established in the constitution, and the maintenance of discipline and observance of the chain of command. Normally, the first condition centres around the notion of defence of the state from external aggression. In addition, the armed forces may be required to perform tasks to aid the civil administration in instances of natural calamities, like floods, cyclones and earthquakes.

Professionalism of the armed forces involve training, motivation and combat readiness and also strict adherence to clearly delineated rules. The military in the bourgeois democratic societies of the West usually performs the above functions and hence can be termed professional. In contrast, the underdeveloped peripheral societies are in general marked by incomplete transition to capitalism as well as in most cases, a non-hegemonic ruling class, usually the petty bourgeoisie. The military in these circumstances does not restrict itself to the constitutionally defined task of defending the state from external aggression and also fails to maintain the rigid discipline and chain of command. The armed forces become interventionist and take command of the state mostly with the aid of the civil bureaucracy and a section of the petty bourgeois politicians, generally from the ruling party which was overthrown. Attempts are made to legalize and rationalize the illegal takeover by extra-legal means, normally by amending the constitution, if it still remains in operation, or by declaring martial law, in which case all civil laws are kept in abeyance and/or made subordinate to martial law. In these situations the regime's interest is perceived to be the the same as the state, and non-conformity with the regime is considered seditious.

The underdeveloped peripheral scenario discussed above throws light on the military involvement in Bangladesh's political process. The military in such a case, far from being "professional", is neither prepared nor interested in roles which are performed by its counterparts in the developed capitalist states. In the following section two differing perspectives on the role of the military in Bangladesh is discussed. One is the dominant perspective of the conventional model, while the other, inspired by the war of independence, was ultimately abandoned in favour of the first.

Role of the Military

The question of the role of the military in Bangladesh has been a matter of considerable debate both within and outside the military establishment. There have been two occasions, a decade apart, where this question was addressed by senior army commanders. The first was soon after independence when the military commanders, Ziauddin and Taher, proposed the strategy of guerilla warfare and self-reliance, and called for the establishment of a "people's army" along the lines of the Chinese Peoples" Liberation Army. Opposing the government policy, favoured by other military commanders, of restoring and rebuilding a conventional army along traditional concepts and practices, these officers argued for the setting up of a "productive army". They believed that such an army would not only be conducive to the deltaic terrain of the country but would also substantially minimize the drainage of national resources that were necessary to maintain a conventional army dependent on imported technology, hardware and foreign assistance. In keeping with their self-reliant strategy, the protagonists of this alternative view advanced the thesis of "soldiers becoming workers", producing their own food and becoming involved in productive work in the villages.

In order to demonstrate the viability of this approach, these officers experimented by cultivating intensive crops. For example they planted 500,000 pineapples in one district. This novel approach involved the physical labour of officers and men daily, earning them the nick name "plough soldiers" (*FEER* 16 August 1974).

As this approach was contrary to the traditions and interests of a conventional army, such innovative ventures met with resistance from the higher echelons of the government as well as the military establishment. The spirit of democratization, egalitarianism and value of physical labour ran counter to the colonial tradition of "hierarchy" and "professionalism", and threatened to undermine the very foundation of the conventional army that the commanders were planning to build. Within six months the "plough soldiers" were stripped of their command in a major reshuffle. Thus a modest and alternative approach inspired by the experiences of the war of independence, to involve the armed forces with national development, was abandoned on orders from the government and the army high command.

The second time senior officers publicly stated their ideas about the role of the armed forces in national development was soon after President Zia's death. By then the idealism of the independence struggle had largely withered and Bangladesh's political process was again faced with issues which had haunted the Bengalis during Pakistan's rule and were thought to have been resolved with the attainment of statehood.[8] The failure of the civilian sections of the petty bourgeoisie under the AL to administer the state had brought the armed forces to power in 1975. By 1981, under General Ziaur Rahman (Zia), the military became deeply entrenched in the politico-administrative processes of the country. The armed forces, accustomed to power and privilege perceived the election of a civilian president, Abdus Sattar, as a threat. Soon after his election the military started asserting its power and again achieved political control when General Ershad staged a coup in March 1982. This was barely three months after President Sattar was elected in a landslide victory.

General Ershad's assumption to power in March 1982 was preceded by a series of events. This ranged from declaration of intent, threat, and finally an ultimatum by the General, with support from the army high command, to alleged acts of sabotage to undermine the government's credibility. After the assassination of President Zia in an army revolt at Chittagong in May 1981, the armed forces high command pledged loyalty to the acting president Abdus Sattar. Within a few days the revolt was suppressed by

General Ershad. This incident strengthened his position and provided him with bargaining power with the government. Soon afterwards General Ershad started pressuring the government on a series of issues. He capitalized on his position and as early as September 1981 expressed reservations about President Sattar's ability to understand the army's corporate needs.

Ershad's increased interest in political affairs was further revealed when, prior to the presidential election, he expressed his apprehension of post-election turbulence if either of the opposition candidates won. This led to speculation about a potential army takeover prior to the elections. Military theorists such as O"Kane (1987) have demonstrated the potential for coups prior to elections when the military believes a power vacuum exists and moves to fill it. Within days after President Sattar's landslide victory, senior army commanders confronted the President in their demand for "a share of power" in the administration (*FEER* 27 November 1981). This incident took place only two days after the newly-elected president categorically rejected any role for the armed forces "in a democratic country" other than defending the frontiers.

The vagueness of the military's "demand" was reflected in the army chief's statement that "What we want is that we must be heard. The government must take into account our views". The General argued that in order to avoid future assassinations of heads of state, the army's role must be institutionalized "for all times to come" (*FEER* 27 November 1981). In stating the army's view, Ershad expressed his belief that the country faced a "deep seated politico-military problem" which needed to be recognized and redressed (*FEER* 19 March 1982). Although the armed forces commanders were not explicit in stating their "demands", subsequent events led political observers to believe that the thrust of the army's demands was directed to (a) having a say in the appointment of cabinet ministers and the vice-president; (b) concurrent appointment of the army chief as the defence minister or alternatively elevation of the three service chiefs to cabinet rank with the right to take part in cabinet discussion and (c) the establishment of a committee of the three service chiefs as a "super-cabinet" in the form of the National Security Council (NSC) with power to veto all government decisions.

Although in January 1982 the president announced the formation of a ten-member NSC with 3 service chiefs, 5 ministers, and the vice president, under his chairmanship, it was rejected by the armed forces. After a series of negotiations the matter was eventually settled in the army's favour when the NSC was reconstituted with the 3 service chiefs, the president and the vice-president. This marked the beginning of another phase of domination by the military, as the entire cabinet was immediately sacked. In accordance with the NSC decision a smaller cabinet was appointed. The admission[9] by the president to the mass media about the inefficiency and corruption of his 72-day old council of ministers only reflected the extent to which the armed forces were prepared to go to achieve power sharing.

In spite of President Sattar's acquiescence to the armed forces successive demands, the military nevertheless resolved to take power. This was evident from the actions of leading army officers.[10] For example, the chief of the general staff and the director general of the defence forces intelligence organization made a trip to Indonesia to be oriented about the administrative apparatus of the military dominated state there and met with senior bureaucrats to discuss future administrative reforms. Thus after having prepared itself for a military takeover it is alleged that the army high command in alliance with its civilian allies engineered the necessary alibi to justify the final takeover just three months after presidential elections.[11]

On 24 March 1982, General Ershad assumed the position of Chief Martial Law Administrator and appointed Justice Ahsanuddin the ceremonial president. Ershad also appointed a cabinet of advisers, dominated by serving and retired military personnel and bureaucrats. In accordance with claims generally made by the armed forces leader after a coup, General Ershad stated that the armed forces seized power because national security was threatened by the economic crisis, unprecedented corruption, and deterioration of law and order. It was also claimed that the new administration would introduce "a unique form of democracy which no martial-law administration anywhere else in the world had been able to do" (*FEER* 16 April 1982). Not surprisingly, however, all political activities were banned, the constitution suspended and parliament dissolved. Regarding economic issues, the government declared its intention to boost the private sector through "liberal and pragmatic" investment policies which included the return of the nationalized industries to their previous owners.

The military regime had been particularly concerned with what was termed "major administrative and social reforms" which involved among other areas, agrarian, administrative, judicial, educational and health services. Needless to say, all such policies have been undertaken to bring about "structural change in the country's economic and social order". Justifying the role of the armed forces in the political process, the general argued that the

Bangladesh armed forces" participation in the war of independence has accorded it a role to fulfil the hopes and aspirations of the people (TV interview, Dhaka, 20 June 1982). Its participation in the war politicized the forces and therefore it should be given an effective role in running the state" (ibid.). He further argued that "with their skill and potentialities the armed forces could replenish the shortfall in the country's administrative, technological and engineering sectors. They should naturally be utilized for rebuilding an integrated powerful and unified nation" (ibid.).

The present regime has now been in power for the past eight years, making military rule in Bangladesh a decade and a half old. Using co-optation and intimidation, the Zia and Ershad regimes have protected themselves from serious challenge by opposition groups. They have managed to obtain external support in the form of foreign aid. The military regimes have also enjoyed monopolistic control over state machineries, legislative, executive and judicial, while exercising exclusive control over the administrative, propaganda and the coercive apparatuses of the state. In addition to their own untapped manpower resources, as claimed by General Ershad, the regimes have had at their disposal a group of pliant politicians, of both right and left wing persuasions, as well as bureaucrats, technocrats, academics, judges, jurists and journalists. The regimes also continued to obtain the World Bank active support and the US Agency for International Development expertise, as well as the support of a large section of the petty bourgeoisie, traders, businessmen and wealthy peasants. In foreign policy the regimes have been successful in rallying support from the Western bloc, the Islamic states, Japan and China. Relations with India and the Soviet Union have also been cordial. In spite of all these favourable conditions, why is it that the "structural changes" promised by the regime have not taken place? The answer necessitates addressing issues which are beyond the scope of paradigms developed on the premise of a clear civil-military dichotomy.

The Military as a Part of the Petty Bourgeoisie

It is a general characteristic of peripheral societies that the army is essentially integrated with the ruling petty bourgeoisie. Political parties, civilian bureaucracy and the military constitute integral elements in the administration of the state on behalf of the ruling class. While there is a constant and unabated sectoral competition among these groups, promotion of petty bourgeois class interest remains their unqualified and prime function.

Some reflection on the petty bourgeois class interest are relevant here. In the developed capitalist countries control over state power by the bourgeoisie was preceded by control over the economy. The bourgeoisie developed the productive forces in agriculture and industry through innovativeness and frugality, organized home markets by creating demands and providing purchasing power to the common people, and protected the market from outside competition. In contrast, however, due to colonial intervention the process of indigenous capitalist development in the peripheral societies have been distorted. In the post-colonial phase the incorporation of these societies into the world capitalist economy and the techno-economic development strategies pursued by these states have essentially given rise to a class which is neither frugal nor nationalistic, but compradore in nature. This unproductive, consumption-oriented class(es), instead of organizing and developing indigenous productive forces and home market, took the role of commission agents with the mission of expanding the operations of international capital in the home country. It is this class which controls the state power in many peripheral societies such as Bangladesh.

The Bangladeshi petty bourgeoisie is by no means the progenitor of the bourgeoisie. It is essentially a hybrid group, a conglomeration of different sectors of the middle class. This group includes, for example, teachers, lawyers, traders and insurance agents. They are neither the capitalists nor the sellers of labour power. As such they lack any coherent ideology and they fail to develop as a class with a sense of a historic mission. The petty bourgeois class is anti-labour and anti-capital. By virtue of its close proximity to political power in the peripheral states it becomes opportunistic, involved in activities like trading, of an essentially illicit type, black marketeering and hoarding, and is dependent on the state for protection and sustenance. Therefore the interest that the political parties and the civilian bureaucracy serve in these states under civilian rule are essentially the same that the armed forces pursue when they seize state power. The degree and the level of control that each of these sectors exercise are empirical questions which depend on conjunctural circumstances.

Crisis in the Petty Bourgeois Rule

Following independence in 1971, the Awami League assumed political-power in Bangladesh. Due to the petty bourgeois class nature of this party it had no interest in initiating any fundamental restructuring of society. No effective steps were taken to develop the productive forces in agriculture since the party did not have a definite strategy on how to initiate land reform. Likewise, the industrial policies that it pursued worked against the development of this sector, being marred through overnight nationalization and the appointment of incompetent political cronies leading to utter mismanagement and widespread misappropriation (Ahmed and Sobhan 1979). This accumulation of wealth in the hands of the people close to the ruling party, coupled with government restrictions on further domestic investment in industries paved the way for a flourishing shadow economy of illegal trading, smuggling, hoarding, speculative business and indenting[12] (Umar 1984). The stagnation in agriculture and anarchy in the industrial sector led to a rapid deterioration of the quality of life for the most of the population. The failure of the regime to effect fundamental changes in the economy and the rampant corruption of the ruling party further eroded public confidence in it. As this crisis intensified, various measures were undertaken to contain it. The regime's alienation from the people was reflected in the necessity to create a paramilitary force, the *Rakkhi Bahini* (the National Guards), and the amendment of the constitution to incorporate provisions for preventive detention and emergency. The declaration of the Emergency in December 1974 along with the suspension of fundamental rights and the subsequent passage of the Fourth Amendment brought about a single party state under the personal stewardship of the "father of the nation", Sheikh Mujibur Rahman. It was under these circumstances that the armed forces seized power in direct collusion with a section of the Awami League.

Bangladesh's one and a half decades of military rule failed to usher in promised changes. The country's economy continues to falter with massive pauperization and landlessness, leading to concentration of land ownership, low productivity in agriculture caused by a lack of investment and the domination of the trading class in the economy leading to near-anarchy. This has undermined the potential for industrial growth, contributed to massive increase in foreign debt and unemployment and a sharp decline in real wages. As a result, the classic pattern of peripheral underdevelopment occurs: while the vast majority of the people suffer, a minuscule minority close to the centre of power prospers.

Regarding the political process, various institutions and practices which are essential for a functioning democracy such as the supremacy of the parliament in law making, separation of powers between the different arms of the state, freedom of the press, freedom of organization and assembly, have all been severely undermined, contributing to a crisis of governance. The most serious casualty of the arbitrary nature of politics has been the principle of secularism, with the regime moving towards religious fundamentalism. The failure of the successive regimes to mobilize the people under their banner had, on the one hand, led them to resort to coercion and on the other, to appeal to obscurantist sentiments. The process of concentration of power in the hands of the chief executive, by emasculating parliament and the cabinet, began during the rule of the AL under Mujib and continued under Generals Zia and Ershad.

The Military in the 1970s and 1980s

By early 1975, with the intensification of the crisis of the petty bourgeois state, senior officers were formally inducted into the ruling party. This move was in effect a recognition of the increasing importance of the coercive apparatus of the state. However, the mid-1970s witnessed the military's predominance in administering the state. The "civilianization" program undertaken by General Zia was essentially directed at replacing the established political parties with a new party, the Bangladesh Nationalist Party, formed at the behest of the armed forces to ensure Zia's own supremacy over state affairs and the promotion of the military's corporate interest. The weakness of the political opposition and the erosion of public trust in political parties provided the military with the opportunity to establish its rule without having to resort to violence and as such it successfully presented itself as a source of stability and order.

In contrast, military rule in the 1980s failed to gain the necessary support from the population. To legitimise its rule the military created a political party, the *Jatiya Party*. There were specific demands from the armed forces chief, General Ershad, to the government to indicate the army's share in the administration with a constitutional guarantee (Ershad 1982). This demand by the armed forces to participate in government was matched by the increasing militarization of different sectors of the state. Of the 64 district police administrators, 53 were military personnel in 1987 while 97 senior positions in the bureaucracy, under the Establishment Division of the Government, were held by army officers. Likewise, while recruitment for government positions was restricted, about 1,500 former army personnel were reappointed (Zaman 1987:3). Invariably there has been an increased number of senior officers to fill positions in the foreign service, state corporations and other government and autonomous bodies. The predominance of military personnel in the administration has resulted in the increasing trend of training army personnel in subjects other than defence, a pattern now common to most Third World armed forces.

The most important feature of the Bangladesh military in the 1980s has been the enmeshing of its interest with other petty bourgeois sectors. By virtue of their location at the commanding heights of the state, military leaders are involved, and in most cases determine the awarding of licenses and contracts for various developmental projects and procurement and distribution of goods for state corporations (Hossain 1987:42). It is now an accepted fact in the trading circles of Dhaka and Chittagong, the two largest cities, that access to senior commanders of the armed forces is increasingly becoming a necessary condition for securing business. The association of retired officers with trading houses and on the board of directors of companies has become a common feature in Bangladesh.

Methods of Military Rule

The failure of the regime to effect any meaningful structural change and to achieve improvement in the quality of life of the majority has resulted in the regimes" alienation from them. These, along with the denial of fundamental human rights have often led to spontaneous outbursts of popular discontent among various sectors of the population. The government has invoked a number of strategies to cope with popular uprising These are. cooptation, repression and ideological manipulation. Here I will briefly deal with the policies pursued in the first two cases and elaborate on ideological manipulation.

Cooptation

The class character of the petty bourgeoisie has made it relatively easy for the military regime to find its apologists among the "middle class", the literati. When Dhaka University students agitated against the government's new education policy in 1984, the General Secretary of the university student's union was inducted into the government with the position of Joint Secretary[13] and was later made a state minister and subsequently appointed to cabinet. Likewise, on two separate occasions key opposition alliance negotiators brazenly accepted cabinet positions, including that of prime minister.

The military regimes have been particularly adept at causing splits in the opposition political parties. Often a faction of the party would join a government sponsored political party. The merging of a section of the BKSAL[14] with the *Jatiya Party* (JP) and induction of a presidium member of one of the two main opposition parties, the Awami League, into its central committee and the breaking up of the other important opposition party, the Bangladesh Nationalist Party, by secretly working with its general secretary are all part of the process of cooptation pursued by the regime.

The composition of the cabinet provides sufficient evidence of the ingenuity of the regime. It has brought together a religious right wing fanatic Maulana Mannan and a one time left-wing trade unionist and firebrand student leader of the late 1960s, Kazi Zafar Ahmed. Along with regular party level contacts the intelligence agencies, including the Defence Field Intelligence (DFI), perform major roles in the negotiations for coopting leaders of opposition parties. Recruitment in the regime sponsored trade union movement, student and youth organizations is similarly achieved.

Coercion

Successive military regimes, like their civilian counterparts, have resorted to coercion and intimidation to bring recalcitrant opposition leaders in line. The harassment of the political opposition by recourse to preventive detention law and interrogation by the intelligence agencies are punishments the regimes" opponents have to endure. The indiscriminate resort to violence in dealing with demonstrators and strikers has become a routine matter[15], and is essentially a reflection of the weakness and insecurity of the regimes. The massacre of scores of unarmed striking inmates in Khulna prison in 1981 is a striking instance of the readiness to make brutal use of force.

Augmenting the armed forces, the paramilitary and police force and their modernization with sophisticated weaponry and telecommunications equipment correlate with an increase incidence of state violence. To control opposition the regimes had enacted new laws, including the Disturbed Area Bill, the Presidential Guards Regiment Ordinance and the Metropolitan Police Ordinance. The military regimes in Bangladesh justified these legislative measures as necessary to maintain order. Such claims are questionable and can in no way be taken seriously given that the executive and legislative functions were in effect vested upon an individual, judges were appointed and dismissed on the chief executive's discretion, and the judgements of the summary military courts, even in civilian matters, were protected by indemnity law. The rise of the intelligence agencies as a bulwark to the armed forces has been one of the hallmarks of the 15 years of military and quasi-military rule. An important feature of these agencies has been their almost overt involvement in civil matters. Their tasks range from the surveillance of opponents of the regime to the recruitment of political allies in the student, trade union and political movements, a point illustrated earlier. As the regimes were essentially concerned with their power base in the military, it was not surprising that the chief executives tended to be more receptive to the military intelligence chief than to their cabinet. It was alleged by former senior state functionaries that there have been occasions when the Defence Forces Intelligence chief was given the final say in sensitive political matters. In the political circles of Dhaka it was common knowledge that the intelligence agencies had a very important input in the appointment of advisers and ministers and other key state functionaries as well in matters like the nomination of the chancellor's representatives[16] in the selection committees of the senior faculty staff of the universities.

Ideological Mobilization

Side by side with such repressive measures, the military regimes of Generals Zia and Ershad have pursued policies aimed at gaining the support of the Muslim majority of the population in the form of a diversionary appeal to religious sentiments. The secular character of the 1972 constitution was terminated by martial law proclamation soon after Zia assumed the presidency, and by an executive decree under martial law that the constitution was amended. The preamble to the constitution was changed by incorporating a phrase eulogizing the glory of Allah. In place of emphasizing the principles of nationalism, socialism, democracy and secularism, as did the original article, the new one pledged the high ideals of absolute trust and faith in the Almighty, Allah. The amendment retained the principles of democracy and nationalism but deleted secularism altogether and qualified "socialism" to mean "economic and social justice". A new article was inserted which read "absolute trust and faith in the Almighty shall be the basis of all actions" of the state. The deletion of the concept of secularism from article 12 of the original constitution which eliminated (a) all forms of communalism, (b) granting of political status to any religion by the state, (c) use of religion for political purposes and (d) discrimination and persecution of persons practising a specific religion, was discarded. The arbitrary amendment to the constitution also emphasized that the state was "to endeavour to consolidate, preserve and strengthen fraternal relations among Muslim countries based on Islamic solidarity".

General Zia's amendment to the constitution was preceded by another. After the second coup in November 1975 President Sayem amended Article 38 of the constitution which restricted individuals from forming or belonging to any religious organizations and societies with political aims and purpose. The new arrangement paved the way for religious fundamentalist elements to stage a come-back in politics. Another proclamation on 23 April 1977 declared that all such amendments to the constitution under martial law were deemed to be valid after its termination and were protected from being challenged in the law courts. Not only were the amendments to the constitution effected by extra-legal means. Constitutional provisions deemed all such "amendments, additions, modifications, substitutions and omissions made in this Constitution by the said Proclamation shall have effect as if (these) were made in accordance with and in compliance with the requirements of, this Constitution".[17] This was an ingenious way to legalize extra-legal action.

Like his predecessor, Ershad pursued a policy of inciting religious fanaticism. His rule was marked by the state patronage of the "holy men". *FEER* (29 October 1982) documents the influence of these spiritual leaders in uniting the top leadership of the armed forces. The regime's failure to attain the people's support prompted it to depend heavily on Islamic fundamentalists. In order to gain the support of the theocratic school, Ershad criticized the progressive elements who had been critical of state patronage of religious fundamentalists. He therefore called on the "true Muslims" to resist such elements. Ershad's repeated assurance that "the ideals and principles of Islam will be maintained...in the constitution of the country", indicated the ideological inclinations of his regime. Its crude manipulation of national symbols of democratic struggle for narrow selfish interests was highlighted when the regime attempted to turn the observance of the "martyrs day" on 21st February[18] into a religious occasion for recitations from the Quran. This was to replace the three decade old tradition of barefoot procession[19] at dawn and painting of *alpana*[20], which were termed "unIslamic" (as did his predecessor in the Pakistani military dictatorship).

The conservatism of the armed forces and their growing involvement with Islamic priests was evident when about 50 key army officers, including the army chief of the general staff, the commander of the strategically important 9th Division, the DFI chief and several other divisional and brigade commanders along with 20,000 troops became disciples of a *pir* (holy man) based in the Faridpur district (*FEER* 7 April 1983). In an earlier occasion the Jessore garrison commander General Shawkat organized the initiation of 15,000 of his men as followers of the same *pir*. General Ershad's January 1983 promise to include the ideals and principles of Islam in the constitution was realised in May 1988 when a bill was introduced in the parliament to amend the constitution to make Islam the "state religion". The President justified the move on the ground that the recognition of a state religion "will enable us to live as a nation with a distinct identity"[21] (*FEER* 23 June 1988).

The principles of state policy as enshrined in the 1972 constitution were reflective of the spirit of prolonged democratic struggle waged by the Bengalis against Pakistani military rule and had been the guiding principles of the armed struggle of 1971. These were not imposed by an individual or a party but evolved as issues of consensus in the course of the struggle for democracy. By abandoning some of these principles and diluting others, the successive military regimes have undermined the consensus of the nation. Such arbitrary exercise of discretion further reverted the process in favour of obscurantist ideals and narrow corporate interests.

The Nineties: Some Speculations

Judging from the experience of the last decade and a half, it is likely that the armed forces will remain in power in Bangladesh in the 1990s. The failure of political parties to articulate popular demand for land, work, adequate wages and fundamental rights has gradually led to their marginalization in the political process. As the parties are led by different factions of the same propertied class, which have a stake in maintaining the status quo, it is only natural that their own interests would be jeopardised if such demands were to be met. The absence of the bourgeoisie as the ruling class has created a structural crisis of the state which cannot be resolved as long as trading capital (and not the industrial capital) enjoys an unquestioned sway. In such a fluid situation where a capitalist class with historic roots is totally absent, it is the petty bourgeoisie who would continue to rule. Such a rule will increasingly be in the nature of crisis management. The armed forces, which is the coercive apparatus of the state, is best suited to perform this task.

What then is the role of the political parties which claim to be engaged in a struggle against the military regime? Essentially their task is to act as a buffer between the increasingly militant population who demand fundamental change and that of the military government (Umar 1989:82). The dominance of the petty bourgeois leadership in the trade union movement and other mass organizations provide them with the opportunity to divert such organizations and movements from becoming further radicalized and to contain them within a framework which does not challenge the status quo. It is in this context that the anti-Ershad campaign currently pursued by the political opposition should be viewed.

In spite of widespread popular desire to bring an end to military rule and to support the anti-government movement, the vested interests of the opposition political leadership effectively undermine any such move. Instead of confronting the military for control of the state apparatus, the opposition pursues a policy of covert collaboration disguised by overt verbal confrontation in the form of reformist demands. Such demands give vent to popular protest while also providing leverage for bargaining with the military administration. For example, the opposition's pressure for the removal of General Ershad is in sharp contrast to the popular demands for a complete end to military rule and all forms of repression. A further instance of this confrontation/collusion strategy is the opposition's paradoxical actions of boycotting the polls one day and participating the next. Likewise, the Awami League's demand for the resignation of General Ershad from the presidency, while themselves retaining their seats in parliament, demonstrates the lack of any serious challenge to the military regime. In spite of some minor conflicts, it is this enmeshing of interests of the civilian and military sectors of the ruling class that will continue to shape the political process of Bangladesh in the 1990s.

Conclusion

The dominant literature on the role of the armed forces in peripheral states attempts to explain military intervention in terms of overt manifestation of sectoral competition among the civil-military elites aggravated by economic and political crises. In a cruder form this literature portrays military rule as the expression of power hungry military officers, individuals or oligarchies. In contrast, it has been argued in this chapter that the military takeovers in Bangladesh are primarily a reflection of chronic crisis in the petty bourgeois dominated rule. This is demonstrated by the fact that each military regime has, after an initial period of direct "emergency" rule eventually adopt indirect rule by embedding their control within the civilian framework. Thus the crisis is more effectively contained by disguising both it and the military regime within the form of parliamentary government. Military rule in this context can thus be best explained as the last resort of the ruling class in order to ensure its continued control of the state. The civilianization of military rule phase of the cycle is therefore to be viewed as a process of partial recovery from the crisis. Likewise, the militarization of civilian rule phase is an indication of the reverse process. In the absence of the emergence of a substantive hegemonic class, either from the bourgeoisie or the working class, the crisis management of the petty bourgeois dominated state is manifested either in tenuous civilian rule with a large dosage of authoritarian content or in "civilianized" quasi-military rule or even in direct military rule.

Notes

    *   I would like to thank Ray Wood for his comments on an earlier draft.
1. I am indebted to Lindquist for the main arguments of this section.
2. Termed by Marx as "India's First War of Independence".
3. It is worth noting that although the war was fought under allied forces no representative of the Bangladeshi resistance was present at the surrender ceremony.
4. General Osmany, the commander of the Bangladesh liberation forces, has been reported as stating that the decision of these elements to switch sides was essentially prompted by the "overkill" policy of the Pakistani forces who attacked the army, East Pakistan Rifles (a paramilitary force) and police barracks at the initial stages of the crackdown. Osmany further observed that had the Pakistani Army been more selective in its dealing with the Bengali politicians then "Bengali personnel in the army might have remained neutral"'(see Lindquist 1977).
5. Being led by the petty bourgeoisie and the short duration of the armed struggle.
6. This assertion is made on the premise that the Bangladesh army was responsible for the assassination of two presidents and organizing a number of coups. It is also credited with several arbitrary amendments to the constitution and has become heavily involved in civilian matters.
7. For an insightful discussion on professionalism of the military in a peripheral state of the Philippines see Selochan, V., (forthcoming), especially chapters 3, 4 and 9.
8. Bengali culture of a secular mould rather than Islam was to be the basis of national identity.
9. Sattar later claimed that he was coerced by the army chief to make such a statement.
10. They were reported to have been involved in preparing a blueprint to form a government after the impending take-over.
11. A recent publication (Islam 1989) by a retired army captain, once based at the Army Headquarters, argues that senior army commanders had a hand in destabilizing Sattar's regime by organizing strikes and demonstrations to paralyse the government. These were funded by close associates of those commanders. Islam alleges that on the one hand, close friends of the generals, who were in most cases retired army officers, had organized a strike by bank employees, while on the other the civilian president was brought under intense pressure by the army high command to effectively deal with the striking employees, thereby further exacerbating the situation. The other incident allegedly precipitated by the army high

command, and which was later frequently used to justify the declaration of martial law, involved collusion of the National Security Intelligence (NSI) organization in setting up a notorious criminal in the official residence of an influential minister in President Sattar's cabinet, who was later "apprehended". While it is difficult to ascertain the validity of such allegations, the release and reinstatement with full arrear pay of the leaders of the bank strike after the assumption of power by General Ershad and their active participation in the government sponsored trade union rallies and the awarding of an ambassadorship to the NSI chief Hakim gives Islam's claim some credence.

12. This involves local companies working as agents for foreign compaies and securing business on their behalf. The local agents receive commission, which ranges from 2 to 10 per cent of the total value of the deal.

13. This position placed him as second in command in the bureaucratic hierarchy of a ministry.

14. This was the acronym for Bangladesh Peasants and Workers Awami League.

15. These are in most cases promptly followed by the formation of enquiry committees whose reports are either never completed or are never made public.

16. The President is the Chancellor of the universities.

17. Paragraph 4 of Section 3A of the Fourth Schedule of the Bangladesh Constitution, amended under Proclamation Order 1 of 23 April 77.

18. An occasion to renew pledges for democratic and cultural rights of the Bengalis. On 21 February 1952 police shot dead several protestors agitating against the national language policy of the Pakistan government to impose Urdu, the language of a small minority, as the *lingua franca* of Pakistan.

19. A Bengali form of expressing protest.

20. A traditional design of ritual-aesthetic value with auspicious connotation.

21. It should be mentioned that there was widespread condemnation of the bill from different sectors of the community. Although about 85 per cent of the population are Muslims, Bangladesh differs from other Islamic countries in the sense that Bengalis are devout Muslims, but they are "relaxed about their religious beliefs".

9

The Military Factor in South Korean Politics

James Cotton

In 1961, and again in 1979-80 the military intervened in the politics of the Republic of Korea (South Korea) with the result that military personnel dominated the administrations that were subsequently established. The coup in office of Park Chung Hee in 1972 was also dependent upon the exercise of military power and was aimed at perpetuating a regime of quasi-military character. Although the present government of President Roh Tae-woo was constituted as the result of national elections in 1987, it is still playing a transitory role since many of its key members formerly served in the armed forces and the connections and loyalties they developed there still provide the framework for their present conduct. This chapter will review the reasons for the original rise to political prominence of the military, and the prospects for this role diminishing given the economic and social transformation of Korea in the last three decades and particularly the adoption (after considerable turmoil and uncertainty) of a democratic constitution in 1987.

History

As in China, so in traditional Korea the military arts were not highly valued according to the standards of the high culture. In practice (during the later Koryo dynasty and on the foundation of its successor, the Yi dynasty) soldiers often stepped in to impose their will upon a disorderly or corrupt political scene, but no cult of the warrior ever emerged to supplant the civilian values of Confucianism. In wars and conflicts (notably the Imjin Wars with Japan in the late sixteenth century) Korea produced valiant and patriotic commanders to be sure, but their successes were often undermined by the endemic bureaucratic factionalism of the royal court which too often paralysed concerted state action even in times of national crisis. Nineteenth century attempts to found a modern military on western lines were destroyed by the annexation of Korea by Japan, which itself induced only a feeble mutiny amongst elements of the small national army.

Japanese annexation did, however, change the standing of the profession of arms for at least some Koreans. On the one hand Koreans served in the Imperial Army or its auxiliaries, some (like future President Park Chung Hee) becoming officers during the second World War. On the other, resistance to the Japanese was conducted in Manchuria and China by a number of ethnic Koreans who served in a variety of military formations generally under the sponsorship of either the Kuomintang or the Chinese Communist Party (the latter providing Kim Il Sung with his initial training in guerilla warfare). From these disparate elements the national armies of the two post-war Korean states were drawn.

The non-military heritage of the traditional culture thus undermined, it was negated almost entirely by the experience of the Korean War. First the exigencies of survival and then the need to guard against the continuing threat of North Korea led to the introduction of military conscription and the creation of a large standing army. Even before the conflict, in becoming the first President, Syngman Rhee had used his connections with the haphazardly recruited para-military and military sectors to good effect against his rivals. Thereafter senior appointments in the armed forces were used to balance rival cliques of officers, and guarantee loyalty to Rhee personally. In an infamous episode in 1952 the political role of the military was underlined when a principled commander who refused to do the president's bidding (Army Chief of Staff, General Yi Chong-chan) was replaced with a more pliant candidate when Rhee met opposition to his wish to withdraw troops from the front line in order to overawe the National Assembly then meeting in Pusan to alter the constitution (Kim Se-Jin 1971:51, 69-71).

From that time the armed forces became, in many respects, a school for development, acting to train and mobilise a whole generation of Koreans, giving them familiarity with the elements of modern technology and of administrative structures. But unlike many developing nations Korea inherited a tradition of over a millenium of cultural, linguistic, and governmental unity as well as of bureaucratic administration. Many of the factors that have led to military interventions in the politics of such nations have not therefore been present in the Korean case. Moreover, the standing of politicians and bureaucrats has been (and still remains to an important extent) high. In 1961 there were many more likely candidates than Korea for the military assuming a political role. The move by the military to centre stage in government should thus be understood in part in terms of the alternatives (or lack of them) to military rule. And the more recent dominance of the military is to be explained as a function of the interests and expectations generated by such a role.

The 1961 Coup and Its Context

There is no doubt that the experience of the military under Rhee reinforced any inclinations that the officer corps might have had to play a political role. They were political participants willy nilly, and privy to the increasing failings and ineptitudes of the Rhee regime. Unhappiness with their position was compounded by the gap in perceptions and experience which existed between middle and senior ranks. Whereas their superiors were often haphazardly trained and rapidly promoted, the by now thoroughly professional elite of younger officers found all too frequently that their way was barred by venal and incompetent placemen. The sense of mission possessed by these younger officers has been traced by Gregory Henderson to the atmosphere of the Korean Military Academy in the 1950s: "In its early years the academy became a kind of island off Korea's moral coast, governed by standards quite different from those of the society around it" (Henderson 1968:353). But there were many obstacles to be overcome on the road to a specifically political role.

In 1960 popular revulsion at Rhee's manipulation of the electoral system led to student demonstrations which, unchecked by the military who refused to intervene, led to the fall of his regime and the coming to power of a democratically elected administration. But though individuals in this administration were often well intentioned, many of the worst features of the political culture conspired to obstruct efficient government. No sooner had the

Democratic Party been elected to office in July 1960 that it split into irreconcilable factions. Prime Minister Chang Myon only retained office by cultivating personal loyalties through a constant turnover of ministers. Hesitant in its treatment of personnel from the Rhee era, the government failed to rally sufficient support either from the electorate in general or influential social groups to ensure its survival. In particular, elements in the military grew increasingly unhappy with its attitude on military questions. Committed at first to a thorough review of senior officers whose conduct had manifestly assisted in prolonging Rhee's personal dictatorship, Chang's administration reneged on its undertakings, touching off several confrontations between middle-ranking and senior officers which sowed the seeds of the subsequent coup. The question of relations with North Korea—at one point policy on this issue seemed almost to be in the hands of student organisations—also excited the military's understandable concern (Han 1974).

The May 1961 coup was undertaken by a group of about 250 officers who were largely graduates of the eighth class of the Officer Training School of what would become the Korean Military Academy, the first to have received formal military education and training. Most were colonels and lieutenant-colonels, including later intelligence chief and prime minister Kim Jong-pil. However, two more senior officers, Major General Park Chung Hee (related to Kim by marriage) and Major General Kim Dong-ha were crucial participants. With the support of around 4,000 troops an almost bloodless coup was effected, the remainder of the armed forces falling into line after some hours of confusion (Jae Souk Sohn 1968; Kim Se-Jin 1971; Lovell 1975).

The ease with which the civilian authority was overcome was due to a number of factors. The original conspirators were but a small group within the military who indeed had been at odds with their seniors concerning the army's political role and reputation. But the coup was made in the name of the Army chief of staff, and his support was eventually forthcoming due to the very little respect held amongst senior commanders for the Chang Myon government. It was also facilitated by the fact that the head of state, President Yun Po-son, not only failed to take any steps to call the armed forces to order (and thereby also deliberately obstructed attempts by the United States commander in Korea to have the rebellion quelled) but actually stayed on in his position until 1962 thereby legitimising the power transfer. The reasons for this must be sought in the fact that Yun was from a rival party faction to Chang Myon, party factionalism not for the last time acting to retard Korean political development.

Soon after seizing power the military revolutionaries made it clear that they were motivated only by the highest ideals. As an officer familiar with the new technology (Park was an artillery specialist and had attended advanced courses on this subject in the United States) and undoubtedly influenced strongly by his service in the Japanese army, Park intended nothing less than to effect a Korean version of the Meiji restoration. He sought a moral, administrative, and cultural renaissance in Korea to deliver it from weakness and undue foreign influence. The bottom line of this transformation was to be economic. Without the economic well being that would flow from Korea becoming an industrial and an exporting nation, none of these other goals would be attainable.

Constructing a political and social vehicle to effect the program of the revolution in order that power could be returned to the civilian sector proved difficult. Senior officers who wished only to clear up the mess and impose order before returning to the barracks had to be shunted aside, and even then divisions within the coterie of leading coup makers constantly threatened to divert their energies. However, in the person of Kim Jong-pil the party of the military revolution possessed a fund raiser and organiser of formidable if unscrupulous talents. The Korean Central Intelligence Agency (KCIA) was established, with Kim who had pursued a career in army intelligence as its head. The KCIA was used as a base from which to dominate the society as well as to facilitate through the provision of funds, personnel and information, the formation of the Democratic Republican Party (DRP). After a complicated series of political maneuvers this became the launching vehicle for Park Chung Hee's first bid for the presidency in 1963, though Kim himself had to retire from the scene for a time as a result of rivalries with other members of Park's clique. Once again conflicts between the remnant factions of the former Democratic Party assisted the, now civilianised, revolutionaries.

The Third Republic: Unstable Quasi-Military Rule

With great dexterity, though only through financial and legal malfeasance, the Park regime enhanced its control over South Korea. Although his program to turn the country into a major exporter soon began to bring results, Park's overall strategy relied upon external linkages at least to secure political funds. Diplomatic relations were opened with Japan, and South Korea entered the Vietnam conflict, both maneuvers bringing directly and indirectly a pay off for the DRP and its leadership (Kim 1975; Kihl 1984).

The Third Republic was a quasi-military regime in the sense that, while the executive absorbed many talented technocrats its leading personnel were individuals of military origins and connections. The regime endeavoured to reinforce its claims to legitimacy by adapting certain elements of still prevalent Confucianism (though shorn of its disdain for military matters) with militant anti-communism (Olsen 1986). In a pattern in keeping with the characteristics of the political culture, and one which is still to be found even in the present, the loyalties of the military were secured by a network of connections and relationships few of which had any formal institutional embodiment. Thus, members of the eighth (KMA) graduating class remained at the centre of Park's court. They developed client relationships with their former juniors in the officer corps, particularly members of the eleventh KMA graduating class. The Park regime also exhibited a strong regional bias, showing preference for individuals from Park's native region of Kyongsang which is in the southeast. The informal and thus ill-defined nature of this network undermined attempts to institutionalise political power (Eugene Kim 1984:24; Huntington 1968:260).

Despite the resources and power Park skilfully accumulated his Third Republic could never claim full democratic legitimacy. A steady economic growth rate of 9 per cent per annum brought a measure of public acceptance, but the regime was never free of reliance upon corruption and electoral manipulations. Moreover, the passage of time produced, as a consequence of rapid economic growth, new classes and demands to which the government failed to respond (Im 1987). The proximate cause of its downfall came, however, from the failings of the DRP. The party established no enduring mass base, and was prone to the same factional disputes as its opponents. Differences on the question of who would succeed to the presidency in 1971 produced an open split between Park and Kim Jong-pil before the constitution was changed to permit the former to run for office again. The manifest unfairness of the 1971 electoral contest between Park and Kim Dae-jung began the process which led to Park's suspension of the constitution, in the name of the Yusin or revitalising reforms in 1972.

The transformation of 1971 and 1972 also had an important security dimension. As has been noted, the 1961 revolution was effected partly to keep Seoul's military and diplomatic preparedness against North Korea intact. From the start Park had maintained an implacable anti-communist stance, often saying that relations between the two halves of the peninsula would never be improved until South Korea's national strength matched or even exceeded that of North Korea. But in 1971 secret overtures were made which culminated a year later in a joint communique issued by North and South together on the principles for national unification. This accord soon broke down in mutual acrimony: at the time of the introduction of the Yusin reforms, Park was insistent that, in an era when further contacts between the two states were likely to take place, South Korea would have to be united in its dealings— otherwise Pyongyang would be able to exploit internal differences for its own purposes. This is an argument which has been heard repeatedly in Seoul and still has its advocates today.

The Return to Military Authoritarianism: Yusin and Chun Doo-hwan

The relationship between the military and the post 1972 Yusin regime was a complex one. On the one hand Park abandoned a number of his original followers when he dispensed with electoral politics (though the DRP continued to contest the mostly irrelevant elections to the National Assembly). By this time, however, many individuals with military backgrounds had made their way into the bureaucracy and business. On the other, and increasingly as time went on, the president resorted directly to the civil use of the armed forces and to all the subtle and unsubtle means of coercion open to the KCIA to repress and contain public dissent. This resort to more authoritarian methods of rule proved only a temporary success. Park's last act under his "emergency powers" as president was to declare martial law in the southern towns of Pusan and Masan on 18 October 1979; this measure failed to stem the tide of popular unrest and he was assassinated one week later by the Director of the KCIA, Kim Jae-kyu.

The assumption by a new military group to political power shortly thereafter is to be understood with reference to the inheritance of the Park era. As a result of authoritarianism the gap between opposition political figures and Park's military and quasi-military heirs was unbridgeable. At the same time there was no clearly dominant group which could have taken power without widespread dissension. The events of 1979 and 1980 may be regarded as a further installment of a pattern of events which could be seen again in 1987 and may be reproduced in 1992 and 1993 when Roh Tae-woo completes the single term of office permitted under the present constitution.

Opposition to Park Chung Hee had produced a number of able and determined figures, most prominent of them being Kim Dae-jung and Kim Young-sam. The conditions of the Yusin period had encouraged the strengthening of the moralistic, hierarchical and even conspiratorial nature of this opposition while it had spawned also a host of more or less radical and fissiparous dissenters. In the vital weeks after Park's execution, when Acting President Choi Kyu-hah procrastinated over the promised introduction of democratisation, the two opposition Kims failed to agree on a common strategy and indeed were still endeavouring to launch their own separate political vehicles when military action swept them aside (Sohn 1988).

Park's heirs were in similar disarray. Kim Jong-pil warred with Lee Hu-rak, who was one of the original coup makers and another former KCIA head, and others among Park's lieutenants over leadership of the remnants of the DRP. Meanwhile, having moved quickly against Park's assassins, Martial Law Commander and Army Chief of Staff Chong Seung-hwa failed to occupy the political space that opened at the top of the political system. This latter act was thus left to others, Major General Chun Doo-hwan, chief of the Defense Security Command arrested Chong on unsubstantiated charges of complicity in the murder of Park on 12 December 1979. Chong subsequently served a sentence in detention and may even have escaped execution as a result of American concern (Peterson 1988:57-8). At the time Chun apparently acted without appropriate authority and in carrying out the arrest blood was shed. Chong later on denounced the "mutiny" of 1979 from the platform of Kim Young-sam's opposition Reunification Democratic Party during the presidential elections of 1987.

Chun had been a loyal follower of the previous president. He was also a graduate of the eleventh class of the KMA, once again marked out from its fellows by virtue of the fact that its members were the first to complete the full four year course of instruction introduced during the Korean War. With a group of his fellow graduates including Generals Chung Ho-yong and Roh Tae-woo, Chun first extended his control to all the most influential military commands. With student demonstrations and public disorder as his cover, he took over the KCIA in April 1980. Shortly thereafter martial law was declared, and a clean sweep was made of the entire political spectrum with the arrest not only of all the key opposition figures but a number of Park's closest associates as well.

This coup by an officer clique was to prove not only less popular but also less bloodless than that of 1961. A popular rising in Kwangju between 18 and 21 May was only suppressed with considerable loss of life, creating wounds in the body politic which remain unhealed. This incident also further complicated the role of the American military forces in Korea since some of the troops used to suppress the rebellion were, nominally at least, under US command. This issue is discussed below.

The 1987 Crisis of Legitimacy and the Civilianisation of the Military

Once again a clique of officers given common identity by KMA class membership, and to a lesser extent regional ties, came to dominate Korean politics. However, from the first there were important differences with the beginning of the Park era.

The success of Park's program had brought into being a Korea vastly more sophisticated and developed than the impoverished nation of 1961. Between 1962 and 1981 GNP per capita increased from US $92 to US $1570. Education, urbanisation and literacy all exhibited a similar transformation. Partly as a result political expectations also came to be vastly different. And the external threat that had been explicitly adduced as one of the original reasons for the foundation of the Third Republic, which was again invoked in 1972, seemed to have diminished if only as a result of the now considerable disparity in size between the two Korean states. The military was also a changed entity, the officer corps in particular being thoroughly professionalized and as a consequence increasingly unhappy with a high political profile.

Perhaps recognising these realities, if only obliqely, Chun was insistent that he would be a single term president, albeit for seven years. His efforts to improve the ethics of Korean politics and otherwise make his mark on the nation's history were rendered implausible by a series of scandals, and even though he presided over a new burst of prosperity he did not win the limited legitimacy that was his predecessors reward in his earlier years. Moreover, there was no abandonment of the engines of coercion inherited from the Park era.

For a time only a number of licensed parties were allowed to share the stage with the regime's Democratic Justice Party (DJP), but consistent with his long term intention to hand an orderly nation back to the civilians, Chun was obliged to lift the prohibition he had placed on genuine political opposition. The superficiality of the consent which he had engineered was demonstrated almost immediately with the strong showing, despite many impediments, of the hastily organised New Korea Democratic Party (NKDP) in the National Assembly elections of February 1985. In substance though not in name, the NKDP was an alliance of the followers of Kim Dae-jung and Kim Young-sam, and the single issue which they were determined to pursue was the fundamental illegitimacy of Chun's fifth republic.

Thus began a prolonged legitimacy crisis which reached its peak in the first half of 1987 and only abated with Chun's departure. For some time it seemed as though Korea would realise the thorough break with its political past which its economic and social conditions would seem to have warranted (Huntington 1984). In the end the political system secured an elected executive in the first really significant political contest for at least sixteen years. But for a variety of reasons as much to do with the failings of the opposition as with the advantages of incumbency enjoyed by the DJP, Roh Tae-woo achieved the presidency (Cotton 1989b; Johnson 1989).

Roh Tae-woo's association with Chun and his era could not have been closer. Their personal connection went back to schooldays, and troops under Roh's command provided the force which backed the coup of 1979. But in 1987, as riot police battled a rising tide of demonstrations which spread beyond the universities to involve significant numbers of the Seoul middle class, Roh despite being Chun's chosen successor as DJP leader broke with the president. He insisted in June that a full acceptance of the opposition's demands for constitutional democratization was the only way to defuse the crisis.

In retrospect Roh's judgement was as correct as his tactics were shrewd. Although the United States enjoyed only a diminished influence in Seoul such a move was in keeping with Washington's urgings. The alternative was a more stringent use of force which would probably have required a declaration of martial law to be effective. This would have been very unpopular with many junior and middle ranking officers, and may have split the military. Even if carried through it would also have prevented Seoul from realising the enormous diplomatic and public relations achievements to be reaped from a successful staging of the Olympic Games in 1988. Roh's estimate of the specifically political impact of his tactics was also accurate. On the one hand he put some distance between Chun and himself while still inheriting the control of the DJP, on the other, he opened the possibility of a split in the opposition camp between the followers of Kim Dae-jung and of Kim Young-sam.

In the event, the personal, ideological, and regional differences in the opposition camp resulted once again in division just at a time when unity would most probably have delivered them office. Running against each other as much as against the DJP, the two Kims along with Kim Jong-pil, who led the revived remnants of the Park political machine, were beaten by Roh Tae-woo who achieved a plurality of the votes in the presidential contest of December 1987. The fundamentally fissiparous nature of the opposition may be judged by the fact that no lessons were learned in this encounter, the pattern repeating itself in the elections to the National Assembly of April 1988. Electoral reform, however, brought an uncertain legacy. With no party commanding a majority in the National Assembly which now had enhanced powers, it was not clear how legislature and executive would interact.

Demilitarising Korean Politics?

So far, Roh Tae-woo has presided over a political system in which democratization has proceeded by fits and starts. However, sufficient changes have been made to the personnel and practices inherited from the Fifth Republic for 1988 to have marked the beginning of a new if still uncertain era in Korean politics. A few examples illustrate this contention.

With the administration only a few months old, the Chief Justice, Kim Yong-chul, stepped down after a petition calling for his removal received wide support from the legal community. For many years the judiciary was an instrument unable or unwilling to check the executive. For example Park was known to detain members of the bench without due process if their decisions displeased him. Of even greater significance, the new standing of the military was shown by the dismissal of the chief of the Army Intelligence Command, and the arrest of two Brigadier Generals under his command after it became known that personnel from that unit were responsible for an assault on a journalist who had written a critical account of the armed forces. Given that the intelligence arm of the military along with the KCIA, which was renamed the Agency for National Security Planning, had previously been able to act as a law unto themselves, this was a significant development. Exemplary treatment was meted out to a number of those closest to the former president. Chun's younger brother was sentenced to a seven-year term of imprisonment for embezzlement and corruption, and several of Chun's associates who were former military men were also disgraced and punished. In fact Chun Doo-hwan himself was forced to offer a public apology for his errors, return his wealth to the state and testify before the National Assembly.

To an extent Roh has been forced to adopt a stern retrospective view by his lack of a majority in the National Assembly since nvestigative panels from the National Assembly have been reviewing the misdeeds associated with the Fifth Republic. Though Roh has since pleaded with the nation that Chun has suffered enough. In addition, such action helped establish his bona fides as a champion of democracy, though some critics have maintained that his connections with Chun being no advantage Roh has been forced through self interest to put as much distance between himself and his predecessor as possible.

In moving to surround himself with new people, however, Roh has been free to employ former military personnel. After working for a time with a cabinet many of the members of which were Chun appointees, Roh instituted a thorough reorganisation of his administration in December 1988. Of the 25 cabinet members, 7 were former officers including two of Roh's classmates from the Korean Military Academy (*FEER* 15 December 1988). Individuals closely identified with Chun have not, however, entirely disappeared from powerful office. In moving in August 1989 to displace critics within the DJP, Roh reinstated as floor leader in the National Assembly and secretary general two individuals, the latter, Lee Choon-koo, a retired one-star general, who had held those same posts during the former administration (*The Korea Herald* 31 August 1989). These developments, though they show the continuing political role of military figures, admit of more than one interpretation. Korean politics, whether government or opposition, is the politics of connections and relationships (Jacobs 1985:chapter 2). Roh's connections happen to be largely military, so his use of them is not necessarily conclusive evidence that he rules in the name of a single and coherent military interest. Indeed, recent personnel changes have confirmed the view that there is a powerful regional factor at work. The upper echelon of the DJP is now held by a group of civilians as well as military personnel known sometimes as the TK faction after Roh's hometown and region of *Taegu-Kyongsang*.

If military personnel are still significant political actors there are clear signs that not all senior military figures are happy with Roh's tenure of power. After an extraordinary incident in which the superintendent of the KMA criticised government policy after snubbing the president at a public ceremony, Roh ordered a reshuffle of top military posts which affected 48 army generals (*The Korea Newsreview* 1 April 1989). More recently there have been moves to restructure the command system of the armed forces in order to ensure loyalty to the head of state (*FEER* 16 November 1989).

Perhaps even more than personnel, policy choices are likely to be the crucial indicator of the character of Roh's administration. A major test for Roh's freedom of action from indebtedness to the military interest, as well as his commitment to thoroughgoing democratization, will be seen in his handling of the security problem. This is an issue of enormous complexity, the difficulties surrounding it compounded by bitter historical experience and intensely held nationalistic sentiments. Here, in brief, the indications are mixed. In 1988 a number of bold statements were made on the need to end confrontation with North Korea. Some of the steps to facilitate this included affirming the right of citizens to debate unification issues which required access to hitherto forbidden materials from and about North Korea. Other forms of new contacts, including freedom to buy North Korean goods were proposed. There were even suggestions that the National Security Law which defines North Korea as an enemy state and decrees harsh penalties for any dealings with it should be amended or even abandoned.

But the realization of such a change of policy entails the overcoming of many obstacles. Dealing with the military interest is the most obvious since the whole rationale of South Korea's powerful and well-funded military forces is founded upon confrontation with North Korea and recent events have shown that the need for vigilance against Pyongyang is no mere relic of history. However, managing a new initiative in relations with North Korea is fraught with difficulties. It is not possible here to develop this argument in full (see Cotton 1989a), but it can be maintained that for a number of years, perhaps since 1973, avenues existed through which North-South Korean relations could have been improved. Such improvement has not been forthcoming because the two Korean regimes have sought different ends. Seoul has wanted incremental and trust-building measures ahead of any grander political union. Pyongyang on the other hand has held out for rapid movement to some form of unification. The domestic dimension to Seoul's preferred policy cannot be denied but it is one which is in keeping with historical realities which tend to be ignored by North Korea. In the case of North Korea the domestic dimension to unification policy is undoubtedly paramount, as it is Kim Il Sung's life ambition and the one achievement that would validate the claims made for his system and guarantee his place in history.

In 1984 and 1985 a number of North-South contacts came to nothing after Pyongyang broke them off most probably for the adverse propaganda impact this would have on the Chun regime. Following the 1988 statements Pyongyang moved to revive these contacts though as in the past while careful to avoid direct negotiations with the executive authorities in Seoul. But the North Koreans also acted to encourage private diplomacy, offering hospitality in Pyongyang to dissidents from Seoul knowing full well that this would be likely to disrupt any improved relations that official contacts would bring. So it proved to be, with the authorities in Seoul obliged to prosecute under the still extant National Security Law a number of individuals who either made the trip to Pyongyang (two indeed returning for the benefit of the television cameras via Panmunjom) or who sought contacts with a view to doing so. Indeed, some commentators in Seoul have characterized 1989 as the year of the regime's manipulation of "national security politics", following the charging of Kim Dae-jung for receiving funds from North Korea via a former member of his party who made a surreptitious visit to Pyongyang.

In short, President Roh's failure so far to match words with deeds in pursuing the policies he announced in 1988, lends credence to the view that he is still to be identified with the narrow security interests from which the DJP sprang. Of course the government's present policy of rigorously prosecuting any individuals who have had unauthorized contacts with the North has its logic. This is intended to send a signal to the North that it will not be permitted to use the reunification issue as a lever to influence Seoul's domestic politics. But if President Roh's much publicised "era of the common man" is truly to be realized no policy or issue can be declared off-limits to debate. Indeed, mutual trust building measures will actually have little real basis if they are constructed entirely by governments, even if the executive must remain ultimately in charge of external policy. And in practice the more people who freely visit Pyongyang, even if they are at first dissidents and radicals, the more the character of both regimes will be revealed. South Korea, with its larger population and immensely more powerful economy has little to fear from such contacts; by contrast North Korea with its rigid social controls and schlerotic socialist economic system may be infected by the very germs of dissent which are carried by such visitors.

It is apparent, then, that Roh's freedom of manuever in this crucial policy area is limited. Nor is there consistent evidence that the government is moving resolutely to dismantle the extensive domestic use of the security apparatus. In an era of transition from authoritarian rule this is not altogether surprising, but the inference to be drawn is that military and security opinion and connections retain a non-institutional but sensitive role in the sixth republic. In an area where Roh might be expected to practise a more democratic style—the organisation and conduct of the DJP—his approach has been somewhat deficient. In 1989 critics of the lack of democracy within the party were quashed, and it was made plain that Roh would himself choose his own successor as party leader and presidential candidate to avoid the internal party dissension that would be the likely product of the employment of any other mechanism.

In a wider sense, to determine the political role of the Korean military in the 1990s is also to seek an estimate of the progress that is likely to be made in further democratization. As has been shown, in 1961 and to some extent in 1979 and 1980, military intervention was facilitated by the failings of the existing political movements. If similar failings are again exhibited the military cannot be expected to vacate the political sphere entirely, even if the likelihood of a further direct intervention is not high given the transformation of the country and the military's perception of its mission.

Successful democratization requires the emergence of political parties which are organisations more durable than mere personality based factions. It requires a settled system of formal and informal rules which exclude no major interests and which are the object of popular confidence and assent. Even this minimal view of democratization has yet to be satisfied in South Korea (Han 1986). Much has changed since the final months of the Chun era and the long term prospects for the political system are undoubtedly hopeful, but it will probably take a change of generations in the political leadership before the triumph of democratization is really assured.

Perhaps the largest obstacle to this progress is the heritage of the past. Despite Roh's efforts his association with Chun and his involvement in the acts of the Chun regime are a matter of historical record. There are some past acts of the Korean state regarding which compromise will be extremely elusive, including many well documented allegations of torture and victimization, and of unexplained deaths while in security or military custody, which occurred during the fifth republic. The publicizing of such allegations has undoubtedly given rise to considerable unease amongst senior members of the armed and security forces. It must also be borne in mind that blameless members of these forces are aware that vigorous and undiscriminating National Assembly investigations may produce a security paralysis which, in the circumstances of continuing confrontation with North Korea, could invite hostile and potentially disastrous intervention. As Roh is assuredly committed not only to avoiding this scenario but also conserving his support from within the military and security sectors he will be hard pressed to protect their interests while meeting the legitimate claims of those with grievances. This issue is further complicated by that fact that the prominence of the two major opposition leaders is largely due to their having been vigorous opponents of authoritarianism since the early 1970s. They will seek to keep past wrongs on the political agenda if only to maintain their predominance.

Military Forces and the Command Structure in the 1990s

Accounting for around 32 per cent of the national budget which is a little over 5 per cent of GNP, South Korea's military forces total 650, 000 men in regular formations. To maintain these forces South Korea employs universal conscription for males of between two to three years, after the completion of which most pass into the eight reserve divisions of the Homeland Reserve Forces. South Korea also hosts around 43, 000 American service personnel, including the Second Division, for the maintenance and support of which the Korean government spent US$2.2 billion in 1988 (*The Korea Herald* 27 October 1989). This degree of military capability is required to meet the threat posed by the forces of North Korea, the command of which is in the hands of an unpredictable and unaccountable leadership. The North Korean armed forces are superior in numerical terms but not in terms of equipment, though there have received some advanced arms transfers from the Soviet Union since 1986.

This degree of military preparedness, which of course is the ultimate guarantee of the military retaining a significant role in Korean society, undoubtedly receives extensive citizen assent. The command structure is, however, the subject of much controversy (Clough 1988; 94ff; Hinton et al, 1988; MacDonald 1988:233ff). Due to the legacy of the Korean War and the existence of the ROK-US Mutual Defense Treaty of 1953-54, the senior US officer in Korea fulfills a number of commanding roles. The most important of these is Commander in Chief, Combined Forces Command, though he is also in charge of the United Nations Command, the main business of which is to maintain the Armistice Agreement. The former places many, though not all Korean forces under his operational control. If any of these forces are detached from this command for civil duties his assent must be sought.

There is no indication that this command structure has acted as a deterrent to military intervention in politics. In 1961 and 1979 the American commander was quite simply incapable of influencing events. Indeed, in the latter case Korean military formations, specifically General Roh Tae-woo's Ninth Division were acting against their superiors who they then displaced by a coup de main (Henderson 1986; Clark 1988). In the suppression of the Kwangju incident the forces initially used against the rebellion whose actions caused considerable bloodshed were not, it has been claimed, under American operational command, though some dispute this. Those employed later were detached from that command in the recognized manner in order to reoccupy the city.

While this command structure is maintained, any overt political role assumed by the military will always entail suspicions of American complicity. In domestic Korean politics this issue has therefore become the focus of criticism from radicals who berate the military with the charge that they are merely serving American purposes rather than those of the nation. Altering the command structure is fraught with all manner of difficulties, not least that it might send the wrong signals to Pyongyang, but it would be an astute move by the military in so far as it would deprive dissidents of one of their chief rallying cries. Negotiations on this issue are being conducted at present.

The Korean Military in the Perspective of Comparative Theory

It has been argued here that to a large extent the military was originally an unlikely candidates for intervention in politics, despite the advantages that the military enjoy as power wielders in developing nations (Finer 1962:6). The failure for complex historical reasons of civilian politics in the context of an extreme security dilemma provoked and provided the occasion for the 1961 coup. Huntington's (1968:194) observation that "Military explanations do not explain military interventions" is correct in this case. However, action by Park in 1972 and by Chun in 1979 and 1980 demonstrate that attempts to transform "military intervention in politics into military participation in politics" (Huntington 1968:243) were a failure. In the sense that there was insufficient energy devoted to creating a formal and institutionalised role for the military in the new civilian politics that was being ostensibly constructed, even though in practice military connections and loyalties were still crucial for the functioning of the political system. Although not a "ruler praetorian army" (Perlmutter 1977:177ff) in the full sense, the military was not displaced from politics or rendered superfluous by Park's initial efforts to create an autonomous political movement. The military role in the transformation of society (Janowitz 1977:156-8), on the other hand, cannot be denied. When Chun was given his opportunity, again by the failings of civilians as well as by the entrenched social power of the military, he did not take over the remnants of Park's political movement but sought to build another.

Yet the inability of the civilians to reap the rewards of mass protest and popular pressure which were a necessary function of the "crisis of legitimacy" created by military intervention (van Doorn 1976:28) points not only to a lack of political institutionalisation which was not unsurprising given the authoritarianism of Korea's recent history, but also to the persistence of old outlooks and styles in the cadre of political leaders who have gained prominence since the 1960s. The years since 1961 have seen the creation in Korea not only of a highly professional officer corps but also the construction of many elements of a civil society of growing sophistication. This transformation, providing its momentum is maintained and it is not disrupted by the growth of wealth inequalities, may be expected ultimately to effect the political culture, though a generation change will be necessary before it will be fully manifest in the workings of political institutions. In the meantime, and given Korea's continuing security predicament, the military will remain important though informal political actors.

10

Military Roles and Relations in Papua New Guinea

Yaw Saffu

Introduction

Civil-military relations are ultimately about the relative political power of the military establishment in a political system. In delineating the relationship, history, constitutional provisions and conventions, military professionalism and values, attitudes of officers and men, wisdom and restraint of politicians, are factors that need to be taken into account. In Papua New Guinea, as in most new states, the historical and constitutional factors are fairly clearcut, compared with issues of attitudes and behaviour.

To explain civil-military relations in Papua New Guinea, this paper looks first at the defence force inherited at independence and at the constitutional basis of the relationship. Then it looks at the roles played by the Defence Force since Independence. After that it surveys flash-points in civil-military relations. On the basis of all the foregoing and on the basis of trends in the political system the paper ends with attempts to suggest pointers to the nineties.

The Origins and Structure of the PNGDF

The present Papua New Guinea Defence Force (PNGDF) has only a tenuous link with the war-time mobilization of Papua New

Guineans into Australian-led Infantry Regiments (Nelson 1980). Demobilization after the war was completed within a few months. The establishment of a defence force in 1950-51 was firmly under the aegis of the Australian colonial power and, without putting too fine a point on it, was intended primarily as part of Australian defence strategy (East 1985). The PNG armed forces had no role in the country's decolonization. Australia's smart decolonization footwork deprived PNG of even a decent nationalist struggle. There was no really large, country-wide nationalist party with depth in society and a place in the hearts of the masses, let alone a nationalist guerrila army. Thus, the military has no legendary, heroic past to exploit in its contest with civilian institutions for power, unlike, for instance, the neighbouring Indonesian army. Its one brief period of glory occurred after independence, when it helped Vanuatu put down a secessionist bid in 1980.

The defence force inherited at independence consisted of 3681 military personnel divided among an army, a navy and an airforce (Mench 1976; East 1985). All the services came under an integrated command. A Brigadier was Commander and six Colonels below him were in charge of headquarters functions such as operations, personnel, and logistics while Lt. Colonels were in charge of the operational units, such as the infantry battalions, the air transport squadron and the patrol boat squadron.

The army, the largest of the services, with just over 3000 officers and men, had two infantry battalions, an engineer battalion, a signal squadron and several logistics units. The First battalion of the Royal Pacific Infantry Regiment (1- RPIR) was based at Taurama Barracks in Port Moresby while 2-RPIR was based at Moem Barracks in Wewak, with a rifle company in Vanimo, at the northern end of the PNG-Indonesia border. The engineer battalion and the signals squadron were based at Murray Barracks, the PNGDF headquarters in Port Moresby. The navy, consisting of one patrol boat squadron and a landing craft squadron and numbering about 400 officers and men, was equipped with five attack class patrol boats and two heavy landing craft. The naval base was at Lombrum, Manus, the most northerly island, while the landing craft squadron was based in the capital. The airforce, the smallest of the services, with about 100 officers and men, operated four Dakota aircrafts and was based at Lae. Recruit training was at Goldie Barracks in Port Moresby. Officer training was at Lae. Advanced training was in Australia.

By 1989, the structure of the PNGDF had hardly changed. What had clearly changed was the composition of the officer corps and the NCOs. On the eve of independences there were 79 PNG officers, mostly junior officers, out of a total officer establishment of

356 (22 per cent). In 1977, two years after independence, there were 306 Australian loan personnel, constituting about 75 percent of the officer corps and 50 percent of NCO's (Mench 1976; *Pacific Defence Reporter* 1978). Four years later, the number of Australian loan personnel had declined to 125 (Hiri 1981). By 1989, there were fewer than forty loan personnel, half of them with the Air Transport Squadron, the rest in advisory roles. From a national officer corps of two Lt. Cols, eight Majors, 22 Captains and forty-seven lieutenants and 2nd lieutenants on the eve of independence, the entire officer corps had been localized, not counting the thirty percent or so who had left the force or died since independence.[1] With the rapid localization also went a speedy indigenization of the barracks culture which at independence was apparently indistinguishable from the genuine Australian article. Indeed, Mench observed that discipline in the PNGDF was stricter and the scope of military regulations more comprehensive than in Australia. By 1989, however, Melanesian culture and *wantokism* had evidently become stronger bases of action and behaviour in the barracks than the codes of military discipline and traditions of Australian military barracks (Mench 1976:148; *Report of Defence General Board of Inquiry* 1989).

There had been proposals and decisions to relocate, expand, reduce, or establish facilities. The most important of these was a September 1983 Cabinet decision which imposed a ceiling of 3050 military personnel (including 300 trainees), and the proposed relocation of several units. However, by 1989, except for the reduction in manpower, few of those had been implemented, either because political will was lacking or because there were no funds. Appropriation for Defence, before the 1983 decision to put the brakes on, was K27.4M or 6.6 per cent of all departmental appropriations. This compared with 5.8 per cent for Primary Industry, 9.6 per cent for Education and 8.9 per cent for Police (*Budget Speech and Related Bills* 1984). Two years later, with a new government in place, the relative appropriations had changed only a little: 6.3 per cent for Defence compared with 4.4 percent for Primary Industry, 7.2 percent for Education and 7.5 per cent for Police (*Budget Speech and Related Bills* 1986).

As Paul Mench (1976b) had discovered a decade earlier, per head of service personnel, the PNGDF cost the tax payer much more than did their African counterparts for instance. Cost was one reason the proposed relocation of the patrol boat squadron to Port Moresby, and the establishment of two forward operation patrol boat bases at Kieta in North Solomons and Wewak on the northern littoral, did not materialize. The proposed relocation of the engineer battalion to Lae, with one engineering platoon permanently located at Vanimo and Kiunga, also did not materialize. Neither did the proposed amalgamation of the recce platoons of 1- and 2-RPIR into a special services unit to be based at Nadzab. The proposed relocation of the air transport squadron from Lae to Nadzab only some 45 kilometres away did not happen. The decision to establish a rifle company base at Kiunga, the mining town on the middle border with Indonesia, was the only one implemented relatively quickly.

The only large capital expenditure on defence undertaken by the PNG government since independence was the purchase of three Israeli Arava light transport aircraft in 1985. The addition of two Dakotas, five Nomad aircraft and four helicopters to the air transport squadron was by courtesy of Australia, through the Defence Cooperation Program. Replacement of the patrol boats with longer range Pacific Class boats in 1987 was similarly arranged. Thus, cost-cutting as an explanation for the 1983 cabinet decision to reduce military personnel is sustainable. But was it also the civilian authorities' undeclared war of attrition on the military? If the 1983 decisions had been fully implemented, the simultaneous effects of reducing the size of the military, dispersing operational units, especially the recce platoons, away from Port Moresby, and seeming to increase the external defence function by spelling it out in realistic detail was compatible with a strategy of occupying the force more fully and also increasing the difficulties for would-be coup makers.

As the above details indicate, the PNGDF is small, particularly in juxtaposition with the Indonesian army, the putative external adversary. Despite carefully cultivated good relations between PNG and her giant neighbour,[2] suspicions about Indonesia, although waning, still persist. The legacy of her expansionist phase in the sixties, the incorporation of Irian Jaya, the consequent activities of the *Organisasi Papua Merdeka* (OPM), the West Irianese Free Papua Movement, which attempts from time to time to operate from PNG territory, a 500-mile land border and occasional incursions by Indonesian armed forces (in hot pursuit of guerrilas, or because the border is not well demarcated, or because navigational instruments failed), still make relations touchy. But if Indonesia is PNG's potential adversary, then, realistically, the PNGDF does not have a credible conventional external defence role, unless it continues tacitly as it originated, as a forward outpost of Australia designed to buy time in the event of an Indonesian military advance.[3]

The Constitutional Planning Committee (CPC), the body which drafted PNG's constitution, agonized over the relevance and cost of the PNGDF (*Constitutional Planning Committee Final Report* 1974). However, because in the end it was inconsistent, it missed an opportunity to be innovative. The Committee was sceptical about an external defence role. It agreed there was an internal security role but it was frankly alarmed by the thought, with all the experience of political role expansion by the African military before it. Even the idea of a civic action role did not seem convincing to the Committee. It therefore asked why the resources in question could not be directed to appropriate civil departments. Despite these underlying reservations, however, the CPC ended up with recommendations which ratified the existence of a conventional military institution within a familiar liberal democratic pattern of civil-military relations.

Sundhaussen (1974) and Mench (1976) advocates an institutionalized but limited political role for the military, such as representation in Parliament and Cabinet, in order, they allege, to stop them from installing outright military rule, since they and others seemed to think military rule virtually inevitable and imminent. In PNG, however, the CPC put the military firmly under the civilian cabinet and gave it no unusual political role. The cabinet (in effect the National Security Council, more or less a cabinet sub-committee) made appointments at the Lt. Colonel rank and above. A Defence Council, made up of the minister for defence, the commander of PNGDF and the civilian secretary of the defence department, was supposed to make the initial recommendations but it was routinely bypassed and overruled by cabinet.[4]

Functions of the PNGDF

The CPC which had articulated such scepticism over a credible external defence role nevertheless argued that for the Defence Force to be competent and professional, which it assumed was what the country wanted, it should be firmly orientated towards external defence. However, it could be predicted that the four functions which the CPC prescribed for the Defence Force would orientate it heavily towards an internal security role rather than external defence. The functions which were enshrined in the Constitution were:

(a) the defence of Papua New Guinea
(b) the fulfilment of international or treaty obligations
(c) the provision of assistance to civil authorities in the circumstances of a state of emergency
(d) the performance of services of a civic nature.

These functions have been endorsed and amplified in all official defence policy statements including the latest, an April 1988 Defence White Paper, approved by the Wingti Cabinet but yet to be tabled in Parliament. The defence of Papua New Guinea has been specified in the White Paper as maintaining an effective "core" force to guard against low level external threats; patrolling Papua New Guinea's international border and carrying out effective maritime survelliance (*Papua New Guinea Defence White Paper* 1988).

So far, the PNGDF has not had to perform under treaty and international obligations, unless joint exercises and war games with friendly countries, Australia, New Zealand, the UK and the US, come under that category. In September 1988, Foreign Minister Somare offered PNG troops for United Nations Peacekeeping Operations. The offer has not been taken up yet. The Defence of the realm has involved the Defence Force in border patrols and the air and maritime elements have helped to protect PNG's marine resources in the economic zone from foreign boats. However, as in the area of civic action programs, lack of adequate funding has restricted achievements. PNG governments evidently believe they get more political mileage by handing out funds to MPs, allegedly for development projects, rather than channeling the funds through the armed forces for civic action projects. In 1988, for instance, a third of the three million kina earmarked for civic action projects was diverted to the National Development Fund (NDF), known as MPs' slush fund, to buy the support of MPs during the run up to the vote of no confidence in July (*The Times of PNG* 14-20 April 1988). The military's internal security role, helping the Police in state of emergency situations and in counter-insurgency operations, as in the North Solomons Province, has appeared to be the primary preoccupation. It has certainly had a higher profile than the other functions.

The PNGDF's Internal Security Role

The PNGDF has been called out four times since independence to help the Police in law and order operations. All these have occurred only since 1984. In that year, when a state of emergency was declared in Port Moresby in the face of a rapidly deteriorating law and order situation, the military was called out to help the police (in Operation Green Beret). In 1987, the defence force was called out again to help the police in Operation Coolex, covering Morobe, Madang and the Eastern Highlands provinces. In 1988, in Operation

LO-MET (Law and Order: Murder, Entry and Tribal Fighting) the Defence Force was called out to help the police restore law and order to the Highlands provinces. Currently the armed froces are involved in counterinsurgency operations in the North Solomons province. That such would turn out to be a major preoccupation of the defence force was widely predicted (Mench 1976; CPC Final Report 1974). On the basis of most demographic, social and political projections, the occasions for such call outs are not going to disappear in the near future (Clifford et. al., 1986; Harris 1988). The Defence White Paper concurs: "The most likely use of the Defence Force within the next decade will be to deal with internal threat situations---public disorder, secession, insurgency, subversion and terrorism" (*Papua New Guinea Defence White Paper* 1988:2). It acknowledges that law and order or internal security is primarily police function but that effort to support civilian authorities to minimize internal security problems contributes to national development.

Yet there is strong evidence for the view that the performance of the internal security role is not popular with officers. During the sitting of the Defence Board of Enquiry, prompted by servicemen's rampage in February 1989, submissions by officers criticized the use of soldiers for what they termed "small-scale emergencie" or "police work" (*Post Courier* 30 March 1989). The point was made most insistently that soldiers are not trained for police role, although that claim is not totally correct in PNG. According to Mench (1976:117), as far back as 1974, 25 to 30 per cent of infantry officer training time was devoted to internal security training. It was also argued that frequent deployment of soldiers under Police officers was likely to lead to a breakdown of the military command structure. The then Secretary of the defence department claimed that such call outs demoralized not only the Defence Force (soldiers' welfare funds had to be raided because call outs were not normally budgeted for) but the Police as well, backing his claim by quoting from a memo from a top police officer (*Post Courier* 29 May 1989).

While large-scale counterinsurgency operations, as in the North Solomons, should be more acceptable to officers as legitimate defence force roles, there is some evidence to suggest that the hearts and minds of PNG soldiers may perhaps be in conflict over their role even in such situations. There have been emotional scenes at the Port Moresby airport involving uniformed men publicly berating the minister for defence, and swearing at him, presumably for being a politician, and, hence, responsible for the North Solomons situation and for the death of the soldier whose body had just been brought. Normal differences between civilian authorities and soldiers in such counter-insurgency situations, with soldiers feeling that they are being unduly restricted from prosecuting the war, have also surfaced. Opportunistic criticisms by opposition politicians, such as Paias Wingti states that "The Defence Force should not be used to fight its own people" (*Post Courier* 8 May 89), serves to fortify beliefs and sentiments that might be lurking among the military that they should have no internal security role.

Flares and Flashes in Civil-Military Relations

There have been a number of incidents originating on both sides of the civil-military relationship which have invariably prompted observers and commentators to ask whether a coup was imminent. Especially those incidents which could be portrayed as acts of sheer indiscipline, or a wanton display of their sense of power by soldiers, have aroused disquiet and provoked speculation. This section presents a survey of incidents in civil-military relations since independence.

The first incident was the so-called Diro Affair in 1977. In August 1977, Brigadier Ted Diro, the first Papua New Guinean Commander of PNGDF, met with leaders of the OPM in Wewak. The government declared the meeting unauthorised. The Irian Jaya/OPM issue has always been a very sensitive issue for PNG governments. Diro claimed he briefed the minister of defence. The government nevertheless decided to reprimand him. Diro meanwhile sought and obtained from his senior officers a pledge of loyalty to himself as commander and then issued a belligerent statement warning the Prime Minister: "I want you to know that the force is becoming sick to death of being made a political football by certain politicians and ex-politicians" (Hegarty 1978). In the same article Hegarty (ibid.) states that relations between the government and military authorities in the preceding weeks had been strained on account of the army's involvement in a community development project associated with a prominent opposition politician.

In 1981, Ted Diro resigned as Commander in order to contest the 1982 elections. Diro's successor, Colonel Gago Mamae, was clearly eligible, being one of the three most senior officers. Although eligible, Mamae was junior to Colonel Ken Noga who was passed over apparently because of Diro's personal antipathies.[5] But as it was the Chan government that made the appointment, a political explanation was evidently given by Pangu leaders. Noga had unsuccessfully contested the 1977 elections as a pro-Pangu candidate. Therefore, when Pangu returned to power in 1982 under Michael Somare, the government moved to replace Gago Mamae, who was only halfway through his term, with Col. Noga. The replacement of Gago Mamae with Noga in turn appeared blatantly political. Mamae immediately resigned and joined Julius Chan's PPP office as an Exeuctive Officer. After unsuccessfully contesting the 1987 elections on PPP ticket he continued to work for Chan.

At the beginning of 1985, Col. Tony Huai, also considered for the Commander's position in 1982, publicly criticised the government's handling of the Defence Force and resigned. Like Brigadier Mamae, Tony Huai also began to work in the PPP's office. When Wingti became Prime Minister in November 1985, after a successful vote of no-confidence against the Somare government, Sir Julius Chan became Deputy Prime Minister. In December, Ken Noga was removed as Commander and replaced with Tony Huai. Political partisanship in top PNGDF appointments was now beyond doubt. Technically, Tony Huai was not even an officer. The Defense Department argued against the appointment but political suitability of the commander appeared to drive every other consideration to the back seat. A report in the *Post Courier* (10 December 1985) indicated that there was a certain amount of resistance to the appointment from senior officers.

Tony Huai's command proved to be eventful. He vowed openly to crush the OPM, and was subsequently accused of imposing a military policy on the civilian authority (*Post Courier* 27 March 1986; 1 April 1986). Huai was opposed to the defense provisions in the Joint Declaration of Principles which Papua New Guinea was negotiating with Australia in 1987. As a result he made a number of secret visits to Indonesia and leaked progress of the negotiations to General Murdani, Commander of the Indonesian Armed Forces, who evidently thanked him in kind (*The Times of PNG* 24 December 1987 - 7 January 1988). For these reasons Huai was dismissed at the end of 1987 and replaced by Col. Rochus Lokinap, the first non-Papuan to the position, a New Irelander from Julius Chan's Namatanai constituency.[6]

At the time of Huai's dismissal, Ted Diro was fighting for his own political survival, having come out very badly in a Commission that enquired into the PNG Forest Industry. Leading a Papuan bloc in Parliament and reported to have good connections with serving officers, Diro fuelled rumours of a coup by making inflammatory speeches, claiming that "all the ingredients for a coup are here" and that he did not want to be blamed when it occurred (*Post Courier*, 16 November 1987). In the aftermath of the Pacific watershed coup in Fiji, when the possibility of a coup in PNG was no longer discussed only by academics and political commentators, Diro's statement aroused much speculation and rumour-mongering. In January 1988, before the rumours could die down, three Colonels, all of them Papuans, were cashiered for reasons which were never satisfactorily explained (Saffu 1988). This added more grist to the coup rumour mill.

The period June 1988 to February 1989 showed the most disquieting examples of sheer indiscipline in the PNGDF as well as acts of insubordination to the civilian authority. The most flagrant exhibition of military disregard for civilian authority so far in PNG occurred in June 1988 (*Post Courier* 14 June 1988). In 1987, cabinet decided to close down Lae airport. After twelve months' grace, all air traffic operations, including the Air Transport Squadron's, were to relocate to Nadzab. For the Defence Force, the move would be an implementation of the 1983 cabinet decision referred to earlier.

On 1 June 1988, the Minister for Civil Aviation duly announced the closure of Lae airport. The same day, the Defence Force authorities flew soldiers from Port Moresby to Lae and literally took over the airport. They put up a barricade around the airport and dared any civil aviation personnel to cross it. Three days later, the Commander of the Defence Force called a press conference to announce the grounding of all defence force planes. After a severe reprimand by the Prime Minister, Brigadier Lokinap claimed that "certain defence force officers went beyond my lawful instructions" (*Post Courier*,14 June 1988). He assured the government and the people of PNG of the force's undivided loyalty. But events from then on suggested that neither he nor the colonels below him could guarantee the loyalty of servicemen because indiscipline had clearly become a very serious problem in the defence force, undermining authority within it and bringing into question its reliability.

In September, drunken officers attacked the National Broadcasting Commission (NBC) studio and stopped a broadcast in progress simply because the previous day an airforce Captain had suffered bruises from fighting an NBC security guard who had prevented him from visiting his estranged wife at the NBC single quarters (*Times of PNG* 27 October -2 November 1988). Two days later, at the Taurama Barracks, more than twenty soldiers attacked a bakery and severely injured three workers after two of their colleagues were refused service after the shop had closed. Two duty policemen who went to investigate were also assaulted by the angry soldiers (ibid). The following weekend, soldiers from the same barracks attacked duty policemen near Murray Barracks when police tried to arrest one of them for drinking alcohol in the street (ibid). This list is by no means exhaustive. In all these instances, soldiers were clearly placing themselves above the law and were using violence to achieve illegal ends, displaying how power drunk they had become. With their access to guns, the attentive public was justified in feeling alarmed.

The most frightening example yet of military indiscipline in PNG occurred in February 1989 when some 300 to 400 soldiers who were dissatisfied with their pay increases defied the orders of their officers and took to the streets. Joined by unemployed youths with their own grievances, they marched on Parliament, damaging vehicles and property and threatening people en route. A panicked government immediately gave in to their demands,[7] but it suspended the commander, the chief of staff and the secretary of the department of defense, and set up a General Defence Board of Inquiry to investigate the rampage and the entire administration and management of the PNGDF including the Defence Department. The findings and recommendations of the Board of Enquiry speak volumes about the present state of the PNGDF and, hence, give strong indications of likely future military roles and relations in PNG.

Pointers to the Future

The Report of the Defence Board of Inquiry portrays a demoralized, discontented Defence Force with discipline problems, poor training and indifferent administration. The 1983 cabinet decision to reduce the PNGDF manpower and underfunding was responsible for a great deal of this unsatisfactory situation. But also implicit on most pages of the report are the consequences of the rapid officer and NCO localization: erosion of professionalism, inadequately trained and inexperienced officers and managerial problems. The report avoids mentioning political manipulation of appointments and the instability at the top of the PNGDF command structure induced by these. A critical review of the Report will aid predictions about the future.

Essentially the report calls for the expansion of the defence force by removing the 1983 ceiling on manpower, as does the 1988 Defence White Paper. Improvements were recommended in housing; transportation; recreational facilities; welfare services; pay; leave entitlements; retirement awards; training facilities; equipment and the calibre of training instructors. The Report comes across as a statement of corporate military grievances and what should be done about them. Yet a great deal of what should be done boils down to increase funding for the armed forces.

It is not likely that the politicians' perceptions of what it takes to get re-elected will include enormously increased spending on defence. Both an expansion and a substantial improvement in the conditions protested about will thus be most unlikely. Also, given the dissatisfaction that exists in the Police and the Corrective Institutions and the very direct way in which dissatisfaction is usually shown in PNG, even by the so-called disciplined forces, no government will be allowed to go very far in meeting the demands of the defence force without substantially increasing its outlay on these other services. Maintenance of relativities is likely to make the attempt at meeting the defence force demands so expensive that the attempt would seem unlikely.

Further, there is almost certainly a difference in perceptions between the military and civilian leaders who have supported the call for an expanded defence force over the role of such an expanded force. The current Minister of Defense, Ben Sabumei for instance, says that the defence force should get an extra 450 recruits next year and then a lower level of increase in the subsequent years. The minister has, however, not indicated his ceiling (*Post Courier* 24 October 1989).8 But what he is talking about really is a nation building brigade or a civic action brigade, anything but a defence force, as the military know it. The defence force, according to Sabumei, "should be carrying out government's development programmes and priorities ... while basic soldiering skills for combat situations should continue to be maintained at respectable levels of competence" (*Post Courier* 14 June 1989). The Defense Minister says there is no need for "large arms spending as PNG faces no threat of armed conflict sufficient to justify large spending on arms or training soldiers. The K30-40m defense budget can be better spent elsewhere in nation building, using qualified resources in trained manpower and equipment we have [in the defence force]" (ibid; *Post Courier* 30 June 1989).

Defense Minister Sabumei's views appear to be representative of the general attitudes and views of PNG politicians. Indeed, the Report of the Defense Board of Inquiry acknowledges that submissions from many citizens questioned the need for a defense force in peace time. But, interestingly, the Report then testily demands that the State of PNG too justify its existence! (*Report of the Defence Board* of Inquiry 1989:53). The Report goes on to indicate acceptance by the military of an expanded civic action role, provided the defense force is expanded and funding is adequate. Two civilians who have, however, worked for long periods in the defense department express scepticism and indicate that at least a massive public relations and propaganda effort will be necessary over a long period before the kind of civic action brigade concept the politicians have in mind would be fully accepted by the military.9 Thus a potential collision course would seem to loom for the future, not only over manning levels, but more importantly, over what the manning is for, and also over the style and conditions of life of increased manpower.

Other recommendations in the Report that do not entail primarily a massive injection of funds into defense nevertheless present their own difficulties. For instance, nationalist sensitivities will probably block any schemes aimed at the reinfusion of needed discipline, professionalism, qualified and experienced instructors and seasoned military managers, through a substantial increase in Australian loan personnel.

With other recommendations such as changes in the command structure, politicians' myopia and a lack of political will could cause delays in implementation and aggravate officer dissatisfaction. Continued use of the criterion of political suitability for appointment and promotion, rather than competence and seniority, could also be a source of officer dissatisfaction. Officers have evidently complained for a long time about the deleterious effects which politically motivated changes at the top have on morale, discipline and efficiency.[10] The desire of politicians to gain political mileage by interfering in operational matters during internal security operations could also provide the military with cause for grievance. For instance, a politician (albeit with a military background) reportedly approved the use of booby traps after the Defense Headquarters had turned down the request from the field commander in the North Solomons operations. Soldiers have since been killed trying to set the booby traps.

Corporate grievances then are likely to persist into the nineties. But will they constitute sufficient grounds for pessimism regarding military intervention in the nineties? So far, corporate grievances have provided the basis for the military's move from influence to blackmail, to use the famous four-step progression of military intervention put forward by Finer (1962) from influence to blackmail to displacement and finally to supplantment. The issues on which the military might move to a more permanent or continuous blackmail stage will increase, compared to the eighties.

In addition to pay and conditions of service, the following are likely to be added to the list in the nineties: the use of the military in internal law and order situations and as a civic action brigade; disgust with corruption among politicians; interference in military affairs, especially politicization of defence appointments and dismissals. However, the underlying consensus and widespread agreement among PNG elites on the economy (essentially pro-private enterprise and capitalism) and on foreign policy (where the underlying consensus is essentially pro-West, suspicious of the Russians and hysteria about communism, in an almost obsolete Cold

War fashion) are not likely to crumble seriously in the nineties. Ideological political basis for military blackmail of civilian authority is thus, in my view, likely to be precluded.

To be able to predict whether the military will move to the higher stages of displacement and, particularly, replacement, beliefs of officers regarding the relative desirability of civilian and military government need to be known. Alternatively, the performance of the civilian authorities must be so abysmal that an impending collapse of the existing system becomes predictable. In PNG, as in most other countries, direct scrutiny of the political beliefs of soldiers is not easy. However, a tradition which has been built up so far provides evidence of a substantial support for civilian supremacy. Disgruntled officers and politically ambitious soldiers have chosen to resign and contest elections rather than plot to overthrow the government. Patterson Lowa, beaten to the Commander's post by Ted Diro, started the tradition, two years after independence. He resigned and stood for Parliament in 1977. He is now a prominent member of the Melanesian Alliance party and Minister for Minerals and Energy. Others followed him, as we have seen.[11] To the extent that the tradition has kept an alternative option open to the ambitious or the disgruntled soldier, to that extent the personal factor, the individual ambition, grievance or fustration, which (Decalo 1976) highlights in the explanation of military interventions in Africa, may be discounted in the PNG situation.

But if the personal factor and corporate grievances may be discounted as triggers for a military takeover in the medium term in PNG, the same cannot be confidently said of the pull factor emanating from the socio-political environment. A serious crisis of ungovernability is looming in PNG. A failure of leadership is the primary culprit. Some leaders choose to follow the grassroots, rather than attempting to lead them, in matters of compensation, for instance, and in the manner of expressing demands, with violence, and in total disregard of the law. Other leaders dedication to their freedom of action, in advancing themselves politically and economically, is such that it is incompatible with organizational cohesion and is detrimental to stability. Above all, most leaders' evident determination to push the adversarial nature of the Westminster system to the limits makes any notion of a national interest or a settled bi-partisan approach to any such national interest a virtual impossibility.[12] There is a real danger of the system collapsing through a lack of effective leadership, a sense of direction and the political will to stop the slide towards ungovernability. The results from all this failure of leadership are a disturbing increase in lawlessness, disregard for authority, indiscipline, instability and violence.

In my view, the most likely scenario for a military intervention beyond blackmail is a political role expansion of the military through their overuse in the circumstances of a crisis of ungovernability induced by the failure of leadership, breakdown of law and order, unsustainable demands for compensation backed by violence, insurgencies and threats of secession. It is the necessary involvement of the Defence Force on a more continuous basis in the efforts to pull the nation back from such impending headlong plunge, the consequential political role expansion of the military and possible fustrations and, almost certainly, the ambitions of conniving politicians, rather than the spread of any strong anti-liberal democratic, anti-capitalist ideology, that could lead to a military takeover.

For the sake of Papua New Guinea, my fervent hope is that this scenario does not materialize because, contrary to the received opinion in Papua New Guinea, I do not know of many Third World countries where a coup is so technically difficult that it can be discounted. And, from the African experience at least, once a coup succeeds technically, chances are very high that it will also be able to survive politically, at least for a while, with the junta being able to draw on the support of malcontents and opportunists.

Summary

The argument of the paper is that the PNGDF ceased to have a credible external defence role when it stopped being a formal colonial institution and a part of the Australian armed forces. Consequently, questions about its relevance and cost were raised. Answers revealed a divergence between civilian and military views. This was shown most clearly in the 1983 Cabinet decision to reduce the size of the defence force and in the recent, 1989 Defence Board of Enquiry Report.

How PNG governments respond to the recommendations of the report, and whether they refrain from further politicization of defence appointments, will determine to a significant extent the future role of the PNGDF. But increasing disregard for authority and an escalating lawlessness throughout PNG society, as the eighties draw to a close, pose the greatest threat to the existing liberal democratic pattern of civil-military relations in the medium term.

Notes

1. The informed estimates are those of an ex-official from the department of defence and some officers.
2. Several agreements had been signed between the two culminating in the 1986 Treaty of Mutual Respect, Cooperation and Friendship.
3 This assumption is widely held among the PNG elite. Ted Diro articulated this in 1978 when he was Commander of the PNGDF. See the *Pacific Defence Reporter*, 1978:263. On the Australian side this assumption would account for a large part of her continuing generosity towards PNG.
4. Interview with former secretary of department of defense.
5. Interview 30 September 1989.
6. Claims that there is a struggle for regional supremacy between the Papuans and the New Guinea Islanders dates from the appointment of Col. Lokinap. Sir Julius Chan is an influential politician in the Wingti government and the Papua New Guinean politician who takes the most interest in the PNGDF. Along with Chan the secretary of defence is a New Irelander with regional ties to Chan, giving rise to conspiracy theories. Diro, Mamae, Noga and Huai are all Papuans. Mench (1976:130-131,153) has shown that Papuans and New Guinea Islanders were over-represented in the PNGDF at independence, while the Highlanders were under-represented. The officer corps and NCOs had been dominated by Papuans. This pattern is changing but very slowly. Recruitment policy has not attempted to reduce past imbalances by positive discrimination. The yearly in-take of recruits is an exercise in equal representation of the provinces to the extent compatible with the criteria of merit, physical fitness and good character references.
7. The government claimed that the pay increase announced by the deputy prime minister to the demonstrating soldiers had been authorized earlier and that it was the defence department's tardiness in implementing the decision that had resulted in the soldiers' frustration.
8. One of Sabumei's predecessors in the ministry, James Pokasui, who was a captain in the army said he would raise the size of the PNGDF to 10,000 if he had his way (interview, 30 October 1989).
9. Interviews 30 October 1989.
10. Interview 30 October 1989.
11. A comparison with the Fijian situation springs to mind. What if Rabuka had obtained the Police Commissioner's job he applied for when, on top of feeling that there was no room for upward movement within the Royal Fijian Armed Forces, he was also threatened with a court martial? A similar tradition might have started in Fiji.
12. I have tried, in recent installments of the PNG Political Chronicle in the *Australian Journal of Politics and History,* to trace the emerging crisis of ungovernability. The February issues of the *Asian Survey* also have

country surveys including PNG which can be consulted. But perhaps the most direct way of coming to grips with the crisis is to read a month's issue of the *Post Courier* or the *Niugini Nius*. The reporters on these papers are nationals, not some prejudiced foreign journalists.

11

The Politicization of Military Professionalism in Fiji

Jim Sanday

Introduction

On 14 May 1987, Lieutenant Colonel Sitiveni Rabuka overthrew the newly elected democratic government of Fiji. The government led by Dr Timoci Bavadra was a coalition of the Labour and National Federation parties. The coalition was officially formalized in December 1986 to contest the April 1987 elections which it won by capturing 28 seats, while the incumbent Alliance government led by Ratu Sir Kamisese Mara, won only 24. Coup leader Rabuka felt that indigenous Fijian interests would be jeopardized by Bavadra's coalition government and used this to justify military intervention in politics. At his post coup press conference, Rabuka gave three main reasons for his intervention:

1. To forestall bloodshed that would ensue from the coalition government's alleged intention to use military force to suppress political agitation by the militant Taukei Movement,[1] which called for the ousting of the Bavadra government.

2. To curb the alleged Libyan and Russian threat to national security.

3. To safeguard indigenous Fijian interests that would allegedly be eroded by the government manipulating the

imperfections of Fiji's 1970 Constitution to undermine these interests.

The first two charges have not been substantiated and can be dismissed as lacking credibility. Subsequent disclosures made by Rabuka to the authors of his biography (Dean and Ritova 1988), that he settled on a military coup when the defeat of the ruling Alliance government was publicly disclosed on 12 April 1987, suggest that the two charges were afterthoughts used to justify political intervention. Underlying Rabuka's third charge was the observation that since Indo-Fijians in Bavadra's coalition government outnumbered representatives of the indigenous community by nineteen to seven, then it was "Indian dominated". That the rights of indigenous Fijians would therefore be eroded was a deduction made and propagandized for public consumption by Bavadra's political opponents. However, a closer examination reveals the misnomer of the "Indian dominated" label. For example, indigenous Fijian interests were protected by racial parity in Bavadra's cabinet. Fijian ministers held all the important domestic portfolios of Home Affairs, Agriculture, Fijian Affairs, Rural Development, Education and Labour. Similarly, the political leadership of the country remained in the hands of native leaders. Ratu Sir Penaia Ganilau remained Governor General, Dr Timoci Bavadra was the newly elected Prime Minister and Ratu Sir Kamisese Mara was the Leader of the Opposition. Indigenous Fijians were also predominant in the upper echelons of the civil service. Of the available 27 senior positions, 11 were held by indigenous Fijians, eight by Indo-Fijians and the rest by other ethnic groups. Indigenous Fijians similarly dominated the Army and comprised half the civil police. While the country may have had greater Indo-Fijian involvement in government than before the elections, the state machinery was certainly not "Indian dominated". Clearly, the coup leader's third charge was based entirely on personal fears that the interests of the indigenous population would be undermined by a coalition government. Whether such fears were justified will always remain a point of contention since the coup denied the coalition the opportunity to demonstrate its effectiveness as a government.

The military coup was widely portrayed in the world media as resulting from racial tensions between indigenous Fijians and Indian-Fijians (referred to as Indo-Fijians). The predominantly ethnic Fijian army is portrayed as intervening in politics to protect the interests of the indigenous population previously represented by the losing Alliance Party. The ethnic explanation of Rabuka's intervention in the context of plural politics is thus used to justify

Rabuka's action by some. For example, Dean and Ritova (1988) and Scarr (1988) rationalise the coup in purely racial terms—Scarr (ibid.) relies heavily on anecdotal evidence and takes for granted the rhetoric of coup sympathisers. A purely ethnic analysis of Rabuka's intervention fails to take into account other factors such as issues of civil-military relations, the influence of social class and the military's position and role within that structure, a position and role that rendered the military susceptible to political manipulation.

This chapter will evaluate the historical development and role of the military in Fiji in the 1980s and speculate on its role in the 1990s. The process of politicization of the armed forces will be the major theme. The development of the military will be traced from its genesis through the various stages of its formation. On the basis of this projections will then be made concerning its role in society in the 1990s. As well as conceptions of military professionalism and prevailing patterns of civil-military relations, the influence of social class and ethnic considerations are examined to clarify the military's role and position in Fiji's rather complex class structure and political economy.

The Origin and Development of the Military in Fiji

Fiji's military traces its origins to 1871 when an armed force was raised to support the government of Ratu (chief) Seru Cakobau who was the paramount native chief and titular head of the pre-colonial government. The Cakobau government was set up in 1871 by sections of the white settler community who were anxious to ensure stability for the establishment of a plantation economy based on the export of agricultural commodities such as coconut oil, cotton and subsequently sugar. Indigenous Fijians were thus introduced to the international capitalist system via a plantation economy which required the alienation of their land and the employment of their labour.

Because the Cakobau government was not universally recognised, a military force was raised to impose its authority throughout the islands. Cakobau's "Royal Army" comprised one thousand men commanded by a British officer with experience in the Crimea and India. While officers and NCOs of the Royal Army were Europeans, the general soldiery was drawn from native tribes loyal to Ratu Cakobau. Operations by the Army included the pacification of rebellious tribes in the mountains and western districts of the island of Viti Levu, which is the largest island in the archipelago. Prisoners taken in these "pacification" operations were often sold as labourers to supplement "blackbirded" [a term used to describe a South Sea Islander kidnapped and sold as a slave] Kanak labour on European owned and managed plantations. These early operations by Cakobau's Army served to forge the role of the military as being one of supporting the authority and interests of the chiefly establishment as well as defending structures created by the state to support a capitalist economy.

Colonialism and the Establishment of an Orthodoxy

At annexation in October 1874, the British inherited the Royal Army, which it continued to employ on pacification operations against rebellious native tribesmen. Again, the main victims of these operations were the tribes in the interior and western districts of Viti Levu, not yet under the domination of eastern-based confederacies. In 1876, the Royal Army was retitled the Armed Native Constabulary (ANC) remaining distinct from the civilian police and retaining its military organization and equipment. The ANC continued to be employed intermittently on pacification operations until it was disbanded in 1905. (See Appendix 1 for a history of the Fiji Military Forces).

Fiji's British Governor, Sir Arthur Gordon, moved quickly after his arrival in 1875 to establish a policy which was aimed at protecting the interests of the native population threatened with the deprivation of their land and labour by unscrupulous sections of the pre-colonial white settler community acting in collusion with some native chiefs. Gordon formulated a "native policy" which was promulgated in the 1877 Native Regulations, and codified in law the Fijian social order as he perceived it to be. Gordon adapted the highly structured social order prevailing in the eastern maritime provinces where social units were vertically integrated under the leadership of hierarchical chiefly dynasties, an order common to most Polynesian societies. This order resembled the Scottish clan system with which Gordon, the youngest son of the fourth Earl of Aberdeen, was familiar and which he used as the basis of his conceptualizations in developing a Fijian orthodoxy (France 1969:169-175). The orthodoxy developed by Gordon was subsequently applied without regard to regional diversity. Thus the legitimacy and strength of one type of Fijian leadership, suitably altered for the purposes of colonial administration, came to be established and supported by colonialism and indirect rule (Sanday 1989:122). This was the basis for later charges of "internal colonialism" raised by some western islanders against the eastern-based chiefly elite. In the context of democratic politics, perhaps the most important legacy of the British policy of indirect rule was that it established a concept of political legitimacy founded on the belief that political leadership is the exclusive preserve of chiefs—invariably the eastern chiefly elite—who were used as agents of indirect rule.

Colonialism and the Development of Monopoly Capitalism

British colonialism encouraged monopoly capitalism in Fiji because there were no alternative sources of revenue available that could enable the Crown Colony to become a self-financing member of the Empire. As a result, state structures supporting the development of a capitalist economy were quickly established. A centralized bureaucracy, a judiciary, legislative council, civil police, and an army were set up to support the capitalist economy based initially on copra, but diversifing, after 1879, to include the large-scale production of raw sugar. Expatriate commercial interests, such as the Colonial Sugar Refining Company of Australia, came to dominate the colony's capitalist economy. Large-scale raw sugar production in the western provinces required cheap plantation labour which the indigenous population could not provide because they were cocooned in village-based subsistence lifestyles by colonial policy, and as a consequence, excluded from the developing cash economy. To satisfy the demand for cheap plantation labour, indentured workers were recruited from the Indian sub-continent. Between 1879 and 1916, over 60,000 indentured labourers went to Fiji. By 1986 the national census put the Indo-Fijian population at 348,704 (48.7 per cent of the total population), outnumbering the indigenous Fijian population of 329,385 (46 per cent). Concomittantly, Indo-Fijians also came to dominate the sugar-based export economy.

The interests of native chiefs in the capitalist economy were enlisted in several ways. For example, they were co-opted into the centralized bureaucracy as agents of indirect rule and were given control of the indigenous economy and access to land rents and royalties. Their access to the latter was entrenched in 1940 by the Native Lands Ordinance which enabled chiefs to draw up to one-third of all land rents. In 1987, the total distributable income derived from land rentals and royalties was estimated at F$7.5 million [US $ 4.9 million] (*Fiji Times* 22 May 1989).

The Role of the Military in the Colonial Capitalist Economy

As the coercive arm of the state, the primary role of the military was the maintenance of the internal stability required for the development of a capitalist economy. Indeed, the roles of the military were defined, in order of importance, as being, to assist the police and civil authorities restore and maintain law and order and to train for homeland defence where resources permit.

In essence, the internal security role required the military to defend state structures established by the colonial regime to support monopoly capitalism. Invariably, this meant the defence of expatriate commercial interests, especially those of large foreign-owned corporations as well as the position and interests of leading native chiefs in the political economy. The organization of the military and the equipment it used, therefore, came to be founded on internal political factors rather than on professional military considerations, since the country's external defense was Britain's responsibility.

In the colony, the ethnic composition of the military reflected the class structure. This structure was characterized by the dominance of expatriate commercial interests and the protection of European privilege. The interests of native chiefs and their position in the political economy came next. At the bottom of this structure were Indo-Fijians and indigenes of commoner status, who were assigned manual labour categories.

Until the 1920s, commissioned ranks in the defence force were dominated by Europeans. After the 1920s, however, selected chiefs with recognized leadership ability were granted army commissions. The rank and file comprised European NCOs while part-Europeans and indigenes dominated the lower ranks of enlisted personnel. The ethnic composition of the military was heavily influenced by the colonial regime's assessment as to the suitability of the islands' main ethnic communities for martial duties. This was based on perceptions of their political reliability and allegiance to those in control of the state apparatus. The order of suitability, which influenced the ethnic composition of the military, was: Europeans, part-Europeans, indigenous Fijians and finally, Indo-Fijians. This was the order of ranking in the military when Japan entered the second World War in December 1941. Where the Indians were concerned, the attitude of the colonial regime towards their recruitment into the military was coloured, to a great extent, by the concept of the "martial races" as it was developed by the British military elite in India following the Indian mutiny of 1857.

Underlying the concept was a belief that the Hindu caste system, with its strict occupational categories, made certain castes in India better soldiers than others. This perception led the British to recruit combat troops from among the recognised martial races of India; the most notable being the Gurkhas of Nepal, Sikhs, Rajputs, Dogras, Jats and Baluchis (Gill 1986). These groups were, however, underrepresented in Fiji. Whatever negative attitude the colonial regime may have had against the military recruitment of Indo-Fijians, was reinforced by the refusal of members of that community to volunteer for military service during World War II. All these factors contributed to the alienation of that community from the military.

War in the Pacific required the expansion and mobilization of the Fiji military. During the war, the islands became an important training base and staging point for US and Allied Forces fighting the Japanese in New Guinea and the Solomon Islands. Lying astride vital sea lanes linking Australasia and the US mainland, Fiji's strategic position in the Southwest Pacific dictated that emphasis be placed on its defence against an anticipated Japanese invasion. The military was quickly expanded and personnel from the New Zealand Army filled most of the important command and staff appointments. The subsequent despatch of two infantry battalions and commando units to Guadalcanal and Bougainville, required additional manpower which was provided, in the main, by indigenous Fijians and other non-Indian ethnic groups. Significantly, the Indo-Fijian community refused to volunteer for war service. Their refusal was couched in anti-colonial rhetoric and they cited, as a matter of principle, pay differentials between themselves and European troops—there were even murmurings of support for Subhas Chandra Bose and his pro-Japanese Indian National Army fighting the Allies in Burma. Nonetheless some Indo-Fijians formed a "Fiji Indian War Effort Committee" which presented a fighter aircraft and two ambulances to the British war effort. As well, it provided cash donations to the Chinese Nationalists appeal and to the Viceroy of India's appeal for the Bengal Relief Fund

Although World War II saw many enlist for military service, ethnic and class considerations continued to dictate the distribution of ranks. For example, although several commoner ethnic Fijians were granted army commissions in the military, they were not promoted above prominent chiefs. The ideology of quasi-feudalism underpinning traditional Fijian society stressed the division between rulers and the ruled, of privileged chiefs and subservient commoners linked by patron-client relationships, customs, traditions and landholding and this was strengthened by war service. But there were other aspects too. The highly structured, hierarchical organization of the military with its warrior ethos, camaraderie and discipline, mirrored in kind the values of Fijian communalism and explains the rapport the indigenous inhabitants have with the military. Following World War II, many demobilised servicemen, armed with values, attitudes and skills acquired from military service returned to their villages to become important reference groups and performed an informal leadership function within village communities. They were, in many respects, a modernizing influence. And many modernization theorists were arguing in the 1950s and 1960s that the military was such a force in developing societies.

Internal Security Operations: Some Political Consequences

On several occasions throughout the islands' colonial history, troops were used to defend the status quo. For example, in 1920 troops were deployed in the Suva and Nausori areas in the wake of the "Indian strike" protesting against poor working conditions and rising food prices. In the 1921 "sugarcane strike" by Indo-Fijian canefarmers, approximately 300 policemen and Special Constables recruited from the indigenous community, were deployed against the strikers. The consequences of this strike on race relations in the colony were far reaching. Gillion (1977:60) records the reaction of a visiting Indian government delegation in 1922:

> The use of Fijians as Special Constables during the past two years has tended to increase their contempt for the Indians whom they were called upon to suppress. At the same time, the Indians have been irritated against the Fijians.

Again in 1943 and 1960, troops were called out to impose order in the canefields following strikes by canefarmers agitating for a more favourable price for sugarcane. It appears that dissension between growers and millers in sugarcane producing countries is typical especially where the latter have a monopoly on cane-crushing. Fiji, where the Australian owned Colonial Sugar Refining Company had the monopoly, was no exception. The Company owned and operated the five sugar mills on the islands at the time and was thus able to dictate milling costs.

Overall, the use of the military to suppress Indo-Fijian demands for democratization and improved labour conditions had several important consequences. For example, it portrayed the internal security problem in the context of a capital-labour conflict that had an overriding ethnic dimension. Indeed, the capital-labour conflict was the most crucial axis of political conflict in the colony. In the 1980s, this conflict came to crystallize the subsequent political alliance between Indo-Fijians, labour, social democracy and the Bavadra-led coalition against exploitative foreign and local capital (the sweat shops of the locally owned garment industry being a case in point), chiefly interests and the Alliance Party. The use of the military to quell domestic dissent also validated, for indigenous Fijians, the negative stereotyping of migrant Indians and the credibility of the "Indian threat" conjured up by economically distraught European businessmen whose commercial interests were increasingly being undermined by the success of Indian retailers. The agitation by Indo-Fijian canegrowers for security of tenure, improved access to land and a better price for sugarcane was often misrepresented to validate the "Indian threat". Increasing political agitation by the Indo-Fijian community for political rights also served to convince the colonial regime that this group was politically unreliable and should not, therefore, be given a role in the military. These sorts of considerations explain why many Indo-Fijians came to see the 14 May 1987 military coup as supportive of unsympathetic foreign interests, as well as the belief held by many leading members of this community that the military coup was externally directed.

Independence and the New Order

At independence, on 10 October 1970, the mantle of national leadership was inherited by the Alliance Party led by Ratu Sir Kamisese Mara, an Oxford educated Fijian chief. With the withdrawal of British colonial authority, political space began to open up, secondary groups were formed, differing interests articulated and new relationships of power and influence developed (Hegarty 1989:1). The role of the Indo-Fijian business class in the economy was strengthened after a rapprochement with some prominent native chiefs and expatriate commercial interests. Members of the ruling chiefly elite and their commoner allies in the bureaucracy formed an indigenous bourgeois class in the newly independent state. This group became a modernising influence committed to the accumulation of capital (Rutz 1987:541). Their access to the economy was enhanced by Alliance government policies which gave the state a greater role in capital accummulation by supplementing and protecting local business interests. The Alliance Party, therefore, came to represent the interests of the Fijian chiefly establishment, privileged sections of the European and part-European middle-class and elements of the Indo-Fijian business community. Political opposition to the Alliance government was from the National Federation Party, which drew its support from the Indo-Fijian community. Politics in independent Fiji was polarised along racial lines and there was little assimilation between ethnic Fijians and Indo-Fijians. Contrasting cultural traditions and attitudes as well as "divide and rule" tactics by the British colonial administration, made assimilation difficult.

Because their stakes in the political game were high, stalwarts of the Alliance party had greater incentive for mobilisation should they perceive the rules of the political game as working to their disadvantage. At the most basic level, these rules were hedged by the tacitly acknowledged assumption that the political ascendancy of indigenous Fijians was the prerequisite for multi-racial cooperation and power-sharing through the important mediating role of chiefs (Norton 1981:317-326). Indeed, it could be argued that that up until the April 1987 elections, stability in independent Fiji was derived from the various compromises made with respect to this fundamental premise of Fijian political life.

Military Professionalism

At independence, the Royal Fiji Military Forces (RFMF) accepted the classical conception of military professionalism. The principal criteria underpinning such a conception were: that the military was subordinate to civilian authority ; its primary function was the management of violence ; the officer corps was professionally trained and motivated ; and, the military remained a distinct institution with separate government regulations guaranteeing its autonomy. This conception derived from the military traditions of Britain and other western industrialised nations. Muthiah (1988:17) and Perlmutter (1980:101), quote Alfred Stepan's assertion that classical professionalism "... responds to threats of external security and is highly specialised, its scope of action restricted, socialisation is neutral and its general attitude is apolitical". Nonetheless the deep entrenchment of the Fiji military in the chiefly system created an underlying structural tension between its "modernising" role and its regime maintenance function which was not, however, made manifest until the victory of the Coalition government in 1987.

In western military tradition the principle challenge for military professionalism is how best to accept and overcome the challenges of war. Capability, readiness and deterrence are some of the key concepts, but performance in combat remains the acid test (Djiwandono and Cheong 1988:10). In the Fiji context, classical conceptions of military professionalism where certain assumptions are made about the professional role of the military, did not apply. Without an overt external threat to national security the challenge of war was not the principal challenge for military professionalism. The principal challenge were the challenges of peace with which many other stable and newly emergent nations also had to contend. Problems of internal security and development, nationalism, disparities in income and expectation levels, along with rapid social and political change, all combine in varying degrees to generate a crisis of modernization that pose unique challenges for military professionalism in developing societies.

Indeed, the crisis of modernization posed important challenges for military professionalism in independent Fiji. Questions of role definition and the relevance of the military to society demanded immediate attention. How best could the military express itself as a symbol of national sovereignty; how could it best contribute to security and development as well as assert its effectiveness as an agent of socio-economic modernization within the ambit of government development policies, were key questions. Given the character of political dissent in Fiji and the polarisation of races, internal security was, not surprisingly, accepted as the primary role of the RFMF. Nation-building and international peacekeeping were secondary roles in which the military was required to develop its expertise. As the roles of the RFMF in pre-coup Fiji evolved, they were defined, in order of priority:

1. To help the Police and Civil authorities restore and maintain law and order.

2. To contribute to the national development effort through active participation in civic action tasks; the training of youth, and resources protection

3. To support the Government's foreign policy objectives with regard to international peacekeeping.

4. To provide a basis for expansion in war or other emergencies.

5. To train for war and homeland defence.

As a result of these roles, the army's engineer corps was expanded to undertake military civic-action programs in rural areas. Three ex-US Navy "Bluebird" class minesweepers were acquired in 1975 to conduct patrols of Fiji's territorial waters. A hydrographic capability was subsequently added to the fledging naval squadron to assist in the charting of coastal waters. Under the aegis of international peacekeeping, Fiji has despatched soldiers on peacekeeping duties with the United Nations in southern Lebanon (UNIFIL); the Multi-National Force and Observers (MFO) in the Sinai Desert; the Commonwealth Monitoring Force in Zimbabwe-Rhodesia, and to United Nations units monitoring the Soviet withdrawal from Afghanistan. A contingent of Fijian policemen also served with the United Nations Transition Group in Namibia (UNTAG).

Politically, the RFMF served the state in several important ways: as the final guarantor of law and order; as an instrument of foreign policy and rural development; as a crucible for citizenship training, as well as providing training in non-traditional attitudes and skills. Prior to the military coup of 14 May 1987, the RFMF was viewed as professional in that it was apparently apolitical, subordinate to civilian authority and performed its duties efficiently. But an examination of the prevailing pattern of civil-military relations confirm a process of politicization taking place that undermined the quality of military professionalism.

Civil-Military Relations: Some Relevant Models

Among the many theoretical models advanced by various scholars for the analysis of civil-military relations, the proposals of Morris Janowitz (1977:183-201) and Eric Nordlinger (1977:10-22) have relevance to the Fiji experience. Janowitz (1977) proposed two models of political-military elites; the "aristocratic" and the "democratic". His models share the same core features to that proposed by Nordlinger (1977) with respect to the latter's "traditional" and "liberal" patterns. The difference in the propositions lie more in their orientations than in their substance. The propositions of Janowitz (1977) are oriented primarily to patterns of civil-military relations prevailing in modern industrialised nations, whereas Nordlinger (1977), is more concerned with those found in developing societies.

In the aristocratic model, Janowitz (1977) records that civilian and military elites are socially and functionally integrated. Like the monarchies of seventeenth and eighteenth century Europe from which the model derives, civilian and military elites share the same aristocratic backgrounds, interests, values and outlooks. Janowitz (1977:187) maintains that:

> The narrow base of recruitment for both elites and a relatively monolithic power structure provide the civilian elite with a comprehensive basis for political control of the military.

In the democratic model, civilian elites exercise control over the military through a formal set of rules which define the role and functions of the military and the conditions under which it may exercise its power. Military officers:

> ...are professionals in the employ of the state. They are a small group and their careers are distinct from civilian careers...The military leaders obey the government because it is their duty and their profession to fight...Professional ethics as well as democratic parliamentary institutions guarantee civilian political supremacy". (Janowitz 1977:188)

Nordlinger (1977:12), maintains that his "liberal" model is explicitly premised upon the differentiation of elites according to their expertise and responsibilities. The model also entails the maximum possible depoliticization of the military. He also argues that his "liberal" model has been most often used to assert civilian supremacy in developing states. He illustrates this by citing the 1961 injunction issued by President Nkrumah of Ghana to Ghanaian military cadets, that "politics are not for soldiers".

In framing appropriate models to explain the Fiji experience, Saffu (1990:159-170) uses the above paradigms as the basis of his hypothesis. His starting point is the 1970 constitution. He points to its "distinct duality" as the locus for the two patterns of civil-military relations that emerged in pre-coup Fiji. He notes:

> On the one hand, it (the constitution) was a liberal democratic document of the standard Westminister variety that Britain usually bequeathed to her colonies at independence. On the other hand, it embodied undemocratic and illiberal provisions such as communal electoral rolls, unequal communal representation, entrenched chiefly-dominated institutions and provisions protecting pre-

democratic customs, customary rights and land" . (Saffu 1990:161).

Saffu (1990), maintains that this duality gave rise to the co-existence of "traditional-aristocratic" and "liberal-democratic" patterns. He argues that the basis of civilian supremacy in the "traditional-aristocratic" model, is:

> ...the harmony of social and political outlooks between politicians and military officers in an essentially pre-democratic political system. Members of the political branch of aristocratic families are accepted as politically legitimate by the military and the church branches of the same network of aristocratic families. Civil-military relations are cosy, intra-family affairs" (Saffu 1990:159).

In the "liberal-democratic" pattern, Saffu (ibid.) ascribes civilian supremacy to:

> ...the democratic belief that civilian politicians have an electoral mandate to rule, and the liberal belief that every major institution under the constitution has its own proper sphere of jurisdiction and relative autonomy demarcated by constitutional provisions, conventions and procedures.

For Saffu, civilian supremacy prior to the coup was predicated primarily on traditional-aristocratic patterns. Moreover, both the traditional-aristocratic and liberal-democratic models were able to co-exist because there was no divergence in the identity of the civilian ruler designated by the models. Saffu's observations can be validated by reference to the tacitly accepted fundamental "rule of the political game" in pre-coup Fiji. This was identified earlier as being based on the assumption that the political ascendancy of the indigenous community was a prerequisite for multiracial co-operation and power-sharing through the important mediating role of chiefs.This was a fundamental assumption underwriting the 1970 constitution and explains the embodiment of "undemocratic and illiberal provisions" in that document. Civilian supremacy in pre-coup Fiji was premised on tacit acceptance of this state of affairs. Traditional-aristocratic patterns of civil-military relations conformed to the "rules" of the game. The pattern had primacy for many indigenous Fijians, their allies of other races including key members of the civilian and military elite. It was sustained because the rigorous hierachy the system embodied provided a source of authority and prestige for the elite (Janowitz 1977:187) and was reinforced by a complex web of blood ties, kinship bonds and marriage links that provided; "...the sinews, the commonality of interests and the harmony of outlooks of the traditional-aristocratic pattern". (Saffu 1990:162).

A key concept of the traditional-aristocratic model was the pervasive belief, held by many within the indigenous population, that political power was the exclusive preserve of chiefs. This reflected the saliency of pre-democratic values that had been sustained by British paternalism and indirect rule, values that were subsequently embodied in the 1970 constitution. Within the indigenous community, the belief encouraged the notion that politics was the business of elites. Such a notion helps explain their low level of political participation. It also suggests that the institutionalisation of civilian control without chiefly participation is much less secure, a factor Bavadra's coalition government appeared to have overlooked in its 1987 quest for power.

Whilst the traditional-aristocratic model may have provided the basis for civilian supremacy, it eroded the quality of military professionalism in at least two ways. By designating the identity of the civilian ruler acceptable to the model, it undermined the apolitical attitude of military professionalism. Secondly, it facilitated the penetration of communal values within the military. Such values, with its cherished ideals and deep-seated antagonisms, retarded the development of a national, secular outlook within the officer corps. It also rendered the military susceptible to political manipulation.

Communalism in the Military

Following independence, manpower for the expanding RFMF was drawn mainly from the indigenous Fijian community, whose warrior ethos and societal structure made them ideal for military service. The ethnic and class identity of the RFMF officer corps was promoted by the appointment of officers from the ruling chiefly class, although educated commoner indigenes and representatives of other ethnic groups, were also co-opted into the officer corps. The chief-commoner cleavage was the dominant split within the officer corps. It was a cleavage that mirrored the class component of Fijian communalism.

Military officers of chiefly background represented and articulated the values and interests of the conservative ruling elite. Swayed by the quasi-feudal values of Fijian tradition, to which they ascribed their political orientations, these officers were socialized in the traditional-aristocratic model of political-military elites. They were the informal agents of political socialization within the military, inculcating their men with political information, values and practices that strongly influenced political orientations and behaviour. Such information implied that the military role was to uphold the status quo in which the chiefs were a privileged elite. By penetrating their subordinates with such information they were also able to obtain loyalty and obedience.

In 1982, chief Ratu Epeli Nailatikau (a son-in-law of Prime Minister Mara) was appointed by the government to command the RFMF. Implicit in Nailatikau's appointment was the government's wish to assert the ascendancy of chiefly interests and traditional values within the military. Nailatikau's appointment also signalled the government's preference for traditional-aristocratic patterns of civil-military relations. The appointment was important in another sense. Symbolically, it completed the ethnicisation of the military ; the RFMF could now be viewed as an ethnic Fijian institution with a respected Fijian chief at its head. The appointment thus confirmed the saliency of communal considerations in the appointment of the professional head of the military. The primacy of the traditional-aristocratic model enabled members of the ruling chiefly elite to prevail over the commoner-based, professional, military-technocratic element from which previous military commanders had been drawn.

The quality of military professionalism was also eroded by the prevalence of patron-client relationships between military officers and influential members of the chiefly hierarchy occupying positions of power. These relationships were founded on tribal relationships and embodied the politics of Fijian communalism. There was, however, a positive side to this relationship as far as the military was concerned. Chiefly connections and social position were important in the sense that it secured the military's corporate interests from the threat of decreased budgetary allocations imposed by the civil bureaucracy on the military. Ultimately, the securing of these interests had to be played out with the compliance of the chiefly arbiters of state power and resources. And the RFMF often used its chiefly connections to secure arbitration in its favour.

Two other factors helped entrench communal values within the military ; the use of Fijian symbolism in military dress, and the condescending nature of chiefly rhetoric. The wearing of the *sulu* [a traditional skirt with serrated edges] on formal occasions, reinforced in the minds of Fijian soldiers that their uniform not only symbolized defence of the country but defence of communal pride and interests (Enloe 1980). Fijian communalism, in particular the values and prejudices underpinning its ethnic and class components, became inextricably interwoven into the fabric of military professionalism. For many commissioned officers and servicemen, military allegiance and ethnic allegiance were perceived inseparably (Sanday 1989:128). Such a perception was reinforced by the condescending nature of chiefly rhetoric which suggested authority over political and military institutions. The rhetoric inferred that it was the historical mission of the RFMF to protect chiefly interests. Britain's legacy of indirect rule was often invoked to remind servicemen that their loyalty to the Crown had always been exercised through their chiefs. In this way, the loyalty of the RFMF came to be defined in racial terms, making the military vulnerable to political manipulation.

Military Intervention in Politics

Elected to political office in April 1987 on a platform that espoused social democratic values, Doctor Bavadra's election victory removed the basis for accepting civilian supremacy in the traditional-aristocratic pattern (Saffu 1990:159). As a result, Bavadra's coalition government could not establish stable relations with the military and representative institutions of the indigenous community. Also, except for the trade union movement, the coalition government could not immediately establish stable relations with powerful social and economic interests in the country. These too were mostly deeply patterned into a system of collaboration with the Alliance political hierachy. In particular Bavadra's pre-election promises to nationalise the gold mining industry and his land reform proposals had created alarm in both the Fijian communal arena and amongst important business interests. For the chiefly establishment, the principle of equitable distribution underlying Bavadra's commitment to democratic-socialism—the depth of his commitment to socialist principles was never tested—represented unwelcome encroachments at important points of their proprietary claim. Bavadra's land reform proposals were especially significant because they would have deprived chiefs of their 30 per cent share of land rents and established the unwelcome precedent of Fijian chiefs being dispossessed by commoners. In the ensuing agitation for constitutional change by the Taukei Movement, democracy came to be labelled "a foreign flower". A situation of disorderly political mobilisation then ensued where institutions for orderly political representation and bargaining became marginalized and politics threatened to spill over from institutional arenas into the streets. To a degree, it had many of the hallmarks of Huntington's (1968:196) description of praetorianism.

Two factors contributed to the rise of interventionist politics immediately following the April 1987 elections. Having polled only 9.4 per cent of the ethnic Fijian vote in communal constituencies (the vote of ethnic Fijians had not, on its own, given a single seat to the coalition) Bavadra's government suffered from a "legitimacy deflation" (Nordlinger 1977:93-95). Another factor was the legacy left by former prime minister and Alliance party leader Ratu Mara, whose capacity to rule was based on a combination of personal and traditional power which contributed to his ability to control dissent. This was manifested in the Alliance party's inability to internalize conflict. Although the Alliance was a political alliance of three ethnically based political associations, there was no regulatory mechanism within the party for dissent to be accommodated and where diverse interests within the Fijian polity could be represented and bargain. This led to the formation of splinter parties externalizing their conflict and fracturing the political unity of ethnic Fijians by appeals to extremist ethnic politics. Thus when Ratu Mara failed to regain power in the April 1987 elections extremist ethnic politics easily overtook the politics of moderation.

Nonetheless by early May 1987, agitation by the Taukei Movement had begun to lose momentum and public support for it appeared to be on the wane. The Taukei Movement alone could not bring about a change in government. For that they needed the support of the military, or elements within it. This occured on the 14 May 1987 when a military coup was staged by politicized elements in the RFMF under Lt Colonel Sitiveni Rabuka. His radical intervention on behalf of the established social order served the interests of the more privileged classes, particularly the Fijian aristocracy. It was therefore not surprising that Rabuka's appeal for support from the traditional chiefly establishment was enthusiastically granted.

At the most obvious level, the coup reflected the failure of the new coalition government to immediately clarify the terms of its relationship with the RFMF and establish a viable alternative to the traditional-aristocratic model that its predecessor in government, the Alliance, had maintained as the basis of civilian supremacy. Significantly, after becoming prime minister, Bavadra chose not to visit the RFMF at its headquarters at Queen Elizabeth Barracks in Suva to provide the necessary clarification that RFMF officers sought with respect to civil-military relations. This should have been an early priority on his agenda. The coup also reflected a refusal by elements within the RFMF to accept the variation on the unwritten Fijian political tradition that Bavadra's coalition government would have demanded—therein lay an important challenge for military professionalism. In the final analysis, the coup confirmed that civilian control of the military in a developing society like Fiji cannot simply be predicated on classical conceptions of military professionalism. Nor can it be based on the various legal guarantees safeguarding the position of the incumbent civilian government. The Fiji experience proved yet again, that civilian control of the military is the result of a long process of indoctrination, socialisation and the direct and indirect manipulation of the values and ambitions of the officer corps. It also proved that civilian control of the military is also dependent on the military's perception of the competence of the incumbent civilian government. The coalition governments inability to assuage ethnic Fijian fears that their rights would be eroded, as well as its inability to establish stable relations with the military and representative institutions of the indigenous Fijian community, was perceived by the coup-makers as a reflection of government incompetence and ineffectiveness.

Tradition: the Legitimizing Mantle

Fijian tradition was used to legitimize the coup, specifically through support given to Rabuka by former Prime Minister Ratu Mara and the Great Council of Chiefs, the highest body charged with safeguarding the interests of the indigenous population. For his part, Ratu Mara joined Rabuka's post-coup Council of Ministers within hours of the putsch and was assigned the foreign affairs portfolio. His immediate identification with those who seized government not only alienated him from the Governor General's initial stand against the coup, but also provided, in the eyes of many members of the indigenous population, the sanction of chiefly *mana* [magico-spiritual powers assigned to chiefs by indigenous folk culture] to legitimize Rabuka's seizure of power.

Governor General, Ratu Sir Penaia Ganilau, isolated and alienated from Ratu Mara and the Great Council of Chiefs because of his opposition to the coup, subsequently sought compromise by accepting Rabuka's demands for the entrenchment of Fijian political supremacy in an amended constitution and by including Rabuka in his Council of Advisors. Rabuka was promoted to the rank of full

Colonel, appointed commander of the RFMF and formally pardoned for his role in the overthrow of Bavadra's government.

The September Coup

On 25 September 1987, Rabuka re-took power to consolidate the gains of the first coup. He felt his objective of amending the constitution to entrench the political supremacy of indigenous Fijians, would be thwarted by the bi-partisan caretaker government that the Governor General had appointed and tasked with returning the country to an elected civilian government. Three days later, on 28 September, Rabuka revoked the 1970 constitution. On 1 October, he abolished the office of Governor General. Then, in a midnight radio broadcast to the nation on 7 October, he unilaterally declared Fiji a republic. He appointed a military government to rule Fiji with himself as head. But in ousting the chiefs from power, Rabuka had unwittingly isolated himself from the legitimizing mantle of Fijian tradition. Alienated from the high chiefs who dominated the ethnic Fijian political system, Rabuka subsequently sought atonement and legitimacy for his actions by surrendering power, on 5 December 1987, to his paramount chief, Ratu Sir Penaia Ganilau, who agreed to become the country's first President. Ganilau appointed Ratu Mara prime minister of an interim government. Mara, in turn, appointed Rabuka Minister of Defence and Security in addition to his appointment as Commander of the RFMF. Rabuka was also formally absolved for his role in overthrowing the governor general's administration. In October 1988, Rabuka was promoted to the military rank of major general.

Post Coup Military: Consolidation and Politicization

The consolidation and politicization of the post-coup military has proceeded in a number of ways. For example, it included an increase in manpower and budget [Table 11.1]. At one point, following the mobilization of army reservists immediately after the coup, the military strength swelled in excess of 6,000 with a corresponding increase in military budget. In 1989, more money was allocated to the military than to the country's health services. The military further consolidated its power in government when four senior officers, including Rabuka, were appointed to cabinet positions in December 1988 with Ratu Sir Kamisese Mara as prime minister. Military officers also commenced training in non-military subjects such as civil-law, political science and some have pursued entrepreneurial activities. The politicization of the military was consolidated by the granting of commissions to political leaders and prominent coup sympathisers.

Table 11.1
Military Budget and Manpower

Year	Manpower Expenditure	Budgetary Allocation (million)	Actual Expenditure (million)	Govt.
1986	2,589	$F16.3	$F16.5	4%
1987	2,588	$F 16.8	$F31.2	7%
1988	3,316	$F 19.8	$F35.2	7%
1989	5,015	$F 29.8	$F34.5	7%
1990	5,015	$F29.3	unavailable	

Sources : *Fiji Government Operating Budget Statements. Report of the Auditor General, 1987 (issued as Parliamentary Paper No 2 of 1989)* and 1988 (issued as Paper No. 22 of 1990. *Canberra Times* 31 October 1990.

Among those who received military commissions were two formers ministers and two former senators from the Alliance party. Within the military, the promotion of officers and NCOs has also succumbed to favouritism and the need for patronage rather than merit. Also apparent, is a trend towards tribalisation within the military where the allocation of senior posts and the recruitment of servicemen increasingly reflect the regional preferences of those now in control of the state apparatus. Here, special advantage appears to be accruing to the eastern maritime provinces of the *Tovata* confederacy, from which hail President Ganilau, Prime Minister Mara and Army Commander Rabuka. All this suggests the subordination of professionalism to military corporatism.

Military Role: The Strategic Choices

In speculating on the future role of the military, three main options come to mind:

Option A. The consolidation of the military as the armed force of indigenous Fijians under the control of the conservative chiefly elite with the military committed to maintaining the political ascendancy and communal prejudices of that elite. Ostensibly, traditional-aristocratic patterns will remain the basis of civilian supremacy.

Option B. The mobilisation of ethnicity by a praetorian military in search of a role relatively independent of the traditional chiefly system.

Option C The transformation of the military into the armed forces of a multi-ethnic Fijian state, with the military strictly committed to purely professional roles related to defence and clearly defined state interests. This option is predicated on the liberal and democratic models of civil-military relations espoused by Nordlinger (1977) and Janowitz (1977) respectively. Here, the military is disciplined by its own professionalism.

Of the three options, the third is obviously the least likely to eventuate in the short term. It would require a depoliticisation of the military and a re-commitment to military professionalism, something for which there is at present no adequate constitutional basis. It is unlikely that either the military commanders or their civilian counter-parts in the new government would agree to the abandonment of the immediate coup objectives that the implementation of "Option C", would signal. This option ceased to be an immediate possibility when Rabuka overturned the Deuba accord between the Governor-General and the Coalition in September 1987.

Not surprisingly, developments to date indicate that Option A is the choice of Ratu Mara's interim government. Option A was also agreed to by Major General Rabuka who resigned from cabinet and returned to the barracks on 5 January 1990 to consolidate his military position. He seemed confident then that the coup objectives of entrenching the political supremacy of indigenous inhabitants would be implemented by Ratu Mara's interim government.

Nonetheless, although he has returned to barracks, Rabuka has indicated that he will not hesitate to intervene again to achieve his coup objectives. By remaining at one remove from government and overtly threatening civilian supremacy unless certain demands are met, Rabuka is signalling the possibility of further praetorian political interventions which in the long term could undermine the traditional-aristocratic pattern of rule he claims to have restored by the coups. Option B could be pursued under a number of circumstances: if Rabuka saw the need to distance the military from the control of the chiefly elite to safeguard his personal interests; or if he, or other military Commanders, moved to protect the corporate interests of the military from chiefly interference; or if the military determined the need to play an independent modernising role free of chiefly constraints. Rabuka has already staked out the third option in rejecting the Deuba settlement in spite of its sanctioning by Ganilau and Mara. More recently, he has supported the corporate interests of the military against the government in rejecting an appeal by Mara to reduce military spending.

The Ideological Underpinnings of the Ethnic Options

Both options A and B complement the notion of Fijian paramountcy being promoted as the new state ideology. We may refer to them, for this reason, as the "ethnic" options. According to the ideology of ethnicity, the rights and interests of indigenous Fijians must prevail over those of other races. It is an ideology that is dominated by feelings of ethnocentric pride and of superiority over other non-indigenous citizens who are perceived as being intrinscally different and alien. In addition, it conveys a claim of propriety to certain areas of privilege and advantage and is based on fear and suspicion that the Indo-Fijian community aspire to political dominance. Moreover, that they secretly covet Fijian land ownership rights, although this is vehemently denied by Indo-Fijian leaders.

Underwriting such an ideology is a conception of distributive justice based on the premise that greater resources backed up by better political access need to be allocated to the indigenous population if political stability is to be assured. This ideology assumes that Indo-Fijians and minority racial groups—such as part-Fijians, Polynesian settlers, Europeans, Chinese and the descendants of Kanak labourers who remain landless—will agree to an enduring political loss to enable the indigenous population to enjoy greater advantages. It is an ideology not shared by many non-indigenous citizens who fear relegation to second or third class citizen status. Nevertheless, in July 1990, the Ratu Mara led regime in Suva promulgated a constitution that entrenches a voting system based on race which will guarantee indigenous Fijian dominance. This will be achieved through the allocation of majority seats in the proposed parliament. Besides inequalities in political structures, the paramountcy of indigenous Fijian interests is also to be articulated in the new constitution through a policy of "positive discrimination". The present leader of the ousted coalition, Adi Kuini Bavadra, who assumed the leadership after her husband's death in November 1989, has described the 1990 constitution as "racist, feudalistic and undemocratic" and has called for a national referendum to determine its acceptability. Although the constitution protects the fundamental rights and freedoms of all citizens, it denies Indo-Fijians and other races parity in political representation with the indigenous Fijian community. This, and the fact that real power will be exercised by hereditary chiefs and representatives of the indigenous community elected to parliament on the basis of a "massive gerrymander", appears to be the principal objections of Bavadra. She has announced her party's intention to boycott national elections expected to be called before the end of 1991.

Some International Reactions

Fiji's constitutional proposals have also been criticized by India's Minister of State for External Affairs, Hari Kishore Singh. On 11 May 1990, the minister told the Indian Parliament (*Lok Sabha*) that his government would alert the international community to what he described as; "... a process of racial discrimination through constitutional changes in Fiji" (*Canberra Times* 12 May 1990). Describing the ruling regime as "illegal", Singh also gave notice of India's intention to put the mattter before the United Nations Human Rights Commission. In addition, he said that India would continue to block Fiji's re-entry into the British Commonwealth from which it was excluded after the coups of 1987. In response, the interim-government ordered the closure of the Indian Embassy in Suva. In a note delivered to the Indian Embassy at noon on 23 May 1990, Fiji's Foreign Affairs Ministry described India's declared intentions as; "...unfriendly and in contravention of international law and practice" (*Canberra Times* 24 May 1990). Reacting to the closure of the Indian Embassy, a statement by a group of Indian cultural organisations in Suva described the shutdown order as; "...unwarranted and provocative". The statement claimed: "This action is clearly aimed at further hurting the dignity and honour of the Indo-Fijian community who have historical, cultural, religious and kinship ties with India. No community can be expected to suffer such humiliation in silence" (ibid.).

The direction of constitutional developments in Fiji was raised in private talks between Mauritian Prime Minister, Sir Anerood Jagnauth, and French President, Francois Mitterand, when the latter visited Mauritius in June 1990 (*Fiji Voice* June/July 1990:6). President Mitterand told his host that he was not fully aware of the situation in Fiji and described the state of affairs as "inadmissable" if indeed the Indo-Fijian population were to be deprived of their rights. Mitterand said that France would continue helping Fiji, but only if human rights were respected. He indicated that he had directed his Foreign Minister to look closely at the Fiji issue (*ibid.*)

On 1 August 1990, Australian Prime Minister, Bob Hawke, told Australian media representatives in Port Vila, Vanuatu, that Australia accepted the reality of the situation in Fiji and; "...despite the flaws of the constitution ... no other constitution was likely to be accepted in the near future" (*Sydney Morning Herald* 2 August 1990). Hawke also called on the coalition to reverse its decision to boycott elections under the new constitution and; "...stay engaged in the parliamentary processes as far as possible".

The Entrenchment of a Political Role for the Military

Several developments point to the entrenchment of a political role for the RFMF in the years ahead. The RFMF has already re-oriented and re-defined its goals to increase its political relevance. For example, where previously it had maintained an apolitical tradition, the RFMF now perceives itself as the legitimate upholder of the constitution and the values it will enshrine. These values include the inalienable right of indigenes to political supremacy and the inviolability of the colonially-constructed, neo-traditional order. In addition to being the final guarantor of law and order, the military, largely through policies that reflect Rabuka's communal values, will now also guarantee an imbalance of power in favour of a chiefly elite. The RFMF also continues to perceive a need to participate in the socio-economic modernization of the indigenous community and has enhanced its developmental role through increased civic-action programs and the use of military transport and naval ships to subsidise the transport costs of rural farmers.

In redefining its goals, the military has the advantage of a favourable socio-cultural environment for goal transformation. For example, the ideology of indigenous Fijian paramountcy has the support of the chiefly establishment which will continue to remain at the forefront in any defence of the established order; rationalizing it as being in the best interests of the indigenous population. Here, Tradition and Culture, in their abstract and undifferentiated form, are imperatives often used to mask vested interests and to defend the status quo. The paramountcy of indigenous Fijian interests, aided and abetted by radical ethnic nationalism operating on the fringe of indigenous Fijian opinion, receives support from sections of the indigenous community who also tacitly support an expansion of military activities and a higher profile for it in politics. Justification for this position is explained in terms of recruitment in the expanded RFMF as a means of alleviating youth unemployment and as a modernizing influence on rural village communities. Also, it provides tangible expression of the indigenous people's control of their own destiny, albeit a control based on coercive strategies to maintain political ascendancy. It also provides the means by which indigenous inhabitants are best able to re-inforce their own position in relation to where real power lies. For Rabuka, at least, radical ethnic nationalism has helped clarify a post-coup *raison d'etre* for the military and elevated the importance of his own position as a power-broker in the current political equation. It has also fuelled his political ambitions. He told *Pacific Islands Monthly* (PIM August 1990:11) that he wanted to become prime minister "To fulfil my objectives and my promises of 1987. My objective was the firming up of the Fijians as the true owners of this country and that we should run it politically, economically and socially."

In a move to establish stable relations with the military power-brokers and with a younger, but more heterogenous entrepreneurial elite now emerging, the chiefly elite has succeeded in pulling both forces into an alliance with it. And around the goals and interests of this new and powerful social group new military goals will be oriented and new patterns of civil-military relations will develop. What is likely, is the fusion of traditional authority with political power and the formation of an integrated elite comprising traditional chiefs as the nucleus, with the military and their allies in the bureaucracy and the Methodist Church, forming a loyal cadre.

Thus at the moment a composite model of civil-military relations appears to exist in which the modus operandi of government is partially based on the primacy of traditional-aristocratic patterns, but supported by a praetorianism that will operate in opposition to it where the corporate interests of the military and the personal interests of the coup-makers are threatened. Liberal-democratic formalities will be accommodated within the model as long as these do not threaten the ascendancy of designated rulers.

Some Problems for the Composite Approach

The collaboration between the chiefly elite and the military in pursuit of ethnic Fijian interests is inherently unstable. The rejection of western forms of democratic rule and the according of legitimacy to "tradition" (including "invented tradition") is based on the misconception that indigenous Fijian society is culturally and politically homogenous. It is not. Traditional mores and values are not constant. An adherence either to option A or, to a lesser extent, the composite model, fails to take into account qualitative changes occurring within the indigenous society. Increasing urbanisation, industrialisation, the mobility of labour and the monetisation of the economy have converted Fijian attitudes and contributed to the decline of "traditional" authority. Tradition alone cannot sustain and regulate native Fijian society. Education and economic factors, for example, have given ethnic Fijians social mobility where they have been denied it by tradition.

It is difficult to see the military agreeing to play indefinitely a political role supportive of a chiefly elite whose authority and influence continue to be eroded by the effects of modernisation. Rabuka, for his part, has already sought legitimation for an independent military role in government by referring to the interests of the Taukei (the Fijian "people of the land"), opening up the suggestion that this might not be co-extensive with the interests of the high chiefly elite. In this regard he could expect a measure of support from many minor Ratus who have already faced down the Governor General (and High Chief) over the consumation and direction of the coups.

Whether the military continues to collaborate with the high chiefs, or whether it follows option B, if its political role is to remain credible, the threat to national security and indigenous Fijian interests will need to be kept alive. This suggests a more internally-directed, political focus for military professionalism in the years ahead. Inherent in such a focus, however, is the danger that professional military standards may continue to erode in the long-term leading ultimately to the absence of a professional officer corps dedicated to military duties. Under these circumstances, Huntington (1957:80-97; 350-373), claims civil-military "fusion" occurs as the military loses its professional autonomy and become identified with a specific set of institutions, a constitutional form, a social class and its associated ideology. In many countries with a history of military intervention in politics, such a conflict in military roles (and a decline in influence in government) have resulted in counter-coups by disenchanted officers seeking a re-definition of military professionalism and a reorientation of military goals.

There will also be problems in securing legitimacy for such a military role from among Fiji's wider multi-racial community which sees the political disarticulation of the military as being a prerequisite for democratic consolidation. Moreover, the military may also not be able to secure universal or adequate allegiance as there exists a critical mass of people in the country who desire a return to parliamentary democracy and see political parties as legitimate institutions for the creation of parliamentary governments. Some have argued the ideology of Fijian paramountcy that is central to the model, tacitly promotes a level of psychological violence against non-indigenes and Indo-Fijians in particular. Undeniably, the ideology has given rise to increased Fijian chauvinism and already some Indo-Fijian families have been the target of politically motivated violence. As well, Mosques and Hindu temples have been firebombed.

A national ideology overtly based on ethnic paramountcy could be expected to produce racial discord in the islands, if ethnic Fijian demands for greater access to political office and the economy spill over into demands for exclusive access. If this occurs, the military could find itself moving increasingly outside the parameters of civil control. The great danger of option B tied, as it would most likely be, to the more radical legitimating promotion of Taukei rights, as against the conservative legitimation of chiefly restoration, is that of a praetorian military acting with unrestrained coercion against sections of the civilian population.

For the United States, Australia and New Zealand in particular, the resumption of defence ties with a regime in Suva that espouses a racially-based state ideology, carries the concomitant risk of relations with India being tested given India's stated intention to isolate the Fiji regime internationally. Australia has suspended its defence cooperation program with the Fiji regime pending the introduction of a constitution "broadly acceptable" to all sections of the population. It has yet to reopen formal defence contacts with the regime in Suva. New Zealand and the United States have also suspended formal defence links and appear to be following Australia's lead in setting the terms for its resumption. Britain, on the other hand, has agreed to provide limited training assistance to the RFMF, while France, Malaysia, Taiwan, South Korea and the Peoples Republic of China, are currently being courted by the regime to provide defence aid. France, in particular, has been singled out by Rabuka (*PIM*:14) as a welcome partner in a defence treaty with Fiji "...if it is in the interest of France to solidify our relationship". Rabuka envisages French help in carrying "...the burden of the security of this country (Fiji)".

There is concern in regional circles that the *quid pro quo* for such a relationship could be French insistence that Fiji drop its objections to the French nuclear testing program in the South Pacific. Two strands of Fiji's foreign policy strategy become immediately apparent here. The first, is a belief that the diversification of external linkages will not only diversify its economic linkages, it will also serve to underwrite regime security and national independence. Secondly, in its relationship with Australia and New Zealand, Fiji seeks to gain a tactical advantage by exploiting perceived policy differences between metropolitan powers—namely, the policies of France *vis a vis* those of Australia and New Zealand, with respect to regional decolonisation and denuclearisation issues. To obtain such an advantage, it appears Fiji is prepared to overlook regional sensitivities towards France.

Some Immediate Challenges

The charting of a course towards a new political compact remains the single most important challenge facing the nation at present. The agenda for successfully resolving these challenges must address the more immediate problems of:

1. How to overcome undue military influence in government/parliament in the future.

2. How to placate radical ethnic nationalism operating on the fringe of indigenous Fijian opinion.

3. How best to reassure the indigenous community, and non-indigenous communities alike, that their interests will be protected.

4. How best to promote the process of democratic consolidation and successfully resolve problems related to the restoration of the liberal-democratic ideal (freedom of expression being a valid example).

5. How best to conduct foreign policy and maintain close relations with democratic countries, at the same time upholding a racially exclusive Constitution that denies half of the population parity in political representation.

Prognosis

In meeting these challenges, the overriding aim must be to strike and maintain a balance among domestic political groups. The key to attaining that balance lies in the politics of conciliation, not the politics of coercion or fear. In any multicultural society, the search for a common solution and peace and prosperity must inevitably require a stable, harmonious relationship among its various peoples; a relationship founded on respect for the culture of the various ethnic groups in the country and based on dialogue and a free exchange of information. This is the enduring lesson for Fiji.

And whither the military? If Fiji is to expect an assured future then the RFMF must accept the primacy of civil power—meaning civilian control of the military and a return to free competition among political parties. The primacy of civil power must be accepted as the fundamental criterion of military professionalism. In establishing new parameters for military professionalism, a recommitment by the military to the ideals of political non-interference, and a pledge to serve the wider defence and security interests of the state and the region—including respect for regional environmental concerns—are the minimum moral adjustments of values required of them.

Notes

1. The Taukei Movement was formed by prominent politicians of the Alliance Party following its defeat in the general elections. The movement openly agitated for the removal of the Bavadra coalition government and called for amendments to the constitution to entrench native Fijian political supremacy. For a discussion of the Taukei movement see Robertson and Tamanisau (1988) and Scarr (1988).

Appendix 1

A Tabulated History of the Fiji Military Forces

1871   The "Royal Army" formed comprising 1,000 men under British officers. Royal Army employed on "pacification operations".

1874   Fiji ceded to Great Britain. Fiji now a Crown Colony.

1872-76   Royal Army continues "pacification" operations against rebellious Fijian tribes.

1876   The Royal Army retitled the "Armed Native Constabulary" of 2,000 men under British officers. "Pacification" operations continue in the Sigatoka area of Viti Levu.

1882 and
1894   "Pacification" operations—Seaqaqa, Vanua Levu.

1905   Armed Native Constabulary amalgamated with the Fiji Constabulary (Police).

1914-18   World War One. Fiji Defence Force formed. Contingents of volunteers sent to France and Italy.

1920   Troops called out in Suva/Nausori areas to restore order following the "Indian strike".

1939-45   World War Two. Fiji Military Forces sent to Guadalcanal and Bougainville with the 14th US Army Corps.

1952-56   Malayan Emergency. 1st Battalion, Fiji Infantry Regiment placed under the command of the 17th Gurkha Division.

1959-60   Military Engineers sent to Christmas Island on "Operation Grapple" (British Atomic Bomb tests).

1970   Independence from Britain.

1975   Naval Division formed (3 x USN "Bluebird" Class minesweepers).

1978	Fiji Contingent to UN Interim Force in Lebanon (one infantry battalion).
1980	Fiji military observer mission Zimbabwe-Rhodesia with Commonwealth Monitoring Force.
1982	Fiji Contingent to Multi-national Force and Observers in the Sinai, Egypt (one infantry battalion).
1987	Two coups in Fiji. Secession from the British Commonwealth
1988	Fiji military observer mission to UN forces in Afghanistan.

References

Adriano, Fermin D., 1984. "A Critique of the Bureaucratic Authoritarianism Thesis: the Case of the Philippines", *Journal of Contemporary Asia* 14(4):459-84.

Ahmed, M. and R. Sobhan., 1979. *Public Enterprises in An Intermediate Regime: A Study in the Political Economy of Bangladesh*. Dhaka: Bangladesh Institute of Development Studies.

Akhtar, Rafique, 1989. *Pakistan Year Book: 1989-90*. Karachi: East and West Publishing Company.

Alavi, Hamza, 1972. "The State in Post-Colonial Societies: Pakistan and India", *New Left Review* 74.

Ali, T, 1970. *Pakistan: Military Rule or People's Power*. Delhi: Vikas.

Almendral, G. N., 1988. "The Fall of the Regime", in A. Javate-de Dios, et. al., eds., *Dictatorship and Revolution: Roots of People's Power*. Manila: Conspectus.

Almonte, J. T., 1986. "Towards Reshaping Philippine Martial Traditions", in M. Rajaretnam, ed., *The Aquino Alternative*. Singapore: Institute of Southeast Asian Studies.

Ambalong, B., 1988. "Military Revolt: An Analysis", unpublished paper. National Defense College of the Philippines. Manila: Fort Bonifacio.

Anderson, Benedict O'G., 1983a. "Old State, New Society: Indonesia's New Order in Perspective", *Journal of Asian Studies* 13(3): 477-495.

_____. 1983b. *Imagined Communities. Reflections on the Origin and Spread of Nationalism*. London: Verso.

Anderson, C. W., 1964. "El Salvador: The Army as Reformer", in M. C. Needler, ed., *Political Systems of Latin America*. Princeton: D. Van Nostrand Company.

Ano Hi Nani ga Attacka (Almanac). 1982. Volume 1.

Arillo, C. T., 1986. *Breakaway: The Inside Story of the Four-Day Revolution in the Philippines February 22-25, 1986*. Manila: CTA and Associates.

Asian Wall Street Journal.

Asiaweek.

Barnds, W. J., 1986. "Political and Security Relations", in J. Bresnan, ed., *Crisis in the Philippines: An Analysis of the Marcos Era and Beyond*. New Jersey: Princeton University Press.

Bauer, R. G., 1973. "Military Professional Socialization in a Developing Country". Unpublished PhD thesis, University of Michigan, Michigan.

Baxter, Craig, 1989. "A New Pakistan Under a Revised Bhuttoism", *Middle East Insight* 6 (4) Winter, 23-27.

Bedlington, Stanley S., 1978. *Malaysia and Singapore: The Building of New States*. Ithaca: Cornell University Press. pp.166-169.

Bello, W., 1986. "Aquino's Elite Populism: Initial Reflections", *Third World Quarterly* July, 8 (3): 1020-1030.

_____. 1987. *Creating the Third Force: US Sponsored Low Intensity Conflict in the Philippines*. San Francisco: Institute for Food and Development Policy.

_____. 1988. "Counterinsurgency's Proving Ground: Low-Intensity Warfare in the Philippines", in M. T. Klare and P. Kornbluh eds., *Low-Intensity Warfare: Counterinsurgency, Proinsurgency, and Antiterrorism in the Eighties*. New York: Pantheon Books.

_____. 1989. 'Democratisation and Stabilisation in the Philippines", *Pacific Focus* 4(1).

Benda, H., 1964. Review of Feith, *The Decline of Constitutional Democracy in Indonesia* in *The Journal of Asian Studies* 23(3):498-456.

Berry, W. E., 1986. "The Changing Role of the Philippine Military During Martial Law and the Implications for the Future", in E. A. Olsen and S. Jurika, eds., *The Armed Forces in Contemporary Asian Societies*. Boulder: Westview Special Studies in Military Affairs.

_____. 1989. *U.S. Bases in the Philippines: The Evolution of the Special Relationship*. Boulder Colorado: Westview Press.

Bonner, R., 1987. *Waltzing with a Dictator: The Marcoses and the Making of American Policy*. New York: Times Books.

Booth, Ann and Peter McCawley, eds. 1981. *The Indonesian Economy During the Soeharto Era*. Kuala Lumpur: Oxford University Press.

Britton, Peter, 1973. "The Indonesian Army: Stabiliser and Dynamiser" in Rex Mortimer ed., *Showcase State: The Illusion of Indonesia's 'Accelerated Modernisation'*. Angus and Robertson, pp. 83-98.

Brzoska, Michael and Thomas Ohlson, 1986. *Arms Production in the Third World*. London: Taylor and Francis, for SIPRI.

Budget Speech and Related Bills, 1984; 1986. Port Moresby: Government Printer.

Bunbongkarn S., 1987a. "Political Institutions and Processes", in S. Xuto, ed., *Government and Politics in Thailand*. Singapore: Oxford University Press.

_____. 1987b. *The Military in Thai Politics 1981-1986*. Singapore: Institute of Southeast Asian Studies.

_____. 1988a. "The Thai Military's Effort to Institutionalize its Political Role", *The Pacific Review* 1(4).

_____. 1988b. "The Military and Development for National Security" in J. S. Djimandono and Y. M. Cheong, eds., *Soldiers and Stability in Southeast Asia*. Singapore: Institute of Southeast Asian Studies.

Burki, Shaid Javed, 1988. "Pakistan Under Zia, 1977-1988", *Asian Survey* 28(10): 1082-1100.

Burma, 1989. Ministry of Planning and Finance, Union of Burma, Report on the Financial, Economic and Social Condition of the Union of Burma, 1989-90 Rangoon: Ministry of Planning and Finance.

Buzan, Barry. 1988. "The Southeast Asian Security Complex", *Contemporary Southeast Asia* 10(1): 1-15.

Canberra Times 12 May 1990; 24 May 1990; 31 October 1990.

Catilo-Carbonell, A. et al. 1985. *Manipulated Elections*. Manila: The University of the Philippines Press.

Chan Heng Chee, 1985. "Singapore", in Zakaria Ahmad and Harold Crouch, eds., *Military-Civilian Relations in Southeast Asia*. Singapore: Oxford University Press.

Chan, Steve, 1990. *East Asian Dynamism. Growth, Order and Security in the Pacific Region*. Boulder: Westview Press.

Chandra, Jeshurun, 1988. "Development and Civil-Military Relations in Malaysia: The Evolution of the Officer Corps" in J. Soedjati Djiwandono & Yong Mun Cheong eds, *Soldiers and Stability in Southeast Asia*. Singapore: Institute of Southeast Asian Studies.

_____. 1980. Malaysian Defence Policy, Kuala Lumpur: Penerbit Universiti Malaya.

Cheng, Tun-Jen, 1989. "Democratising the Quasi-Leninist Regime in Taiwan", *International Journal* 41(4):471-499.

Clark, D. N., 1988. "Interpreting the Kwangju Uprising", in D. N. Clark, ed., *The Kwangju Uprising. Shadows over the Regime in South Korea*. Boulder: Westview Press.

Clements, Kevin, 1989. "Common Security in the Asia-Pacific Region: Problems and Prospects", *Alternatives* 14(1).

Clifford, W. L., Morauta and B. Stuart, 1986. *Law and Order in Papua New Guinea*. Port Moresby: Institute of National

Affairs and Institute of Applied Social and Economic Research.

Clough, R. N., 1987. *Embattled Korea: The Rivalry for International Support*. Boulder: Westview Press.

Cohen, Stephen P., 1971. *The Indian Army: Its Contribution to the Development of a Nation*. Berkeley: University of California Press.

_____. 1984. *The Pakistan Army* Berkeley: University of California Press.

_____. 1987. *The Security of South Asia: American and Asian Perspectives*. Urbana, USA: University of Illinois Press.

_____. 1988. "The Military and Indian Democracy", in Atul Kohli ed., *India's Democracy*. Princeton: Princeton University Press.

Collier, David, ed., 1979. *The New Authoritarianism in Latin America*. Princeton: Princeton University Press.

Constitutional Planning Committee Final Report, 1974. Port Moresby: Government Printer.

Corpus, V. 1987. Silent War. (Manuscript).

Cotton, J., 1989a. "North-South Korean relations: another false start?", *The World Today* 49:104-8.

_____. 1989b. "From Authoritarianism to Democracy in South Korea", *Political Studies*, (37):244-59

Crossroads to Reform. 1985. Unpublished RAM paper.

Crouch, Harold. 1978. *The Army and Politics in Indonesia* Ithaca: Cornell University Press.

_____. 1983. "A strict division", "Time to consolidate on a new front line", "Counter-insurgency: less emphasis, fewer demands", *FEER* 20 October 1983.

_____. 1984. *Domestic Political Structures and Regional Economic Co-operation*. Singapore: Institute of Southeast Asian Studies.

_____. 1985a. "The Military and Politics in South-East Asia", in Ahmad Zakaria and H. Crouch eds.,. *Military-Civilian Relations in South-East Asia*. Singapore: Oxford University Press.

_____, 1985b. *Economic Change, Social Structure and the Political System in Southeast Asia*. Singapore: Institute of Southeast Asian Studies.

_____. 1986. "The Missing Bourgeoisie: Approaches to Indonesia's New Order", in D.P. Chandler and M.C. Rickleffs, eds., *Nineteenth and Twentieth Century Indonesia: Essays in Honour of Professor J.D. Legge*. Victoria: Monash University, Centre of Southeast Asian Studies.

_____. 1987a. "After the gold rush: the politics of economic restructuring in Indonesia in the 1980s", in Richard Robison, Kevin Hewison and Richard Higgott, eds., *Southeast Asia in*

the 1980s: The Politics of Economic Crisis. Sydney: Allen & Unwin.
_____. 1987b. "The Politics of Islam in Southeast Asia", *Flinders Asian Studies Lecture 18*. Adelaide: Flinders University of South Australia.
_____. 1988. "Indonesia: The Rise or Fall of Suharto's Generals", *Third World Quarterly*. 10(1)
_____. 1990. "After Suharto What?", *The Independent Monthly*. February.
Cumings, Bruce, 1988. "Power and Plenty in North-East Asia: the Sources of US Policy and Contemporary Conflict", in Andrew Mack and Paul Keal, *Security and Arms Control in the North Pacific*. Sydney: Allen and Unwin.
Daily Express.
David, V. M. 1987. "Defend Government Kung-Fu Style", unpublished paper. PC. GHQ, Manila: Camp Crame.
Dawn (Karachi).
de Dios, A., 1988. "Intervention and Militarism", in A. Javate-de Dios, et. al. eds., *Dictatorship and Revolution: Roots of People's Power*. Manila: Conspectus.
de Dios, E. S., 1988. "The Erosion of Dictatorship", in A. Javate-de Dios, et al. eds., ibid.
de la Torre, E., 1987. "On the Post-Marcos Transition and Popular Democracy". *World Policy Journal* Spring 4 (2): 333-351.
Dean, E., and S., Ritova. 1988. *Rabuka: No Other Way*. Sydney: Doubleday.
Decalo, S., 1976. *Coups and Army Rule in Africa: Studies in Military Style*. New Haven: Yale University Press.
Deger, Saadet, 1986. *Military Expenditure in Third World Countries. The Economic Effects*. London: Routledge and Kegan Paul.
Downes, C. J., 1985. "To Be or Not To Be a Profession: The Military Case!", *Defense Analysis September* 1 (3): 147-171.
East, C., 1985. "PNGDF: colonial legacy or independent force?" *Pacific Defence Reporter* 12(5): 11-13,60.
Enloe, C. H., 1977. "Malaysia's Military in the Interplay of Economic and Ethnic Change", in J. Lent ed., *Cultural Pluralism in Malaysia*. Dekalb: Northern Illinois University, Center for Southeast Asian Studies.
_____. 1978. "The Issue Saliency of the Military-Ethnic Connection: Some Thoughts on Malaysia", *Comparative Politics* 10:2, (January).
_____. 1980. *Ethnic Soldiers: State Security in Divided Societies*. Athens: University of Georgia Press.

Ershad, H. M. 1981. "On the Role of the Armed Forces", *Bichitra* December. Dhaka.
Evans, Peter, Dietrich Rueschemeyer and Theda Skocopol, eds., 1985. *Bringing the State Back In*. Cambridge: Cambridge University Press.
Far Eastern Economic Review (*FEER*) [various editions].
Feith, Herb, 1962. *The Decline of Constitutional Democracy in Indonesia*. Ithaca: Cornell University Press.
_____. 1981. "Repressive-Developmentalist Regimes in Asia", *Alternatives* 7(1).
Fiji Government Operating Budget Statements, 1987, 1988, 1989. Suva: Government Printer.
Fiji Voice, June/July 1990. Sydney: Fiji Independent News Service.
Filio, C. P., 1986. "Understanding the Aquino-Enrile Controversy Through the Concept of Functional Loyalty". Unpublished paper.
Finer, S. E. 1962. *The Man on Horseback: The Role of the Military in Politics*. London: Penguin.
_____, 1982. "The Morphology of Military Regimes", in Roman Kolkowicz and Andrzej Korbonski, *Soldiers, Peasants and Bureaucrats: Civil-military Relations in Communist and Modernizing Societies*. London: Allen and Unwin.
Foucault, Michel, 1980. *Power-Knowledge*. Hassocks: Harvester Press.
France, P., 1969. *The Charter of the Land: Custom and Colonization in Fiji*. Melbourne: Oxford University Press.
Fry, Greg, 1990. "Peacekeeping in the South Pacific: Some Questions for Prior Consideration", *Working Paper 1990* No. 7. Canberra, Dept of International Relations, Research School of Pacific Studies, Australian National University.
_____. ed., 1991. *Australia's Regional Security*. Sydney: Allen and Unwin.
Funston, John. 1980. *Malay Politics in Malaysia*. Kuala Lumpur: Heinemann.
Garcia, J. Z.,1978. "Military Factions and Military Intervention in Latin America", in S. W. Simon, ed., *The Military and Security in the Third World: Domestic and International Impacts*. Colorado: Westview Press.
Ghai, Y., 1987. "The Fijian Crisis: The Constitutional Dimension", *The Minority Rights Group Report*. No. 75:9-13.
Gibbons, D. S., and Zakaria Haji Ahmad. 1971. "Politics and Selection for the Higher Civil Service in New States: The Malaysian Example", *Journal of Comparative Administration* 3 (November).

Gill, V., 1986. From Professionalism to Politicisation: the Military in Pakistan, Oslo: *International Peace Research Institute Report 12/86.*
Gillion, K. L., 1977. *The Fiji Indians: Challenge to European Dominance 1920-1946.* Canberra: Australian National University Press.
Girling, J. L. S., 1985. *Thailand: Society and Politics.* Ithaca: Cornell University Press.
Gregor, A. James, 1979. *Italian Fascism and Developmental Dictatorship.* Princeton: Princeton University Press.
Guyot, James F., 1974. "Ethnic Segmentation in Military Organisation; Burma and Malaysia" in C. M. Kelleher ed., *Political-Military Systems: Comparative Perspectives.* Beverly Hills, California: Sage Publications.
_____. 1989. "Burma in 1988: Perestroika with a Military Face". *Southeast Asian Affairs.* Singapore: Institute of Southeast Asian Studies.
Hak-Kyu, S. 1988. Political Opposition and the Yushin Regime: Radicalisation in South Korea, 1972-79. Oxford University: DPhil thesis.
Halliday, Fred and Maxine Molyneux, 1981. *The Ethiopian Revolution.* London: Verso.
Hamilton, Clive and Richard Tanter, 1987. "The Antinomies of Success in Korea", *Journal of International Affairs* 41(1).
Harris, B. 1988. The Rise of Rascalism. Port Moresby: *IASER Discussion Paper No. 54.*
Hashmi, Bilal, 1983. "Dragon Seed: Military in the State", in Hassan Gardezi and Jamil Rashid, eds., *Pakistan: The Roots of Dictatorship, The Political Economy of a Praetorian State.* London: Zed Press.
Hawes, G. 1989. "Aquino and Her Administration: A View from the Countryside", *Pacific Affairs* 62(1):9-28.
Hayes, Peter, Lyuba Zarsky and Walden Bello, 1986. *American Lake. Nuclear Peril in the Pacific.* Harmondsworth: Penguin.
Heeger, G., 1974. *The Politics of Underdevelopment.* New York: St Martin's Press.
Hegarty, D., 1978. "Political Chronicle of Papua New Guinea", *The Australian Journal of Politics and History.*
_____. 1989. "Stability and Turbulence in the South Pacific", *Working Paper No. 185.* Canberra: Strategic and Defence Studies Centre, Australian National University,
Heinze, R. I., 1974. "Ten Days in October: Students vs Military: An Account of the Student Uprising in Thailand", *Asian Survey* June.

Henderson, G. 1968. *Korea: The Politics of the Vortex*. Cambridge: Harvard University Press.
_____. 1986. "Why Koreans Turn Against Us", *The Washington Post*, 1 July.
Hernandez, C. G. 1985a. "The Philippines", in Ahmad. H. Zakaria and H. Crouch, eds., op.cit.
_____. 1985b. "The Philippine Military and Civilian Control: Under Marcos and Beyond", *Third World Quarterly* 7 (4): 903-919.
_____, 1986. "Reconstituting the Political Order", in Bresnan, J., ed., *Crisis in the Philippines: An Analysis of the Marcos Era and Beyond*. New Jersey: Princeton University Press.
_____. 1987. "Towards Understanding Coups and Civilian-Military Relations", *Kasarinlan, Philippine Quarterly of Third World Studies* 3 (2).
Hinton, H. C., et. al. 1988. *The US-Korean Security Relationship: Prospects and Challenges for the 1990s*. Washington: Pergamon-Brasseys.
Hiri (The Official News Magazine of the Papua New Guinea Government).
Horowitz, Donald L., 1980. *Coup Theories and Officers' Motives. Sri Lanka in Comparative Perspective*. Princeton, NJ: Princeton University Press.
Horowitz, I. L., 1981. "Military Origins of Third World Dictatorship and Democracy", *Third World Quarterly* 3(1): 37-47.
Hossain, M. 1987. *Bangladesh's Ruling Class and the Political Situation of the Last Decade*. Dhaka: Society Printing. (In Bengali).
Huntington, S.P., 1957. *The Soldier and the State*. Cambridge MA: Harvard University Press.
_____. 1968. *Political Order in Changing Societies*. New Haven: Yale University Press.
_____. 1984. "Will more countries become democratic?". *Political Science Quarterly*, (99):193-218.
IDS, Bulletin, 1985. *Special Issue on Disarmament and World Development* 16(4).
IISS, International Institute for Strategic Studies. *The Military Balance 1975-76; 1978-79; 1979-1980; 1981-82; 1990-1991*. London: Brassey's.
_____. 1989. *Strategic Survey 1988-89*. London: Brassey's.
Im, Hyug Baeg, 1987. "The rise of bureaucratic authoritarianism in South Korea", *World Politics* (37):231-57.
Islam, M. S., 1989. Politics of Soldiers, Vol. 1, London: East-West. (In Bengali).

Islam, S., 1986. "Rise of the Civil-Military Bureaucracy in Bangladesh", *Asian Thought and Society* 11(31): 28-36. Hong Kong.
Jackson, Robert. 1975. *South Asian Crisis*. London: Chatto and Windus.
Jacobs, N., 1985. *The Korean Road to Modernization and Development*. Urbana: University of Chicago Press.
Janowitz, Morris, 1964. *The Military in the Political Development of New Nations*. Chicago: The University of Chicago Press.
_____.1977. *Military Institutions and Coercion in the Developing Nations*. Chicago and London: The University of Chicago Press.
Jenkins, David, 1984. *Suharto and His Generals: Indonesian Military Politics 1975-1983*. Ithaca: Cornell Modern Indonesia Project, Cornell University.
Johnson, C.,1989. "South Korean Democratization: The Role of Economic Development", *The Pacific Review* 2(1):1-10.
Karp, Aaron, 1990. "Military Procurement and Regional Security in Southeast Asia", *Contemporary Southeast Asia* 11(4).
Khan, Ayub, 1967. *Friends Not Masters*. Karachi: Oxford University Press.
Khin Nyunt, 1989a. *Burma Communist Party's Conspiracy to Take Over State Power*. Yangon: News and Periodicals Enterprise.
_____. 1989b. *The Conspiracy of Treasonous Minions within the Myanmar Naing-ngan and Traitorous Cohorts Abroad*. Yangon: News and Periodicals Enterprise.
Kihl, Y. W., 1984. *Politics and Policies in Divided Korea: Regimes in Contest*. Boulder: Westview Press.
Kim Eugene, C. I., 1971. "The Military in the Politics of South Korea: Creating Political Order", in M. Janowitz and J. Van Doorn, eds., *On Military Intervention*. Rotterdam: Rotterdam University Press.
_____. 1984. "Civil-Military Relations in the Two Koreas", *Armed Forces and Society* 11:9-3.
_____. 1988. "The South Korean Military and Its Political Role", in I. J. Kim. I. J. and Y. W. Kihl, eds., *Political Change in South Korea*. New York: Paragon House.
Kim, J. A., 1975. *Divided Korea: The Politics of Development, 1945-1972*. Cambridge: Harvard University Press.
Kim, Se-Jin, 1971. *The Politics of Military Revolution in Korea*. Chapel Hill: University of North Carolina Press.
Klare, Michael, I., 1972. *War Without End. American Planning for the Next Vietnams*. New York: Vintage.

_____. and Peter Kornbluh, 1988. eds., *Low Intensity Warfare. Counterinsurgency, Proinsurgency, and Antiterrorism in the Eighties.* Pantheon: New York.

Kraprayoon, S., 1990. "The Military and National Development" in P. Natiyakul, ed., *Applied Psychology for National Security* 33. Bangkok: Chaoprayd.

Kullavanij. P. 1986. *The Role of the Military in National Development.* (in Thai). Bangkok: National Defense College.

Lande, C. H., 1986. "The Political Crisis", in J. Bresnan, ed., op.cit. New Jersey: Princeton University Press.

_____ and R. Hooley, 1986. "Aquino Takes Charge", *Foreign Affairs* 64 (5):1087-1107.

Liefchultz, L., 1979. *Bangladesh: The Unfinished Revolution.* London: Zed Press.

Lindquist, A., 1977. "Military and Development in Bangladesh", *Institute for Development Studies Bulletin* 9(1):10-18. Sussex: The University of Sussex.

Lissak, M., 1975. "Center and Periphery in Development and Prototypes of Military Elites", in K. Fidel, ed., *Militarism in Developing Countries.* New Jersey: Transaction Books.

_____. 1976. *Military Roles in Modernization: Civil-Military Relations in Thailand and Burma.* Beverly Hills: Sage Publications.

Looney, Robert E., and P.C. Frederiksen, 1990. "The Economic Determinants of Military Expenditure in Selected East Asian Countries", *Contemporary Southeast Asia* 11(4):265-277.

Lovell, J. P., 1975. "The Military and Politics in Postwar Korea", in E.R. Wright, ed., *Korean Politics in Transition.* Seattle: University of Washington Press.

Luckham, A.R., 1971a. "A Comparative Typology of Civil-Military Relations", *Government and Opposition* 6(1).

_____. Robin, 1971b. *The Nigerian Military. A Sociological Analysis of Authority and Revolt 1960-67.* Cambridge: Cambridge University Press.

_____. Robin, 1979. "Militarism and International Dependence: a Framework for Analysis", in J.J. Villamil, ed., *Transnational Capitalism and National Development.* Hassocks: Harvester Press.

_____. 1987. "Disarmament and Development. A Survey of the Issues", *Working Paper No. 22.* Canberra: Peace Research Centre, Australian National University.

Luttwak, E., 1968. *Coup D'Etat: A Practical Handbook.* London: The Penguin Press.

Macdonald, D.S., 1988. *The Koreans: Contemporary Politics and Society*. Boulder: Westview Press.

Mack, Andrew and Paul Keal, 1988. *Security and Arms Control in the North Pacific*. Sydney: Allen and Unwin.

Mackenzie, A. 1987. "People Power or Palace Coup: The Fall of Marcos", in M. Turner, ed., *Regime Change in the Philippines: The Legitimation of the Aquino Government*. Canberra: The Australian National University, Department of Political and Social Change, Monograph No. 7.

Maizels, Alfred K. and Michito Nissanke, 1986. "The Determinants of Military Expenditure in Developing Countries', *World Development* 14(9).

Manila Bulletin.

Manila Chronicle.

Maniruzzaman, T., 1987. *Military Withdrawal from Politics: A Comparative Study*. Cambridge: Ballinger Publishing Company.

Maung Maung, 1969. *Burma and General Ne Win*. New York: Asia Publishing House.

McCoy, A. W., 1987. "After the Yellow Revolution: Filipino Elite Factions and the Struggle for Power", in P. Krinks, ed., *The Philippines Under Aquino*. Canberra: The Australian Development Studies Network.

_____. 1988. "RAM boys: The Politicization of the Philippine Armed Forces". Paper presented at the Asian Studies Association of Australia Conference at the Australian National Unversity, Canberra, February.

McDougald, C. C., 1987. *The Marcos File: Was He a Philippine Hero or a Corrupt Tyrant?*. San Francisco: San Francisco Publishers.

Mench, P., 1976a. "The Roles of the Papua New Guinea Defence Force", *Development Studies Centre Monograph No.2*. Canberra: Development Studies Centre, Australian National University.

_____. 1976b. "The Defence Forces of Small States: A Comparison of Defence Statistics in Twenty Six States in Tropical Africa, PNG and Fiji", *Occasional Paper No.5*. Canberra: Development Studies Centre, Australian National University.

Migdal, J. S., 1988. *Strong Societies and Weak States: State-Society Relations and State Capabilities in the Third World*. Princeton: Princeton University Press.

Miranda, F. B., and R. F. Ciron, 1987. "Development and the Military in the Philippines in a Time of Continuing Crisis", *Social Weather Stations Occasional Paper*. Quezon City.

Moore, Mick, 1990. "Economic Liberalisation Versus Political Pluralism in Sri Lanka?", *Modern Asian Studies* 24(2):341-383.
Muego, B. N., 1987. "Fraternal Organizations and Factionalism within the Armed Forces of the Philippines", *Asian Affairs* 14 (3):150-162.
Muslim (Lahore).
Muthiah, Alagappa, 1986. US-Asean Security Co-operation: Limits and Possibilities. Kuala Lumpur: Institute of Strategic and International Studies.
_____. 1987. "Malaysia: From the Commonwealth Umbrella to Self-reliance" in Chin Kin Wah, ed., *Defence Spending in Southeast Asia*. Singapore: Institute of Southeast Asian Studies.
_____. 1988. "Military Professionalism and the Developmental Role of the Military in Southeast Asia", in Soedjati Djiwandono and Yong Mun Cheong, eds., *Soldiers and Stability in Southeast Asia*. Singapore: Institute of Southeast Asian Studies.
Nation (Lahore).
National Operations Council. 1969. *The May 13 Tragedy*. Kuala Lumpur, Government Printer.
Nelson, H., 1980. "Hold the Good Name of the Soldier: The Discipline of Papuan and Guinean Infantry Battalians, 1940-1946,". *The Journal of Pacific History* 115(4).
Nemenzo, F., 1986a. "A Season of Coups: Military Intervention in Philippine Politics", *Diliman Review* 34 (5-6): 1 and 16-25.
_____. 1986b. "A Nation in Ferment: Analysis of the February Revolution", in M. Rajaretnam, ed., op.cit.
_____. 1987. "A Season of Coups. Reflections on the Military in Politics", *Kasarinlan, Philippine Quarterly of Third World Studies*. University of the Philippines. Reprinted in Philippine Studies Newsletter, October 1987.
_____. 1988. "From Autocracy to Elite Democracy", in A. Javate-de Dios, et al., eds., op.cit.
New Straits Times (NST)
Nordlinger, Eric. A., 1977. *Soldiers and Politics: Military Coups and Governments*. Englewood Cliffs, New Jersey: Prentice Hall, Inc.
Norton, R., 1981. "The Mediation of Ethnic Conflict: Comparative Implications of the Fiji Case", *Journal of Commonwealth and Comparative Politics* 19(3):309-328.
O'Donnell, Guillermo, 1973. *Modernisation and Bureaucratic Authoritarianism: Studies in South American Politics*. Berkeley: University of California Press.

_____. 1978. "Reflections on the Patterns of Change in the Bureaucratic Authoritarian State", *Latin American Research Review* 12(1).
O'Kane, R. H. T., 1987. *The Likelihood of Coups*. Aldershot: Avebury.
OECD, 1989. Organisation for Economic Cooperation and Development, Financing and External Debt of Developing Countries 1988 Survey. Paris: OECD publication.
Olsen, E. A., 1986. "The Societal Role of the ROK Armed Forces", in A. Edward, E. A. Olsen and S. Jurika, eds., *The Armed Forces in Contemporary Asian Societies*. Boulder: Westview Press.
Overholt, W. H., 1986. "The Rise and Fall of Ferdinand Marcos", *Asian Survey* 26 (11): 1137-1163.
Pacific Island Monthly, August 1990.
Papua New Guinea Defence White Paper, 1988. Port Moresby.
Pauker, G.J., et. al., 1973. *In Search of Self-Reliance: U.S. Security Assistance to the Third World Under the Nixon Doctrine*. Santa Monia: Rand Corporation, R.-1092-ARPA.
Perlmutter, A., 1977. *The Military and Politics in Modern Times*. New Haven: Yale University Press.
_____. 1980. "The Comparative Analysis of Military Regimes: Formations, Aspirations and Achievement", *World Politics* 33.
Peterson, M. 1988. "Americans and the Kwangju Incident: Problems in the Writing of History", in D. N. Clark, ed., *The Kwangju Uprising: Shadows over the Regime in South Korea*. Boulder: Westview Press.
Philippine Situationer, 1989, 1 (7).
Poole, F., and M. Vanzi,. 1984. *Revolution in the Philippines: The United States in a Hall of Cracked Mirrors*. New York: McGraw-Hill Book Company.
Post Courier. Port Moresby.
Pye, Lucien, 1962. "Armies in the Process of Political Modernisation", in J.J. Johnson ed., *The Role of the Military in Underdeveloped Countries*. Princeton, N.J.: Princeton University Press.
Rau, Robert L., 1986. "The Role of the Armed Forces and Police in Malaysia", in Edward A. Olsen & Stephen Jurika, Jr. eds., op.cit.
Report of the Auditor General (Fiji) 1987. *Parliamentary Paper No.2 of 1989*. Suva: Government Printer.
Report of the Auditor General 1988 (Paper No 22), Suva: Government Printer
Report of the Defence General Board of Inquiry into the Administration and Management of the Papua New Guinea Defence Force Department, 1989. Port Moresby.

Rizvi, Hasan, 1986. "The Civilianization of Military Rule in Pakistan", *Asian Survey* 26(10):1067-1081.
_____. 1984. "The Paradox of Military Rule in Pakistan", *Asian Survey* 24(5):534-555.
_____. 1988. "National Security, Domestic Politics and the Military", *Defence Journal* 14(12): in *Strategic Digest*, April 1989, 409-415.
Robertson, R., and A. Tamanisau, 1988. *Fiji: Shattered Coups*. Sydney: Pluto Press.
Robison, Richard, 1985. "Class, Capital and the State in New Order Indonesia", in R. Higgott and R. Robison, *Southeast Asia*.
_____. 1986. *Indonesia: The Rise of Capital*. Sydney: Allen & Unwin.
_____. 1988. "Authoritarian States, Capital-Owning Classes, and the Politics of Newly Industrialising Countries", *World Politics* 41(1).
Rodriguez, F. C., 1985. *The Marcos Regime: Rape of the Nation*. New York: Vantage Press.
Ross, Andrew L., 1990. "Growth, Debt and Military Spending in Southeast Asia", *Contemporary Southeast Asia* 11(4).
Rouquié, Alain, 1981. *La Politique de mars. Les Processus Politiques dans les Partis Militaries*. Paris.
_____. 1987. *The Military and the State in Latin America*. Berkeley, Ca., University of California Press.
Rutz, H. J., 1987. "Capitalising on Culture: Moral Ironies in Urban Fiji", *Comparative Studies of Society and History* 29(3):533-557.
Saffu, Y., 1988. "Political Chronicles of Papua New Guinea", *The Australian Journal of Politics and History*. (34) 3.
_____. 1990. "Changing Civil-Military Relations in Fiji", *Australian Journal of International Affairs* 44(2):159-170, Canberra: Australian Institute of International Affairs.
Samudavanija, Chai-Anan, 1982. *The Thai Young Turks*. Singapore: Institute of Southeast Asian Studies.
Sanday, J., 1989. "The Coups of 1987: A Personal Analysis", *Pacific Viewpoint* 30(2):116-131, Wellington: Victoria University Press.
_____. (forthcoming). *Fiji: Anatomy of a Crisis*. Canberra: Strategic and Defence Studies Centre, Australian National University.
Santos, A. L. and L. Domingo-Robes, 1987. *Power Politics in the Philippines: The Fall of Marcos*. Manila: Center for Social Research.
Scarr, D., 1988. *Fiji: The Politics of Illusion*. Kensington: University of New South Wales Press.

Schirmer, D. B., and S. R. Shalom,. eds., 1987. *The Philippines Reader: A History of Colonialism, Neocolonialism, Dictatorship and Resistance*. Quezon City: Ken Incorporated.

Selochan, V., 1989. *Could the Military Govern the Philippines?* Quezon City: New Day Publishers.

_____. (forthcoming). *Professionalization and Politicization of the Armed Forces of the Philippines*. Ithaca: Cornell University Press

Shultz, R. H., 1989. "Low-Intensity Conflict", *Survival* 31(4):359-374.

Silverstein, J., 1977. *Burma: Military Rule and the Politics of Stagnation*. Ithaca and London: Cornell University Press.

_____.1990., "Civil War and Rebellion in Burma", *Journal of Southeast Asian Studies* 21(1).

Simon, S. W,. ed., 1978. *The Military and Security in the Third World: Domestic and International Impacts*. Boulder: Westview Press.

SIPRI, (Stockholm International Peace Research Institute) *SIPRI Yearbook 1988*: World Armaments and Disarmament. Oxford: Oxford University Press.

_____. 1990. *SIPRI Yearbook 1990*. Oxford: Oxford University Press.

Sklar, Richard, 1987. "Developmental Democracy", *Comparative Studies in Society and History* 29(4).

Smith, Chris, 1990. "Indigenous Defence production. The Failure of Policy Implementation", *IUMDA Newsletter*, 2 and 3, Delhi, Information Unit on Militarization and Demilitiarization in Asia.

Snider, Lewis W., 1990. "The Political Dimensions of Military spending and Debt Service in Southeast Asia", *Contemporary Southeast Asia* 11(4).

Soedjati Djiwandono & Yong Mun Cheong, 1988. "The Military and Development in Southeast Asia: Perspectives from Observers and Practictioners", in *Soldiers and Stability in Southeast Asia*. Singapore: Institute of Southeast Asian Studies.

Sohn, J. S., 1968. "Political Dominance and Political Failure: The Role of the Military in the Republic of Korea", in *The Military Intervenes. Case Studies in Political Development*. New York: Russell Sage Foundation.

Steinberg, D. I., 1989a. "Crisis in Burma", *Current History* April 1989: 185-188 and 196-198.

_____. 1989b. "Afterwards: Forty Plus One", in Josef Silverstein, ed., *Independent Burma at Forty Years: Six Assessments*. Ithaca: Cornell University Southeast Asia Program.

Stepan, A. 1973. "The New Professionalism of Internal Warfare and Military Role Expansion", in *Authoritarian Brazil: Origins, Policies, Future*. New Haven: Yale University Press.

_____. 1988. *Rethinking Military Politics: Brazil and the Southern Cone*. Princeton: Princeton University Press.

Sudsapda, M. 1989. *Mathichon Weekly*.

Suk Joon Kim, 1990. "The Rise of the Neo-Mercantile Security State: State Institutional change in South Korea", *Pacific Focus* 5(1):11-148.

Sundhaussen, U., 1974. "What Role for the Army?" *New Guinea*. (8) 2.

_____, 1982. *The Road to Power: Indonesian Military Politics 1945-1966*. Kuala Lumpur: Oxford University Press.

Sungjoo, H. 1974. *The Failure of Democracy in South Korea*. Berkeley: University of California Press.

_____. 1986. "Political institutionalization in South Korea, 1961-1984", in Scalapino, R. A. and J. Wanandi, eds., *Asian Political Institutionalization*. Berkeley: University of California, Institute of East Asian Studies.

Sydney Morning Herald, 2 August 1990.

Tanter, Richard, 1981. "The Militarisation of ASEAN: Global Context and Local Dynamics", *Alternatives* 7(1).

Tapol, 1987. *Indonesia: Muslims on Trial*. London: Tapol.

Taylor, R., 1985. "Burma", in Zakaria Ahmad and Harold Crouch, eds., op.cit.

_____. 1987a. *The State in Burma*. London: Honolulu: University of Hawaii Press.

_____, 1987b. "Burma: Defence Expenditure and Threat Perceptions", in Chin Kin Wah, ed., op.cit

_____. 1988. "The Sangha and Sasana in Socialist Burma", *Sojourn* (1) 26-61. February".

_____. 1989. "Burma's National Security and Defense Posture", *Contemporary Southeast Asia* June. 11(1): 40-60.

The Economist.

The Financial Post.

The Korea Herald (Seoul)

The Korea Newsreview (Seoul)

The Nation. 28 November 1986 and 26 January 1990.

The New Yorker.

The POOP, 1987. Philippine Armed Forces Alumini. January-February.

The Rank and File, 1988. September and November.

The Royal Thai Army 1983. The Army's Position in the Constitutional Amendment Problem (in Thai). Bangkok. February.
The Royal Thai Army, 1951. *The Army Day 25 January 1952* (in Thai). Bangkok.
The Times of PNG. Port Morseby.
Tin Maung Maung Than. 1988a. "Burma in 1987: Twenty-Five Years after the Revolution", *Southeast Asian Affairs.* Singapore: Institute of Southeast Asian Studies.
Trimberger, Ellen Kay, 1978. *Revolution from Above: Military Bureaucrats and Development in Japan, Turkey, Egypt and Peru.* New Brunswick, N.J.: Transaction Books.
Umar B. 1989. *Military Rule and Politics in Bangladesh.* Dhaka: Pratik. (In Bengali).
Umar, B. and Muhammad, A., 1988. *Religious Fundamentalism and Communalism in Bangladesh* (in Bengali)Dhaka: Sanskriti Prokashon.
Umar, B., 1979. *Imperialism and The General Crisis of the Bourgeoisie in Bangladesh.* Dhaka: Progoti Prokashon.
Van Doorn, J., 1976. "The Military and the Crisis of Legitimacy", in G. Harries-Jenkins and J. van Doorn, eds., *The Military and the Problem of Legitimacy.* London: Sage.
White, Gordon, ed., 1987. *Developmental States in East Asia.* London: Macmillan.
Wise, W. M., 1987. "The Philippine Military After Marcos", in C. D. Lande, ed., *Rebuilding a Nation: Philippine Challenges and American Policy.* United States: The Washington Institute Press.
Woddis, J., 1977. *Armies and Politics.* London: Lawrence and Wishart.
Wolpin, M. D., 1983. "Sociopolitical Radicalism and Military Professionalism in the Third World". *Comparative Politics* 15(2):203-221.
World Bank, 1989. *World Development Report.* Oxford: Oxford University Press.
_____. 1990. *Annual Report.*
WPD, 1989. *Working Peope's Daily.* Yangon. 28 July.
Yasmeen, Samina 1985. Chinese Policy Towards Pakistan 1969-1979, Ph.D Thesis, University of Tasmania, Hobart.
_____. 1990a. "Recent Changes in Pakistan: An assessment", paper presented at a conference Recent Changes in South Asia: Various Perspectives, organized by the University of Western Australia and Curtin University, Perth, 17 August 1990.

_____. 1990b. "The Elections of 1990: An Assessment", *Indian Ocean Review*.

Yitri, M., 1989. "The Crisis in Burma", *Asian Survey*, June. XXIX(6): 543-558.

Yongchaiyuth, C., 1987. "Politics in the Eyes of the Military", Royal Thai Army (in Thai).

Zakaria Ahmad, 1981. "The Bayonet and the Truncheon: Army-Police Relations in Malaysia", in Dewitt Ellinwood & Cynthia Enloe eds., *Ethnicity and the Military in Asia*. New Brunswick, N.J.: Transaction Books.

Zakaria, Ahmad., 1985. "Malaysia", in Zakaria Ahmad & Harold Crouch eds., op.cit..

_____. 1987. "The Police and Political Development in Malaysia", in Ahmad Zakaria ed., *Government and Politics of Malaysia*. Singapore: Oxford University Press.

_____. 1988. "The Military and Development in Malaysia and Brunei, with a Short Survey on Singapore", in J. Soedjati Djiwandono & Yong Mun Cheong, eds., *Soldiers and Stability in Southeast Asia*. Singapore: Institute of Southeast Asian Studies.

_____. 1989. "Speech to Class 8", *Lakthai*. August.

Zaman, H. 1987. *Army Rule and the Socio-Economic Reality of Bangladesh*. Dhaka: Dhanshish. (In Bengali).

Ziring, Lawrence. 1971. *The Ayub Khan Era: Politics in Pakistan 1958-1969*. Syracuse University Press.

_____. 1980. *Pakistan: The Enigma of Political Development*. London: Dawson and Westview, London.

Praise for
*The Military, the State, and Development
in Asia and the Pacific*

"This volume is both expert and timely. As we move towards the twenty-first century it is imperative to understand the role the armed forces are likely to play in their respective countries and in the region as a whole."

—Desmond Ball,
The Australian National University

"I welcome this volume as both timely and of key importance."
—General P. C. Gration, AC, OBE,
Chief of the Australian Defence Force

As the threat of the cold war in Europe recedes, other parts of the globe are drawing the attention of Western policymakers and security specialists. Asia and the Pacific make up one such region, and this book provides an up-to-date, comprehensive analysis of the region's armed forces and their political role in this potentially volatile part of the world. Each chapter has been prepared by a distinguished country specialist who provides a balanced examination of the present state of affairs and considers probable developments into the next decade.

Viberto Selochan is a research fellow at the Centre for the Study of Australia-Asia Relations at Griffith University in Queensland, Australia.

For order and other information, please write to:

Westview Press
5500 Central Avenue
Boulder, Colorado 80301

ISBN 0-8133-1111-X